Soft Skills

Personality Development in the AI age and beyond

4th Edition

Prashant Sharma

www.bpbonline.com

Fourth Revised and Updated Edition 2026

First Edition 2021

ISBN: 978-93-65894-660

Distributors:

BPB PUBLICATIONS
20, Ansari Road, Darya Ganj
New Delhi-110002
Ph: 23254990/23254991

DECCAN AGENCIES
4-3-329, Bank Street,
Hyderabad-500195
Ph: 24756967/24756400

MICRO MEDIA
Shop No. 5, Mahendra Chambers,
150 DN Rd. Next to Capital Cinema,
V.T. (C.S.T.) Station, MUMBAI-400 001
Ph: 22078296/22078297

Published by Manish Jain for BPB Publications, 20 Ansari Road, Darya Ganj, New Delhi-110002 and Printed by him at Repro India Ltd., Rewari.

www.bpbonline.com

Dedicated to

My Parents

My Wife and Children

My Clients, Partners, Team and Students

and

For all the people from small towns, who have the talent but lack the exposure and self- belief. I hope this book can be the medium for change in your life and encourage you to realize your true potential. May you all achieve the dream life you have envisioned for yourself.

About the Author

Leadership & Business Coach| Master Facilitator | Mentor| Ed-tech Entrepreneur | Board Member

Prashant Sharma is an accomplished ICF-Professional Certified Coach (PCC), seasoned Executive Coach, and Training Facilitator with extensive corporate and entrepreneurial experience. As the founder of First Personality, a leading organization providing leadership development and training solutions across India and globally, Prashant has been dedicated to transforming thousands of individuals and organizations by unlocking their potential.

In his career spanning almost three decades, life as a corporate executive and entrepreneur has been a great teacher, and Prashant is determined to share this teaching with everyone who comes into contact with him. He has seen life up close and personal. Through downs in business and life and struggles. And Thrived!

Prashant conducted his first training program in 1996 when he was invited by the New Delhi YMCA to lead a course in Public Speaking & Effective Communication. The Times of India, too, has recognized this achievement.

Prashant is a First Prize Diploma holder in Public Speaking from the Nazareth's Speakers Academy, Mumbai, and a B.Com from the Sydenham College, Mumbai. Upon completion of his Master's in Management from the University of Massachusetts, USA, he returned to India to be part of the Indian post-liberalization story. He has co-founded two successful start-ups. One of his companies was among the first to introduce barcoding in India, in the pre-Internet era. In his other venture, a design and export business, he employed nearly 200 people at its peak.

His first job was with the TATA group in Taj Group of Hotels as Duty Manager, which made him realize the disparity between the soft skills of the average Indian vis-a-vis the people in the West. Prashant rightly predicted that this lack of soft skills would be a great hindrance to the employability of our Indian graduates and founded his Personality Development training start-up. He has been an entrepreneur with international exposure to diverse verticals, greatly adding to his knowledge and expertise. This entrepreneurial experience has helped him sharpen his sales and marketing instincts. Prashant brings over 28 years of

expertise in designing and delivering impactful leadership development programs. His dynamic approach integrates innovative training methodologies, strategic coaching, and comprehensive program management to drive tangible results.

Prashant develops and delivers his own content. His trainings are based entirely out of his extensive real world professional experience backed by solid management concepts. His programs are based on his in-house developed Learning-Internalization-Feedback-Evaluation (LIFE) Model.

Prashant has worked with some of the world's leading corporations. He has coached and trained thousands of professionals, offering bespoke solutions for complex business challenges.

His clients are based worldwide, and this enables him to incorporate global best practices in his sessions.

He has over 2500 hours of Executive consulting and Business coaching with senior corporates and entrepreneurs across verticals to enable them get the visibility, recognition and growth that they deserve. He has deep Experience in Training and Facilitating diverse cohorts: College Graduates to First Time Managers to Lateral and Mid-Managers level, right upto CXO level Consulting and coaching.

Prashant is a storyteller. His effortless and engaging style, peppered with real life personal experiences of different people and different cultures, makes his delivery different from others. He has actually experienced everything he talks about, and that's what attracts others towards him for mentorship.

Prashant is a regular guest panellist in top leadership and HR forums such as Times Ascent.

In 2013, Prashant was nominated by the Govt. of India to train UPSC-qualified IAS/IFS/IPS Services Officer Trainees in Soft Skills. He is also on the visiting faculty panel of Premier Govt. training institutions like INGAF (Min of Finance), SBI Training Academy, etc.

He conducts training programs in all formats: Online, In-person as well as Outbound.

Prashant says: ***"Experience Life! Experience hardship. Letdowns and challenges build resilience. Diverse interests increase your luck surface area. This is the growth mindset of good professionals and great leaders."***

Acknowledgement

This book is the result of the support, constructive advice, and good wishes of several individuals. I would like to extend my heartfelt thanks here.

To my parents Wng. Cdr. O.D Sharma, a self-made towering personality, and Sudesh Sharma, the best learner I know. For their unwavering support in more ways than I can count. Their tremendous faith in me has been a constant in my life. They have given me the values that shaped my personality and, in turn, enabled me to influence others positively. They have allowed me to live the life that I chose, to carve my own path and made me safe in the assurance that I would always have their support.

To my wife Bhavna, who has literally been the wind beneath my wings. Her brilliant psychology-related inputs and perspective on life have made a huge difference in the quality of my training and writing. Putting up with an entrepreneur's timings and erratic lifestyle is not easy, and for that, I am grateful to her. She keeps egging me on, like a marathoner nearing the finishing line, and for her motivation, patience, perseverance, and steady belief in my abilities. And for her finally understanding that the weekly off is not quite that!

To my children, whose innocence has provided valuable insights into the potential of the human mind.

To Manoj Sharma for his guidance and encouragement. A special mention to Gaurav Mishra, Asit Sait, and Ajay Kadyan, and all my other friends and family for providing me with the rocket start to my training career.

For my clients and the participants of my trainings, all brilliant professionals and human beings, whose feedback and enthusiasm have been the fuel that drives my training wagon.

I also thank the Publisher and the whole staff at BPB Publications for supporting this book through its journey across multiple editions. Especially Mr. Manish Jain and Varun Jain for making sure the book took the shape that I had envisioned for it.

And finally, to the Almighty for giving me the wisdom to share knowledge and ignite the spark.

Preface

We have transitioned from the information age through the influencing age to the intelligence age. From Volatile-Uncertain-Complex-Ambiguous (VUCA) to Brittle-Anxious-Non Linear-Incomprehensible (BANI), the world is constantly changing. This is a unique period in the working world when different generations are working together. Gen-X, Millennials, Gen-Z, and soon Gen-Alpha, bringing cultural challenges. Dealing with these differences is a major challenge for the leader in this AI age.

Over-reliance on AI has made us lazy, even unethical. When robots can brush your teeth and agents can represent you at your own birthday party, how can a book help? As AI becomes ubiquitous in our lives, it becomes critical to ask: Are soft skills really necessary? Who needs dictionaries or paid apps? Is there any point in learning about any other culture or language when there is GenAI? Who needs Google when Perplexity can be your personal valet? Why bother reading when an AI LLM tool can create a 10-minute audio and video podcast of a 200-page company report or thick textbook?

These are all pertinent questions. The answer in a nutshell:

AI might give us efficiency, but empathy and personal connection will be humans' differentiator. Technology might help us translate text, but only humans can translate feelings.

Feelings are central to the building of emotional quotient. People with people skills will be required to provide context to the data that AI generates.

That is where this book becomes relevant. This book is a result of experiences and a demonstration of how experiences help. AI spits out cookie-cutter, generic answers. These responses might not be relevant to you or your life. That is where the personal coaching that this book provides helps. A coach who can provide personal experience. Learning from another's experience can help you save time, money, and effort.

Are people with dynamic and brilliant personalities born with these people skills, or can we all acquire the soft skills required to build a commanding personality? The answer is that, given high-quality training and practice with a professional, we all can acquire important soft skills to succeed in life. Through this book, the author, who is a soft skills training expert, shares his over three decades

of industry and corporate coaching and training experience to help the reader attain these soft skills in an accelerated time frame.

With AI becoming the go-to source of information and data generation, it is essential to be cognizant of using AI tools appropriately. A new chapter on using AI for powerful communication has been added to give the reader a guide to using AI to enhance their communication and language skills.

This book also introduces the reader to the all-important art of storytelling, specifically performance storytelling; the art of promoting yourself and your skills. When there are multiple candidates for fewer vacancies, candidates have to hard sell themselves. Storytelling helps people, especially introverts or those with shy personalities, who find it difficult to talk about their achievements. Using AI for communication and performance storytelling helps highly skilled people with sharp technical skills who do not get recognition and visibility due to their inability to promote themselves.

As WFH becomes the norm, building a strong online presence has become a necessity. Remote work has become normal, and remote teams meet online, in informal locations where it is challenging to maintain meeting formality. Whereas virtual meetings used to be a small percentage and mostly optional, these are common now. In such a scenario, it becomes essential to build online presence skills. The chapter on building a high-impact online presence has been added to give the reader a competitive advantage in this new virtual online space.

Living as we are in an intensely competitive environment where Performance = Power, the ability to communicate effectively and work cohesively has become a necessity. With AI creating job disruptions and such a huge amount of young people competing for limited jobs, the need to rise above one's peers is crucial. Competition is a way of life! Soft skills help a person become successful. They are the vital difference between success and failure.

The foundation of personality development is good people skills. If you are able to communicate well with anyone, anywhere, anytime, without fear or hesitation, you can influence other people. This is nothing but leadership, the most sought-after soft skill.

Students have a good theoretical knowledge base and learn from sound academic textbooks and teachers. However, only a select few students are truly employable and job-ready when they finish their education. While they have a lot of technical knowledge, when it comes to taking initiative or showing leadership, a majority of our students are found wanting. Lack of employability skills, specifically soft skills, is the single biggest headache for recruiters today.

Start-up entrepreneurs and seasoned business people alike find themselves struggling to make an impact on prospective clients, even though they have the best products and services.

Working executives go through the corporate grind, struggling for visibility, recognition, and growth.

And the common factor in every situation? Lack of soft skills!

The increased focus of the media and the internet in our lives has ensured that every person has access to the same information. In such a scenario, how does one get ahead? The answer lies in the development of effective soft skills as demonstrated below:

Better Soft Skills and Communication Skills
↓
Self-Confidence
↓
Influence over other People
↓
Leadership Skills
↓
Success (Professional & Inter-Personal)

Most individuals find out through bitter struggle and hardship that real-world experiences are different from their academic experiences. Students, especially those coming from vernacular or non-English backgrounds, struggle in the absence of mentorship and guidance from Industry professionals.

This book aims to be the professional guide, coach, and mentor to all those who want to upgrade their soft skills to get a head-start in their careers. The author wishes that the present generation should not wait to graduate and begin their professional journey to learn these skills. This book is designed to give all individuals the all-important personality development soft skills required by them to become successful and powerful personalities.

Written by an experienced corporate and industry professional and soft skills trainer who has been an executive, entrepreneur, coach, and master facilitator for 30 years, this book has been designed to be a bridge between academic curriculum education and the industry.

Effective communication and personal development training concepts given in this book impart knowledge that is geared towards enhancing their soft skills and enabling them to develop a co-operative mindset.

Through this book, anyone wishing to develop powerful personalities will be able to have lucrative career choices and attain life success. They will develop well-rounded personalities; attain self-confidence and an ability to successfully overcome any challenge that life throws at them.

Chapter 1: Introduction to Soft Skills - This chapter explains why soft skills are critical for both personal development and professional success in today's fast-changing world. It provides the connection between personality development and soft skills, clearly differentiating them from hard or technical skills. The chapter bridges the gap between campus learning and corporate expectations by highlighting real industry needs. Readers are introduced to the most essential soft skills required for life success, along with practical ways to develop them. A global perspective, case study, reflective questions, applied exercises, and vocabulary-building tools ensure learning is practical, relevant, and actionable.

Chapter 2: Emotional Intelligence - This chapter looks at how emotions influence our day-to-day choices, actions, and reactions, and inter-personal relationships. It explains why EQ often wins over IQ to navigate real-life challenges and conflicts. The reader is guided to see self-awareness and emotion management as best practices that can be developed with practice, not a fixed trait. The role of empathy and social skills in building trust, motivation, and cooperation is explored through everyday situations. By the end of the chapter, readers gain deeper Insight into what it truly means to act with emotional maturity.

Chapter 3: Self-image Management - This chapter focuses on how first impressions and perceptions about people are formed long before they speak or act. It explores practical ways to strengthen self-belief and project confidence in everyday interactions. Readers are guided to reflect on their strengths and limitations to create a powerful Personal Brand. The idea of Leadership Presence is highlighted to show how credibility, composure, and influence are built over time, both offline and online. The chapter also emphasizes the role of language, expression, and online visibility in creating a lasting professional impression.

Chapter 4: Building High-performance Teams - This chapter explains how people work better when they function as a team rather than as individuals. It helps the reader understand the importance of collaboration, cooperation, and coordination. The chapter shows how teamwork and trust can lead to better results in studies, work, and relationships. It also explains how disagreements can

be handled calmly instead of turning into arguments. Finally, readers learn how basic negotiation skills can help them reach win-win solutions while maintaining healthy relationships.

Chapter 5: Time Management and Goal Setting - This chapter helps understand how to use time more wisely instead of constantly feeling rushed or stressed. It explains why time often feels scarce and how small daily habits can either help or hold us back. Readers learn practical ways to overcome procrastination and stay focused on important tasks. The chapter shows how clear goals can turn hard work into real progress. One gains valuable tools to effectively balance work, studies, personal time, and leisure.

Chapter 6: High-Impact Communication Skills - This chapter introduces communication frameworks as everyday habits that affect how we work and connect with others. It explains how and why miscommunication takes place and strategies to avoid the same. sometimes misunderstood. Readers learn how small changes can make virtual and physical conversations clearer. The chapter offers practical tips to improve speaking, listening, and writing skills. It also highlights basic rules that help messages sound respectful in tone. Attention is given to communicating with people from different cultures and backgrounds. The chapter also helps readers recognize common Indian expressions that may cause confusion and how to express ideas more clearly.

Chapter 7: Communication in the AI Age - This chapter introduces powerful insights into using AI as a helpful support in everyday communication. It explains how AI can assist in composing messages that are clear, confident, and easy to understand. Readers learn the importance of using AI responsibly, with honesty and ethics. The chapter presents AI as a practice coach that can help improve communication skills. It also shows how AI can be used to prepare for crucial conversations and meetings and help frame prompts to respond more politely to others. Readers learn how technology can support better listening and relationship-building.

Chapter 8: Presentation Skills and Public Speaking - This chapter introduces the fundamentals of speaking without hesitation in any situation, with clarity and confidence. It helps the reader overcome common fears related to public speaking and provides practical ways to manage them. Readers learn how to prepare content that is well-structured and easy to follow. The chapter explains how careful preparation improves both delivery and impact. The reader also learns how platform presence and body language influence how the presentations are

received. Presentation frameworks are shared to help plan and deliver technical data in a manner that leaves a strong and positive impression.

Chapter 9: Non-Verbal Communication - This chapter helps students understand how messages can be effectively communicated without words and through actions. It explains the importance of non-verbal cues such as posture, facial expressions, and gestures in everyday communication. Readers are introduced to subtle elements like silence and personal space, which often speak louder than words. The chapter shows how mindful body language can strengthen confidence and clarity. Equal importance is given to Active listening as a relationship-building, empathetic skill. The reader learns how paying attention improves understanding and reduces conflict.

Chapter 10: Building Online Presence - This chapter focuses on communicating effectively in virtual and online settings. It helps readers understand how to remain visible and recognized while working remotely. The chapter explains how to create a strong first impression during online interviews, meetings, and presentations. Readers learn how executive presence and personal branding translate to the digital space. Practical guidance is shared on appearing confident and natural on camera. The chapter also covers planning and delivering engaging online presentations and pitches.

Chapter 11: High Performance Leadership - This chapter explains leadership as a quality that can be practiced in everyday life, not just through fancy titles. It encourages readers to notice leadership traits in people around them and learn from their actions. The chapter explores how effective leaders motivate and influence others through behavior and attitude. Readers are guided to develop professionalism as a showcase for their skills and abilities. The chapter also highlights what it takes to perform consistently well in academic and work settings. Creative thinking is introduced as a skill that helps individuals stand-out and solve problems.

Chapter 12: Meeting and Business Writing - This chapter introduces the core principles of effective written communication used both in academic and professional settings. It helps readers understand how clear language improves understanding and credibility. The chapter focuses on building strong writing skills for everyday business communication. Readers learn the basics of correct and professional English usage. Practical guidance is provided on writing emails that are clear, polite, and outcome-focused. Insights are provided on how thoughtful communication creates a positive impression in meetings and important conversations.

Chapter 13: Etiquette and Grooming Habits - This chapter introduces etiquette and manners as everyday habits that shape how we are perceived positively by others. It explains why respectful behavior is important in academic, social, and professional settings. Readers learn how good manners build confidence and create positive relationships. The chapter offers practical guidance on developing polite and considerate behavior in daily life. Attention is also given to personal hygiene, appearance, and grooming as part of self-respect and professionalism leading to success. Readers understand how good etiquette supports a positive first impression.

Chapter 14: Resume Writing and Job Applications - This chapter helps the reader understand why a well-prepared resume plays an important role in career opportunities. It explains the importance of a Resume to convey one's skills clear and practical manner. Readers learn how to present their knowledge, education, and experiences in a structured and effective way. The chapter highlights common mistakes to avoid while preparing resumes. Guidance is also provided on writing clear and polite covering letters and job applications. Students are introduced to using AI tools appropriately to improve clarity and presentation.

Chapter 15: Personal Interview and Group Discussions - This chapter prepares the reader to approach job interviews with confidence and clarity. It explains what interviewers generally observe while assessing candidates. Readers are guided through a time-tested checklist to help them prepare systematically. The chapter introduces common types of interview questions and how to respond appropriately. Attention is given to proper interview preparation, etiquette, and professional conduct. Practice exercises and role-play activities help readers apply what they learn. The chapter also offers guidance on participating effectively in group discussions.

Chapter 16: Performance Storytelling and The Art of Promoting Yourself - This chapter introduces performance storytelling as a way to present one's skills with clarity and confidence. It helps readers learn how to speak about their achievements without exaggeration or discomfort. The chapter provides neuromarketing: psychology-based insights into how people naturally respond to stories and well-structured messages. Readers gain insight into how decision-makers notice, remember, and evaluate you and your pitches. Attention is given to matching personal strengths with current industry expectations.

Coloured Images

Please follow the link to download the
Coloured Images of the book:

https://rebrand.ly/0c9e4f

We have code bundles from our rich catalogue of books and videos available at **https://github.com/bpbpublications**. Check them out!

Errata

We take immense pride in our work at BPB Publications and follow best practices to ensure the accuracy of our content to provide an indulging reading experience to our subscribers. Our readers are our mirrors, and we use their inputs to reflect and improve upon human errors, if any, that may have occurred during the publishing processes involved. To let us maintain the quality and help us reach out to any readers who might be having difficulties due to any unforeseen errors, please write to us at:
errata@bpbonline.com

Your support, suggestions and feedback are highly appreciated by the BPB Publications' Family.

Piracy

If you come across any illegal copies of our works in any form on the internet, we would be grateful if you would provide us with the location address or website name. Please contact us at **business@bpbonline.com** with a link to the material.

If you are interested in becoming an author

If there is a topic that you have expertise in, and you are interested in either writing or contributing to a book, please visit **www.bpbonline.com**. We have worked with thousands of developers and tech professionals, just like you, to help them share their insights with the global tech community. You can make a general application, apply for a specific hot topic that we are recruiting an author for, or submit your own idea.

Reviews

Please leave a review. Once you have read and used this book, why not leave a review on the site that you purchased it from? Potential readers can then see and use your unbiased opinion to make purchase decisions. We at BPB can understand what you think about our products, and our authors can see your feedback on their book. Thank you!

For more information about BPB, please visit **www.bpbonline.com**.

Join our Discord space

Join our Discord workspace for latest updates, offers, tech happenings around the world, new releases, and sessions with the authors:

https://discord.bpbonline.com

Table of Contents

Chapter 1 Introduction to Soft Skills

Power Skills for Success in the AI age

LEARNING MILESTONES

This chapter will enable you to:

- Appreciate the need for developing your soft skills in the AI era
- Develop soft skills for working effectively with changing demographics
- Recognize that personality development equals soft skills
- Differentiate between soft skills and hard skills
- Master the soft skills for better employability and success
- Explore the first steps to acquire soft skills
- Learn new business phrases and build your vocabulary

Expert Quotes

"The best Communicators use AI as a Partner...not a Replacement."

1.1 Importance of soft skills in the AI age

Case in Point

You are creating a slide deck for an upcoming very important presentation. Google, ChatGPT, or other LLMs are open on different screens. It's all coming together beautifully.

The day of the presentation arrives. You begin. You are in full flow. You present the figures and data with pride. Slide after slide of complex numbers wrapped in beautiful graphs, infographics, and visuals, so wonderfully prepared by AI tools.

But it's not landing! You can see that there is no impact!

The first person closest to you takes out her phone to check something.

Someone in the back yawns.

The senior stakeholder, who was leaning forward, now leans back and rubs her eyes. You panic.

And that's when you remember what's missing.

A story to put the figures in context. You tell them of a time when you experienced the problem that your presentation is attempting to solve.

Someone says: Yeah...happened to me too.

The audience is back!

You end with a bang.

Commitments are made to meet again next week to review your proposal.

So what just happened here?

When there was dependence only on the AI tools to make the presentation, the machine processed your data. But that did not touch the audience. It was a bland dish without taste. Your story added the missing ingredient. And you yourself thought of it. You thought on your feet! Using your experience, your knowledge. Your exposure. Your ability to pivot to the changed environment.

These are the crucial soft skills that elevated your presentation from boring to great!

This is the reason why soft skills are more important now than ever.

In this AI age, the ability to probe, to ask the right question to guide the AI to arrive at the right answer, will be our key differentiator. The availability of AI by itself does not provide a competitive advantage. It's the use of soft skills to drive AI that will provide the competitive advantage. AI will only deliver the information. Our soft skills will help us arrive at Key Insights to arrive at accurate, reliable, and ethical solutions.

OpenAI CEO Sam Altman recently said: "...determining the right questions to pose will surpass the importance of just finding the answers". If the key to finding the answer is available to everyone, then the only 2 things separating us from the machine are curiosity and critical thinking: key soft skills. Asking the right question or prompt, Engineering becomes as critical as the race to the answer, as the wrong question can lead to ethical, compliance, and wrong paths.

Till now, software coding has been a factor in the instructions we give to the computer. With generative AI, it's the same principle except now the language will be your language skills, whether English or any other language that you speak.

1.2 Developing soft skills to work effectively with changing demographics

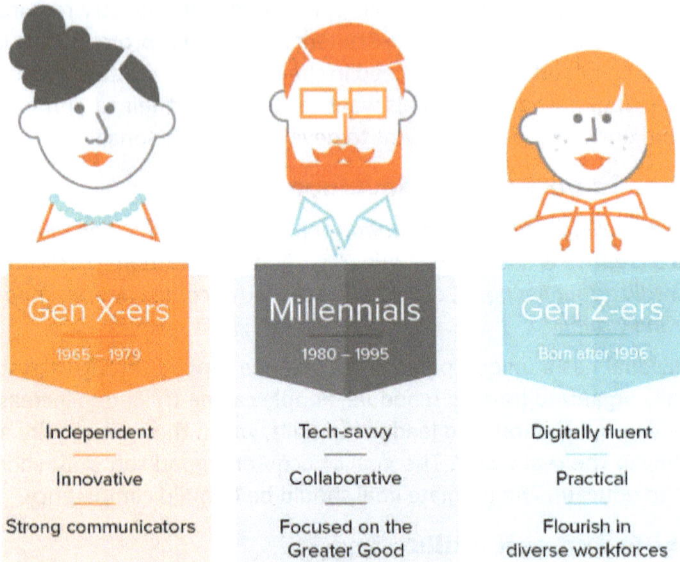

***Figure 1.1**: How generations redefine the workplace*

Do you know of a person who changes their job every 11 months? Or prefers to text rather than take your call? Or how about that senior manager who insists on working from the office rather than WFH?

This is a unique time in history when different generations are working together in the same workplace: There are Gen-X professionals in their late forties and early fifties. There are millennials in the age group of 30-45. Then the Gen Z age 22-30. And the Gen Alpha who are in high school and junior college now are about to enter the workforce.

Every generation brings with it its own mindset, experiences, and way of life. More than socio-economic differences, generational shifts have gained more importance in setting professional culture and behavior rules.

For e.g., the much misunderstood and aligned Gen-Z is often stereotyped in a certain way. There is often a clash of cultures across generations and age groups that causes conflict.

None of this is intentional. It's just the way it is.

Considering these generational differences, it becomes even more important to navigate the quirks and qualities of different generations.

Good soft skills involve respecting and working with differences. Not just tolerating it. Soft skills enable us to enhance our people skills to work effectively with different generations. To leverage the strengths, the knowledge, and experience of each generation is the essence of good people skills.

1.3 Personality development, meta skills, and soft skills

Due to the disconnect of the academic curriculum with industry requirements, it is a fact that a majority of college students and young professionals lack the communication or soft skills to succeed in the Real World. At the same time, it is also a fact that almost all individuals want to succeed in their careers and lead a fulfilling and enriching life. They want to develop their personalities!

What then is personality development?

Personality development means enhancing soft skills, which enables you to develop a creative & cooperative mindset, choose and attain a career of your choice, realize your life goals, and finally help you become a well-rounded and popular individual.

Every individual has a unique persona that can be tapped through a systematic and logically organized training schedule. People can be trained to increase their grooming, communication, and leadership skills, which they can acquire and use immediately in the real world. The goal of acquiring good soft skills should not simply be to educate. The ultimate goal should be to build competency.

Meta skills and soft skills

One would do well to acquire meta skills and soft skills.

Meta-skills are overarching abilities that support the development of other soft skills and are particularly crucial for team performance. As technology evolves, specific job skills change, but meta-skills like self-awareness, emotional intelligence, and communication skills remain valuable because they make individuals versatile and help develop a growth mindset.

These meta skills are the foundation for Soft Skills that enable us to acquire leadership skills and communicate better. People develop better inter-personal skills, which have a positive effect on their personality.

Those equipped with meta skills have powerful personalities and are generally perceived to be more knowledgeable and well-informed than others. They radiate self-confidence and a positive mental attitude. They are able to see the positive aspects of life and view problems as opportunities. They view the glass as half-full rather than half-empty.

***Figure 1.2**: Your outlook shapes your outcome*

They live an enriching life and finally build a successful career.

The positive mental attitude that students attain by developing their communication skills gives them the confidence to not just become better communicators but also better human beings.

1.4 Soft skills v/s hard skills

"Having hard skills gets you hired. Lacking soft skills gets you fired."

Jaspree Bindra, the founder of AI & Beyond, says: "Many of our core assumptions around our knowledge, education, and skills will need to change, as we become co-creators with AI and orchestrators of AI agents. For one, the questions we ask will become far more important than the answers we give."

If ChatGPT can give us all the answers, then the solution becomes a commodity, something accessible to everyone. In this situation, our ability to think critically and frame the right prompts becomes more critical than our hard skills.

Hard Skills are the technical skills acquired through formal education or on-the-job experience.

However, research done by Harvard University shows that 85% of job success comes from having well-developed soft skills, while only 15% of success is based on technical skills. In other words, most students and professionals spend only 15% of their lives trying to acquire skills that account for 85% of their success! That, in a nutshell, exposes the lack of preparedness of individuals in their soft skills. Students spend their entire education learning by rote, without any idea of applied knowledge, to acquire technical skills. It is essential that the technical education imparted in the college should be given a corporate and industry-oriented perspective.

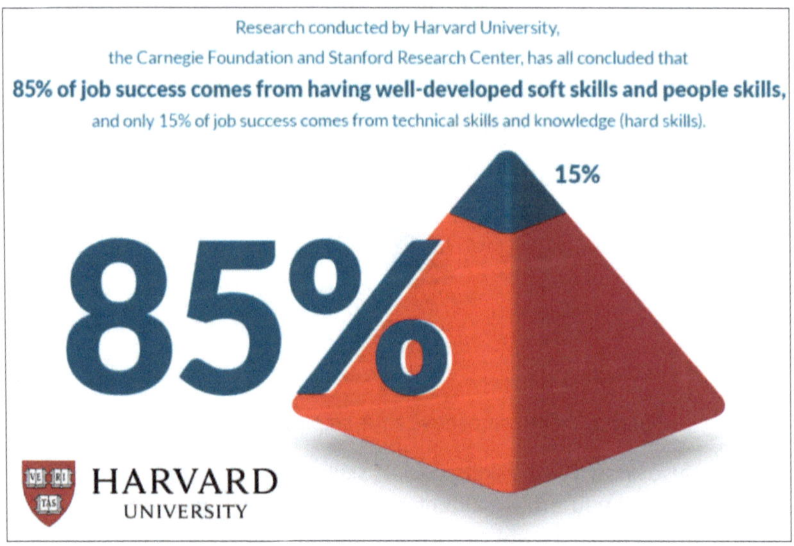

***Figure 1.3**: Hard skills get you hired. Soft skills get you promoted*

1.5 Industry need: from campus to corporate

Industry leaders and corporate experts all agree on one thing: that Lack of `employability' skills in job applicants is the single biggest headache for recruiters today. The time and budget spent on training are only shrinking, and companies now want to hire candidates who can hit the ground running and perform from Day 1!

According to a survey report by *Wheel box: `India Skills Report 2025'*, India's national employability rate stands at 54.81%.

Summary of in-demand skills

This year's survey results reflect a clear trend toward prioritizing foundational soft skills like ethics, collaboration, and problem-solving, alongside key competencies like digital literacy, management, and cognitive skills. As the workforce continues to evolve, employers are increasingly looking for well-rounded candidates who can adapt to change, communicate effectively, and contribute to the overall success of their teams and organizations.

In-demand skills are no longer confined to technical expertise alone, with a strong focus on emotional intelligence, self-efficacy, and leadership abilities across industries.

SOURCE: WHEEL BOX: INDIA SKILLS REPORT 2025: *Unlocking Indian skills for the world*

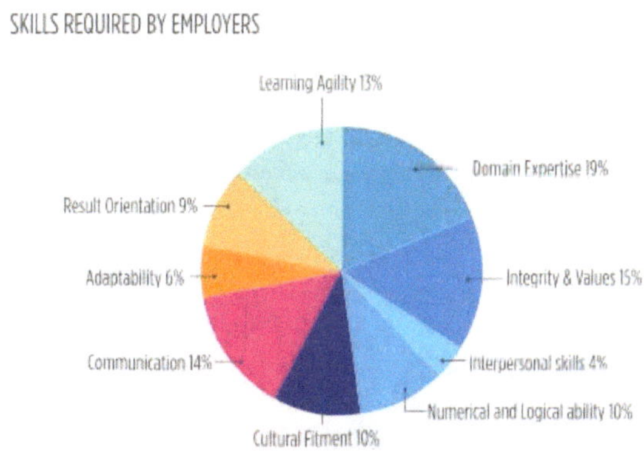

***Figure 1.4**: The competitive edge employers value most*

Soft skills are also known as life skills, people skills, or relationship skills. Whatever the name, whether you are a student or a professional, it is almost essential that you have to communicate or interact in public at some point or another. Whether it is presenting your project work, interacting with your bosses, clients,

or teachers, appearing for group discussions or job interviews, or excelling in the real world, people from all streams need the all-important `soft skills'.

1.5.1 The most important soft skills required for life success

We all want to develop our personalities. But which aspect of personality should we focus on? The answer lies in a holistic development covering the four pillars of human development. These four pillars are:

a. Physical,
b. Mental,
c. Spiritual,
d. Emotional.

A good personal development program is a 360-degree learning program that helps an individual to become happy, confident, and eager to face the challenges of daily life with a Smile! People with dynamic personalities are able to thrive in an atmosphere of discussion and debate on a variety of subjects, which helps them to speak more confidently on a wide range of subjects.

While there are innumerable soft skills, the book has highlighted only those soft skills that corporate experts, business leaders, entrepreneurs, and leading management thinkers have thought as crucial to Professional and personal success.

Mastery of these soft skills, as detailed in the book, will lead to personality enhancement.

Graphical Representation of these all-important Soft Skills:

***Figure 1.5**: Your personal development compass*

1.6 The first step towards soft skills:

Lao Tzu said: "The journey of a thousand miles begins with a small step."

People from all vocations and all professions should aim to develop their soft skills. Doctors should display empathy and kindness in dealing with sick patients, irrespective of their workload. Lawyers need to develop the ability to be non-judgmental and display a lack of prejudice when dealing with their clients. Engineers and other people employed in technical fields must develop the ability to look beyond their numerical ability, tools, and systems, and develop interpersonal skills and the ability to get along with others. Those employed in the service industry need to display positive body language, perfect etiquette, and professionalism. Students should become better listeners and develop relationship skills with their peers, teachers, and parents. Even homemakers need soft skills to maintain an atmosphere of peace and harmony in their households.

Figure 1.6*: The need for soft skills*

However, the fact remains that acquiring soft skills is not easy. It is not an event that takes place all of a sudden. It is not a pill or medicine that one can take. Instead, acquiring soft skills is an ongoing process of self-improvement and self-management. Our education system has drilled into us the ability to work within a structured system. However, in the real world, the ability to think out of the box is crucial for success.

So, let's begin the process of developing soft skills without delay! **The first step is the hardest.**

Based on the author's long corporate and business experience, here are the first steps to acquire soft skills. The book will elaborate on the most crucial soft skills that the reader should study to develop a powerful personality:

- **Read:** Reading newspapers, blogs, articles, and books. Don't just think of reading as a simple act of reading. Treat reading as if you are having a cup of tea with an expert. And that expert (the author) is giving you all the wealth of experience in a short time and helping you to avoid costly mistakes.

***Figure 1.7**: Learning is lifelong, location is irrelevant*

- **Observe:** learn from others' experiences. Don't repeat their mistakes.
- **Write:** Write down anything that inspires you. A habit, a gesture, an act that you observe in another person on social media, or in a movie, YouTube, TikTok, real life, just about anywhere.
- **Listen:** to podcasts, to others, especially mentors or more experienced people. Listening involves not just one's ears, but one needs to listen with one's entire mind.
- **Appreciate others:** Complement them on their achievements. Appreciate life and its gifts. Be thankful for the present and hopeful for the future.
- **Growth mindset:** Don't just think, act now! Learn and Adapt! Take the plunge and fight your inner demons. Conquer your fears.
- **Speak:** to an expert about any issue or problem in your life. Learn to be more open about your feelings and share your thoughts, and in return, you will receive a wealth of information from others.
- **Internalize soft skills:** The soft skills so acquired should become part of your basic nature. You should act, appear, and practice the habits so acquired. These should not appear artificial, else you will be called a `fake'.
- **Train yourself in soft skills:** For example, if you are scared of public speaking, take a professional course. Explore online programs if distance or cost is an issue. Steven Covey, in his book 'The 7 Habits of Highly Effective People,' talks about acquiring a habit: `Sharpen the Saw. ' This means keeping your skills active by constant training and staying ahead of the curve. The training needs to be an iterative process, which means that through continuous contact programs and re-training sessions, the learning remains fresh and relevant.

Remember: Soft skills are not inborn! Soft Skills can be acquired by training combined with Practice.

1.6.1 Global Perspective

India's strong IT/ITES backbone gives it an advantage in adopting digital communication. And taking advantage of this, many partnerships and business models are being developed both by the public sector and the private sector to develop India's soft skills potential.

The **SANKALP (Skill Acquisition and Knowledge Awareness for Livelihood Promotion Programme)** aims at providing job-ready training to 350 million Indians. Apart from this, the government would set up 100 India International Skills Centers that will conduct advanced courses in foreign languages to help youngsters prepare for overseas jobs.

There are many other such initiatives in the pipeline. Visit the Skill India website for more details, or visit a skill development center in your area to see how you can upgrade your skills.

Soft skills form the backbone of these initiatives, with the partners to encourage them to develop soft skills along with technical skills.

However, we cannot wait for the benefits to trickle down the channel. The responsibility for developing soft skills remains with the individual.

1.7. Summary

It's a very competitive world out there, and only the truly motivated and driven individuals will be able to get ahead of the pack and beat the competition. This is because when it comes to choosing between two equally technically qualified individuals, soft skills are the differentiating factor between success and failure.

Soft skills are the backbone of life success.

Without soft skills, personality development is not possible. The book demonstrates how the reader can acquire Soft Skills to overcome setbacks, challenges, and economic headwinds with determination and courage. How can even a person with limited exposure and limited means become the personality that everyone looks at and says Wow!

Whether you realize it or not, your mind has a secret invisible board. On one side are the letters **PMA** (**Positive Mental Attitude**), and on the other are the letters **NMA** (**Negative Mental Attitude**). Soft skills help us to focus on our strengths, the positives, and work on eliminating the negatives.

Soft Skills give rise to a positive attitude that naturally attracts the good and the beautiful.

Your success, health, happiness, and wealth depend on how you use soft skills and develop a strong and impactful personality!

Business is not just done B-to-B or B-to-C. Professional success results from P-to-P (People to People)

Knowledge Check:

1. What is the difference between Hard Skills and Soft Skills?
2. How can Soft skills increase employability in the era of Artificial intelligence?
3. What is the Industry requirement for Soft Skills?
4. List the three Verticals of key soft skills with two examples of each.
5. What are the ways in which soft skills can be learnt?

Additional resources for self-development

Resource blog on soft skills: http://www.coachprashant.com

Case in Point

"You are a failure! You will never succeed in life," shouted Sudhir's father! "Get out of my house!" His mother pleaded with her husband to be soft on their only son, but he wouldn't have any of it. "I never want to see your face again."

Sudhir hung his head in shame and sobbed silently. Realizing that his father would not relent this time, he picked up his bag and left the house with his mother sobbing behind him. Not having anywhere to go, he went and sat in the nearby bus stand when a car stopped by. It was Rahul, his close friend, a rising star in his MNC job.

Rahul, an IIM-A graduate, asked him: "Hey, long time no see, my friend! Where have you been?" Sudhir tried to hide his face, but Rahul insisted that he sit in the car.

"What happened?" he asked.

Sudhir said, "My father caught me drinking during the day again. I was fired from my job due to my alcohol problem, and I was depressed. I was never successful at what I did in life, and look where it has brought me. I don't have a future. Whatever, I have tried my hand at business, work, and relationships, and I have been a failure. I don't know what I should do. The future looks so bleak."

Rahul said: "Success? Do you know what success is? Just because you experienced some failure early in your life, you got scared. You ran away from adversity and failure. You couldn't accept challenges. That's why you are in this state. You know I can tell you so many things about success if you will listen."

"Surely," said Sudhir, "I want to know."

Rahul said. "Let me tell you about successful people:

1. They are strong technically. But they are also stronger in their `Soft skills.'
2. They give the best to whatever they do. Successful people don't make excuses and keep learning from their mistakes.

3. They don't make shortcuts. They put in a lot of hard work and effort.
4. They do smart work more than hard work. They think creatively. Think with your head, not with your hands. Rickshaw pullers use their hands. You have been hired to use your brains. Think!
5. Remarkably successful people habitually do what other people won't do. They go where others won't go because there's a lot less competition and a much greater chance for success.
6. Average success is often based on setting average goals. Don't be average! Set your goals high and work backwards from that.
7. Character: Successful people follow their moral compass and do what is right.
8. Vision: People who are successful have the ability to think beyond the tip of their nose. They bear short-term pain for long-term gain.
9. Persistence: When the going gets tough, the tough get going. No slacking, no sitting. Only hardcore action is the mantra for successful people.
10. Learn from their mistakes. Only a fool makes the same mistake twice.
11. Mentor and teach others. Successful people believe in setting systems, sharing knowledge, and learning from others.

Seven habits of highly successful people

"That's all fine," said Sudhir. "But what about at work? How do I get successful at work? I never seem to hold on to a job. I don't seem to have a goal in mind. Look at you! We started our careers together, but look where you have reached. I feel like a loser."

Rahul said: "There are seven habits of highly effective people, especially helpful for one's corporate career.

The Seven Habits (excerpts from The Seven Habits of Highly Effective People, Dr. Steven Covey):

1. **Be proactive.** I recommend an attitude of taking charge and taking action instead of thinking.
2. **Begin with the end in mind.** Covey recommends formulating a "personal mission statement" to document one's perception of one's own purpose in life.
3. **Put first things first;** Prioritizing work that is aimed at long-term goals, at the expense of tasks that appear to be urgent, but are in fact less important. Delegation is presented as an important part of time management.

4. **Think Win/Win** describes an attitude whereby mutually beneficial solutions are sought, that satisfy the needs of oneself as well as others, or, in the case of a conflict, both parties involved.
5. **Seek First to understand, then to be understood**. Thoroughly listening to another person's concerns instead of reading out your own autobiography results in increasing the chance of establishing a working communication.
6. **Synergize** describes a way of working in teams.
7. **Sharpen the saw** focuses on balanced self-renewal. Joining a training program like those conducted by First Personality can easily keep your body and mind active.

Asking the right questions

Rahul continued: "Why can't I get a job?" "Why am I always so broke?" "Why can't I have better relationships?" These seemingly valid questions can cause difficulties in your life and your success. If you want to get a job, make more money, lose weight, or achieve any other worthwhile goal, it's time you start asking better questions.

A much more effective strategy is to ask **solution-focused questions**. Instead of "Why can't I get a job?", the following are much better questions because they lead directly to solutions:

- What can I do to make a positive and lasting impression during my next interview?
- What would I have to do to get a job in the next 30 days?
- How can I become more qualified than any of the other candidates?
- What other skills do I have that I can emphasize that will make up for my lack of experience?
- What five things can I do to stand out from the 100 other applicants?

Can you see how asking these kinds of questions will lead to dramatically different answers and results?

Figure 1.8: *The foundation of success is self-belief*

Asking "What can I do to get a job?" versus "Why can't I get a job?" isn't just a play on words or the latest pop-psychology trick. It's an effective strategy to solve a problem because when you start asking **solution-focused questions**, you tend to start finding solutions.

Successful people ask solution-focused questions. You too must do the same, Sudhir!"

Rahul said, "I know whatever I am saying, you will forget very soon. I will tell you one trick to remind you of the solutions and things we have discussed today.

Trick: Wear a rubber band on your wrist. Every time you ask a problem-focused question, give yourself a snap and rephrase the question. It might take a few days or even weeks to break the habit, but before long, I guarantee that you will have a bruised wrist and a lot fewer problems."

"Wow", said Sudhir, "I will do this immediately! I feel good already. I am going home, and apologize to my parents. Then I am going to call my old boss and request him to give me one more chance."

"Keep me updated on your progress," said Rahul. "All the best. Remember: If you really want to do something, you'll find a way; if you don't, you'll find an excuse."

Applied knowledge:

1. Describe the qualities that Sudhir lacked that made his life so difficult.
2. What are some solutions that Rahul suggested that you can apply in your own life?
3. Think of some solution-focused questions that you can ask yourself for a real-world problem that you are facing.

Build your vocabulary

Learn and use the Words and Business phrases used in this chapter to improve your Spoken English Skills:

- **Make the cut:** To get Shortlisted
- **Persona:** The aspect of someone's character that is presented to or perceived by others.
- **Pivot:** To make a fundamental change in a plan, strategy, product, or business model because the current approach is not yielding the desired results.
- **Holistic:** Taking into account an overall, 360-degree approach. Not just focusing on one aspect but on the entire issue as a whole.
- **Ahead of the curve:** Beating the competition. Being in fashion, up-to-date with the latest trends, fashion, or technologies.
- **Hit the ground running:** Start something without delay or wasting time.

Chapter 2 Emotional Intelligence

Managing Self for Awareness, Empathy and Personal Transformation

LEARNING MILESTONES

This chapter will enable you to:

- Understand what is emotional intelligence?
- Learn how EI helps us at in all areas of life.
- Understanding the relationship between IQ and EQ.
- Know how EQ can be a powerful personal transformation tool.
- Find out how social skills and empathy can be strong motivational tools.
- Master the art of becoming an Emotionally Intelligent.
- Acquire new business phrases and build your vocabulary.

Expert Quotes

"A Growth Mindset is loving challenges and seeing them as opportunities to grow stronger" - Carol Dweck

"Feel your emotions, but don't let them rule your actions."

"Winners don't have the best of everything...They make the best of everything" – Anthony Robbins

2.1 Essentials of emotional intelligence

Emotional Intelligence (EI) is the ability of individuals to be aware of their own emotions and feelings, the ability to control their own emotions, and use this to recognize and guide others' emotions and actions. EI is a collection of feelings, emotions, skills, and characteristics that drive performance and success. EI simply means to use emotions intelligently according to your advantage.

The knowledge of EI is extremely essential as it is now clear that technical skills alone cannot provide professional and personal success. High EI is a great predictor of high performance. There is a direct link between EI and earning potential.

The study of EI was a result of a problem that challenges almost everyone: Why do people with the best education and technical skills and knowledge often perform poorly in their careers? And how is it that some people who appear `average' or even mediocre can end up becoming such great leaders and managers? The answer was that these average people had a high degree of Emotional Intelligence that enabled them to influence others.

Mahatma Gandhi was a lawyer with average legal skills. His first public speaking opportunity proved to be a disaster in court and became the father of our nation! Common people in pressure situations become heroes. While they go forward and tackle situations head-on, others shrink with fear or shy away. Different strokes for different folks: It all depends upon their EI.

Case in Point

In the business world, we have seen great startups like Apple & Uber being built by single persons, from scratch. Steve Jobs at Apple and Travis Kalanick at Uber are examples of positive-thinking entrepreneurs with a huge intellectual capacity who built billion-dollar companies due to their sheer tenacity and brilliance. However, both of them had to be removed from their own companies. The boards of companies that they owned asked them to leave due to their poor people skills. Although they had great IQs, they lacked emotional intelligence. Travis has admitted his failure in developing EI and admitted to taking professional help from coaches and mentors to develop his EQ.

***Figure 2.1**: Steve Jobs and Travis Kalanick: When brilliance is disliked due to low EQ*

Day after day, we encounter fights, conflicts, and misunderstandings between people everywhere. And these conflicts are resolved by people whom we perceive to be leaders. Leaders with EI. When you have high EI, it is far easier to solve complex problems and deal creatively with challenges of an ever-changing, dynamic environment.

In our pursuit of gaining the best education and intellectual knowledge, we put in the same effort to develop our **Intelligence Quotient** (**IQ**). However, in our desire to acquire soft skills and develop dynamic personalities, it becomes more important to develop EI. We need to have a high **Emotional Quotient** (**EQ**) along with a high IQ.

- **90% of top performers have high EQ.** Emotional intelligence correlates strongly with workplace performance. (TalentSmart)
- **EQ accounts for 58% of job performance.** It's one of the strongest predictors of success across industries. (Forbes)
- **People with high EQ earn $29,000 more annually.** Better interpersonal skills translate to higher salaries. (TalentSmart)
- **Students with high EQ perform 11% better academically.** Emotional regulation improves focus and learning outcomes. (Journal of Educational Psychology)

2.2 Intelligence quotient (IQ) or emotional quotient (EQ)?

For all practical purposes, we have two brains, or two minds. One brain is the rational brain, and the other is the emotional brain. Both the rational brain (IQ), which gives rise to reason, and the emotional brain (EQ), which gives rise to gut feeling, are important; they need not be mutually exclusive. In other words, a person needs both IQ and EQ to develop their personality.

The New Paradigm urges us to harmonize head and heart – *Daniel Goleman*

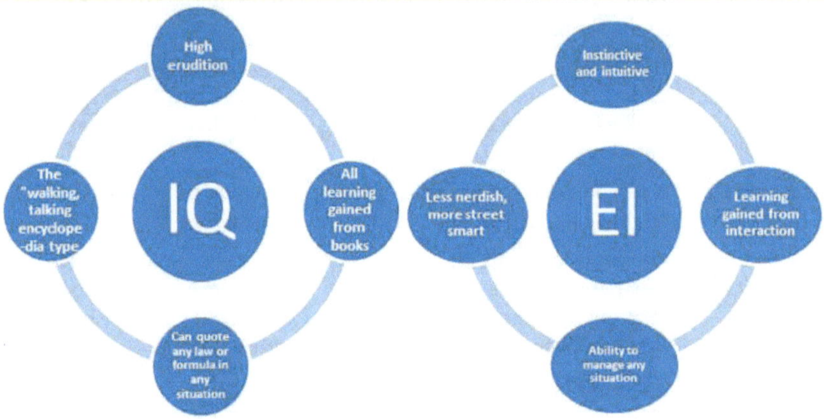

***Figure 2.2**: IQ opens doors. EQ builds influence*

However, there are fundamental differences between the two, and hence the consequences arising from both are different. A student who tops the university in math may find that number crunching in a regular banking job as a financial analyst is not their cup of tea! That student with a high IQ who could crack mathematical equations in their sleep is now unable to get along better with their boss. They cannot work in teams, are unable to think out of the box, and insist on applying theoretical concepts to solve basic human relation problems. They get defeated by failure easily and constantly let their teams down. What use then is their high IQ?

Case in Point

Often, we meet friends from school who were the school toppers. Our parents would give us examples of those students' ability to get good marks. You, however, played sports, participated in extracurriculars, and travelled with your parents, visiting new places. However, now, after meeting them, you realize that those toppers' personal growth has been unidimensional. They are good at memorizing books. But when it comes to applied knowledge, you are far superior. And this shows up in the lack of their professional growth. In the pursuit of getting good marks or coming first in class, they lost sight of learning. Cramming or learning by rote replaces an understanding of the basic concepts. Hence, while you are chosen to be in high-profile teams due to your EI, your old school friend's IQ has proved to be of less importance.

Does that mean that IQ is unimportant? Not at all! The theory and technical skills that account for 15% of our future success are an important and necessary step towards passing entrance and competitive exams. Credentials and Certifications do provide credibility in the initial phases of one's career. Exams are used as a filter to separate high-IQ individuals from others. If one is not part of the successful pool of candidates, there is little chance of getting more opportunities.

Cracking that entrance exam is an essential way to go to acquire & display EI: Soft skills that will account for 85% of your success.

Item	EQ	IQ
Signifies	Ability to manage self and others' emotions.	Intellectual Ability to learn.
Measured by	A person's relationship skills, ability to get along, and other soft skills.	Numerics generated by standardized tests.
Development	Constantly develops through experience, understanding, human relationships, and sensitivity. Acquired over a period of time.	Generally, remains the same throughout one's life span. A person is generally born with it.
Application	Creative thinking, innovation, management, leadership, collaboration, and networking	Technical expertise, academic excellence, and logical and linear thinking.
Characteristics	A professional with a multi-dimensional personality who is flexible in approach, cooperative, thinks out of the box, and proactive in solving human problems.	A highly gifted and talented but rigid professional with a one-sided personality.
Importance in career	EI is directly linked to pay and promotion. Lack of it gets you fired.	The first step. Gets you hired or placed in the shortlist or team.

2.3 Components of emotional intelligence

While EQ as a concept had been proposed earlier, it has been brought into focus by Dr. Daniel Goleman in his book *Emotional Intelligence: Why it can matter more than IQ*. A link to the audiobook has been given at the end of this chapter, and readers are well advised to listen to it with attention before beginning their journey towards acquiring soft skills.

Goleman researched that EI, rather than cognitive ability, was the reason for 90% of the difference between star performers and average performers in companies. As a result, he has proposed a group of five skills comprising emotional Intelligence that can take average professionals to the next level of greatness:

1. **Self-Awareness:** Honestly recognizing feelings within, as they happen.
2. **Self-Regulation:** Taking control of your emotions and thoughts.
3. **Personal Motivation:** Being driven to achieve, for the sake of achievement.
4. **Empathy:** Being sensitive to others' feelings while making decisions.
5. **Social Skills:** Managing relationships to influence people in the desired direction.

These five components can be grouped under two different clusters:

Personal Transformation	Social Relationship Management
• Self-awareness • Self-regulation, Self-management • Personal motivation and growth mindset • Strong value system	• Empathy • Relationship skills

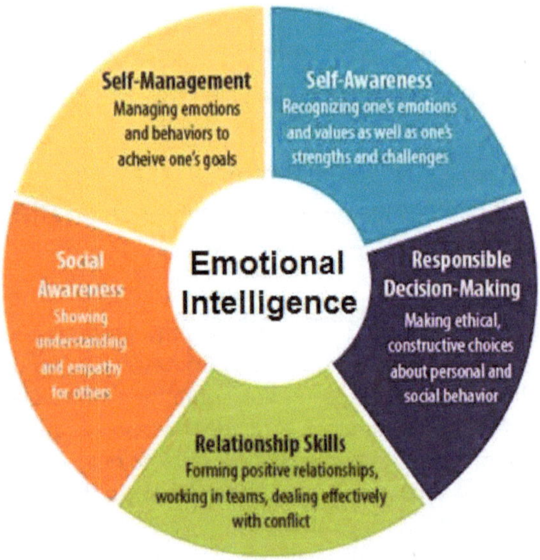

***Figure 2.3**: Components of Emotional Intelligence*

2.4 Applying emotional intelligence at home and work

A. **Personal transformation skills first involve focusing on oneself in order to influence others:**

1. **Self-Awareness**

It is the ability to be honest with oneself and identify, understand, and evaluate personal feelings. To have a deep understanding of one's emotions, feelings, values, and needs. And to use this awareness to understand others' feelings and the impact of one's emotions on their environment.

Self-awareness is concerned with knowing about your own state of mind and capabilities, preferences, resources, and perceptions.

As you become more self-aware, you are able to be in better touch with your own feelings.

People with a heightened self-awareness are neither pessimistic nor overtly optimistic. Rather, they are candid with themselves and with others, at work and at home.

By becoming Self-Aware, you gain ownership of Reality – Deepak Chopra

People with strong self-awareness:

1. Are honest about their areas of improvement and weaknesses without getting defensive.
2. Are self-confident as they voice their opinions even if unpopular and are open to receiving feedback.
3. Are able to perceive situations accurately & are sensitive to changes in their environment.
4. Are willing to take risks for what they believe to be right.
5. Believe that they are the best person for that job and present themselves accordingly.
6. Make decisions in tune with their values and beliefs.
7. Have a self-deprecating sense of humour, i.e., display the ability to laugh at themselves.

Case in Point

Radhika is the daughter of a self-made, wealthy entrepreneur with deep connections. Her father forced her to study Commerce in her undergrad. He wanted her to be a Chartered Accountant, something he never could be. She graduated, and after her B.Com, her father got her a job as an Articles clerk at a Big Four accounting firm. In her vacations, prior to her joining, Radhika did a lot of soul searching and realized that accounting is not to her interest. She just couldn't imagine a future working with figures, finances, and numbers. Instead, she found herself excelling at Art. She spent the vacation going to art galleries and studying the works of the Masters. She explored post-graduation

programs in Design and finalized one. She revealed her plans to her parents, who were very angry and disappointed! They did everything they could to force her to change her mind, but she stood her ground. She went on to study Art and Design, and today she is the leading Art Historian in her field.

2. **Self-Regulation (also known as Self-Management)**

It is only human to feel angry, sad, lonely, happy, joyful, hopeful, etc. On any given day, we experience multiple emotions. There is little that we can do when emotions rise inside of us. However, there is a lot we can do to manage these emotions. Every emotion need not be displayed or shown. This is called Self-management. Regulating oneself involves being a master of one's own mind rather than being a hostage to one's emotions. It means taking control over fear, anger, and anxiety rather than them taking control over you.

Self-management is important because when people are able to better manage their emotions, they behave and react appropriately depending on the situation.

People who are good managers of their emotions:

1. Are adaptable and open to change and don't panic when faced with sudden disruptions in their lives.
2. Deal calmly with stress and display calmness, impulse control, and restraint.
3. Display intention and productivity, and behave in a fair, reasonable, and rational way.
4. Stick to their ethical values and confront others due to a lack of them.
5. Have attention to detail and are organized and careful.
6. Adapt plans, behavior, or approaches depending upon the situation.

Case in Point

Adi, a manager, has entrusted an important client presentation to Yusuf, whom he feels is ready for such an important task. On the day of the presentation, Yusuf gets very nervous, makes various errors, and delivers a mediocre presentation. The client leaves without a promise of a sale. Adi, in the past, has displayed extreme anger by kicking chairs and screaming and shouting at the person at fault. However, he has matured as a manager and now practices self-regulation. Today, he first asks his entire team, including the trembling presenter, to leave for the day. He then closes his eyes and takes 10 deep breaths. He then proceeds to write an email to the client acknowledging gaps in the presentation and explaining the presentation pitch, without making excuses for his team. He does not send the mail immediately; instead, he sets it for auto sending the next morning at 9 a.m.

He then switches off the lights and leaves for the day. The next day, he meets Yusuf in his office, and they go over the problems in the presentation and how Yusuf can improve for the future. At the end of the day, the client writes to Adi appreciating his honesty and his care for his team.

2.5 Importance of ethics and values

***Figure 2.4**: Ethics and values*

2.5.1 A strong value system

Those who have a high level of Emotional Intelligence also have a strong value system and a strong code of ethics.

Values are a set of beliefs because of which we behave in a particular manner. For example, honesty, integrity, respect, professionalism, and reliability are values that help us to admire a person as a great professional!

People with a strong set of values:

1. Tend to do what they believe is right.
2. They believe in those values and rarely compromise on those.
3. They make choices and decisions based on their values.

Case in Point

A person who believes in Respect for other genders as a personal value will never put themselves in a position where they get accused of sexual harassment.

#meetoo

4. They demand those same set of values from others.
5. They care about their professional image and the company's image so that their value system is consistent with that of their organization.
6. They lead by example. First, they practice those values, and then they compel others to follow them.

Case in Point

John is a newly appointed Team Lead. He is now managing a team of 4 software engineers. The project deadline is coming close, but he finds that his team members are not punctual with their work. He shouts at them, threatens them, gives them warnings, but nothing seems to be working. Then one day, his manager asked him what time John reported to work daily. John

was shocked when he realized that he himself was oversleeping many days and then making excuses just because he thought, as a Team Lead, he could come late. But what he didn't realize was that his team was simply observing his unpunctuality and following the same set of values.

2.5.2 A strong code of ethics

Ethics are the set of rules that govern the behaviour of a person. How people behave in times of stress, temptation, anger, and opportunity is determined by their ethical beliefs. Ethics determine a person's integrity. How sincere a person is in his/her job or performance is a function of integrity.

Integrity is doing the right thing when no one is watching.

Ethics determine what is right or wrong in an organization. What is acceptable and what is not? It demands a high level of self-management.

Case in Point

OftenSoft is a fast-growing IT/ITES company. Post-COVID, it started a policy that allows its employees to work from home (WFH) on any 7 days of the month. After a 6-month review, it was found that the productivity went down by 25%! Projects were being submitted late, and most employees were often unavailable for calls and meetings.

Their HR manager resigned and joined another company called GlobalLife, located close by. He was amazed to hear that the employees of Globallife had 15 days of WFH! Here we go again, he thought!. Same old problems. But he was further amazed when he saw the numbers. Productivity was actually up, and the client's satisfaction rate was very high. He enquired from the MD. The MD told him that before they implemented the WFH policy, they ensured that all employees agreed to a code of ethics and conduct. This code of ethics mentions that employees must be available and work from home in the same manner as they would if they were on campus. Timelines and commitments must be adhered to without compromise in the levels of professionalism.

Due to this strong code of ethics, the employees were able to work from home and yet gave their best output. A win-win for all.

2.5.3 Growth Mindset & Personal Motivation

When the going gets tough, the tough get going!

Motivated People are natural Leaders. They don't wait for life to happen to them. They have a Growth Mindset to actually do something to make their lives better. And in this way, they make others' lives better, too!

They are driven to achieve beyond their own expectations- and others' expectations of them. They set the bar higher and higher each time, breaking their own records. Failure for them is a problem to be dealt with and learned from.

The thrill of achievement drives them. The excitement of doing something path-breaking, something innovative, and having the courage to change something

that drives them. Motivation comes from within, but it forces the person to act! Traits of motivated people are:

1. Passion for their work.
2. A desire to surpass all expectations.
3. See failure as an opportunity to improve.
4. Show exemplary commitment to completion of the task.
5. Show tenacity. Do not take no for an answer.

Case in Point

Col. Sanders had an idea to make fried chicken using his own recipe. At age 65 he was said to have been rejected by almost 1000 banks to fund his idea. Armed with the belief that he could make the best fried chicken in the country and just $ 105 of social security in his pocket, he was motivated and started a movement called KFC, which has more than 18000 restaurants in more than 100 countries today!

***Figure 2.5**: Colonel Sanders is the perfect example of relentless persistence*

Case in Point

Ray Croc was a traveling salesman who kept getting rejected by restaurant owners for his milkshake machine. However, he didn't give up and kept travelling across the country trying to sell his gadget. On one such sales call, he came across an outlet run by two brothers called McDonald's. He was hooked by their idea of an assembly line approach to fast food and wanted to take their franchise, but they kept refusing him. Finally, he convinced them and started McDonald's all over the USA and eventually around the world. Today, McDonald's needs no introduction. All because of one man who was motivated enough to believe in his idea.

***Figure 2.6**: Ray Kroc identified opportunities invisible to most*

2.5.4 Social Skills and Social Awareness

This component involves using one's emotions to guide and influence others to admit one's point of view. Individuals with social awareness can negotiate effectively, create lasting networks, and navigate through company politics and the conflicting agendas of others successfully. The characteristics of socially aware individuals are:

Empathy

Become the kind of Person who spreads sunshine and joy wherever you go!

NOT whenever you go.

Empathy is perhaps the most visible characteristic of emotional intelligence. People with empathy are able to put themselves in others' shoes. Feel their pain, anxieties, insecurities, anger, joy, whatever they are feeling. Not just feel, but also take action to address those feelings. That is empathy. Empathy involves hearing `unspoken' thoughts of others and picking up their emotional cues.

A professional who shows empathy is rarely caught off guard when the emotions of the team boil over. When there are fights, escalations, and discord, the empathetic manager is able to solve these conflicts by showing empathy.

People who show empathy are good business leaders, get prominence in society, and become effective parents and role models who understand that personal success and group success are inseparable.

However, empathy does not mean always accepting what others say. Rather, empathetic leaders consider others' feelings to make intelligent decisions, not emotional ones.

Case in Point

Bob, a Finance Manager, was extremely good at his job. However, in his appraisal, he always received feedback that his style of working was very `cold'. His team members felt that he was not very approachable and receptive to their ideas and suggestions. He would show visible irritation if any of his team members asked for leave or were late in submissions.

After his last appraisal, the HR Head called and advised Bob to develop more empathy. He tried to be empathetic, but it appeared artificial and fake to him. He just didn't know how to connect to his team.

He voiced his concerns to the HR Head, who asked him to do a simple exercise at home for 7 days:

Put on your favorite show. Turn off the sound and watch it to see if you can identify the expressions, moods, and nonverbal clues of the actors. All this on silent mode! Try to follow the story and guess the dialogue just by watching their expressions. After a week, Bob reported that he was able to follow the story and make out what the actors were saying. Now the HR Head told him to do the same activity with his team. Watch out for their body language and non-verbal clues.

And incredibly, he could pick up so many emotions just by watching them from afar. He developed empathy for them by understanding what they were feeling inside.

Traits of empathetic professionals are:

1. They don't shy away from showing `tough love'. i.e., make hard decisions or speak bluntly for others' benefit
2. Leaders with empathy are good listeners: not just listening with their ears, but reading others' body language.
3. They are able to preempt conflict or pressure situations before they occur.
4. They are proactive about solving their team's or group's needs.
5. They are able to use this understanding of their group to their advantage and make decisions accordingly.
6. They make good friends, coaches, or mentors.
7. They are able to perform very well in a cross-cultural environment.

***Figure 2.7**: Empathy goes beyond words*

Relationship and Networking Skills

Relationship skills are `People Skills'. Also known as Social skills. It is the ability to get along with others in teams at work or in personal life. It's not just about being friendly or nice to people. Rather, it is friendliness with a purpose in order to get a defined result. People with good relationship skills are able to create lasting and mutually beneficial networks.

Social skills are a sum of all other components of Emotional intelligence. People who are good at self-awareness and regulation can control their own emotions and motivate themselves to empathize with others. This leads to them being good listeners and good sounding boards for others. They are able to help others by understanding their needs. People with good Social skills display the following traits:

1. **Organizational Awareness:** They understand workplace politics, hidden agendas, and dynamics between team members. They know who the decision makers are, what the issues are that are affecting performance, and the organizational culture. They use this to navigate their way through the maze of organizational hierarchies to reach the top.

***Figure 2.8**: Don't hand over your strings for someone else to pull*

2. **Service Orientation:** They understand others' requirements, match their products or services with others' needs, and ensure client satisfaction.
3. **Rapport:** They are able to find common ground and create a network that they can tap into whenever required. They have the contacts to get the job done at the right time.

***Figure 2.9**: Right people, right vibe, right help when needed*

4. **Popularity:** People gravitate towards them in times of need. They are like magnets that attract others and help them with or without any motive. This ability is very helpful in creating a support base that can propel them towards the realization of their goals.

Case in Point

Kabir is a competent and popular colleague. Just 2 years into his job, he is known for his helpful nature. His team leader, Noor, is very happy with him. However, she feels that Kabir lacks initiative and needs more push than the others. This is preventing Kabir from getting promoted. One evening, before

leaving, he sees Noor sitting at her desk, looking worried. He asks her if all's well. She replies that her boss has asked her for a feasibility report on a new AI tool by the next morning, and she doesn't even have an idea about it. Kabir goes online and immediately sends her a detailed file on the technology. It is complete as a report in almost all respects. Noor is stunned. She asks him how he had it? Kabir replies that he spends the time commuting on his way to home and to work, surfing tech blogs, and is very aware of the latest LLMs. A friend of his who is a consultant shared this report with him and told him to do the same. Noor makes a few changes and sends it to her boss. She is very thankful. But more importantly, she now views Kabir in a new light. The fact that he makes an effort to update his skills is a huge plus in his favor, along with the fact that he selflessly shared the information with her, which made her look good. Kabir is now on the fast track!

2.6 Five steps to improve Emotional intelligence

All of us possess Emotional Intelligence. However, having a higher degree of EI than others enables them to get ahead in Life and become leaders. However, Life Success lies in constantly learning new ways of developing EI. Through organized training coupled with practice, the EQ can be enhanced. Becoming emotionally intelligent is a journey that starts and ends with the self. The process is tough as it takes experience, effort, time, and commitment. But the benefits of developing EI are well worth the effort. The relationships and goal achievement that result make the entire journey of EI wonderful.

Here are five easy and practical ways to develop EI:

1. **Reflect**: Take time to pause, think, and journal your thoughts. Slow down and take breaks from social media. Write down your thoughts and reflect on your actions. Look out for self-limiting beliefs and negative patterns that recur in your life. Use reflection to learn from past experiences to grow for the future.

2. **Practice acceptance:** Accept the consequences of your own actions. Don't give anyone else control over your emotions. Accept that others will not always act in the manner you desire and conduct your life accordingly. Once you are freed from this dependence on others' approval or reactions, you will be able to fully focus on your own progress and your own life. Take charge and act maturely.

3. **Practice positivity**: Positive thoughts and affirmations give rise to positive actions. This has been proven countless times over the history of humans. Beware of the downward spiral of negative thoughts leading to negative self-esteem. Instead, be an optimist and focus on your strengths and improve your weaknesses. Anger, hate, jealousy, and other negative emotions are chains that prevent you from swimming successfully towards your life. Instead, set positive goals that lead to proactive and productive action. Believe in the principle of good karma, wherein good deeds and actions will be returned to you.

4. **Never stop learning**: Add life to your years, not years to your life! Acquiring new skills and adopting new ideas lead to positive change in habits, beliefs, and actions. You are able to handle the ups and downs of life changes and disruptions with ease. You are always updated, thereby having better relationships and networks. Share knowledge and pay it forward. This means developing and educating others without a motive. Acknowledge and reward others' strengths and accomplishments.

5. **Lead by example**: You can influence others only if they see you `walk your talk'. Practice what you preach and raise your hand to go first. This will not only give you confidence but also inspire confidence in others as well. Leadership is nothing but paving the way for others to walk on. True leadership-whether professional or personal comes from action, not reaction.

2.7 Summary

Emotional Intelligence can be developed at any stage of life, helping one to lead a life of joy and success. But first, one must introspect and look within to see if there is a bias towards a specific negative mindset, and then accept the need to change that viewpoint for better results.

Once a person realizes that success is being blocked by their own mindset and attitude, slowly but surely, there is a change in thought: The personality changes from `lose in some situations' to `win in all situations'. This is what the world calls a `well-rounded personality'. It is never too late to develop EI. Rather, acquiring new skills and developing your EQ is a lifelong process.

Remember, leaders in all spheres of life and other legends have won many victories purely due to a high level of Emotional Intelligence.

Knowledge Check:

1. Define Emotional Intelligence. How is it useful?
2. Explain the difference between IQ and EQ.
3. Explain how Emotional Intelligence can be applied in daily life? Give examples.
4. What are the five components of Emotional intelligence? Give two characteristics of each.
5. What is the importance of Values & Ethics? Give one example of each, and how you can apply it in your daily life.
6. What are the attributes of people with great social skills?

Additional resources for self-development

- The ultimate guide to Emotional Intelligence: Daniel Goleman, *Emotional Intelligence: Why it can matter more than IQ*: **https://www.youtube.com/watch?v=YWbUUUBIGN4**

- Carol Dweck, the author of Growth Mindset: **https://youtu.be/-71zdXCMU6A?si=7YTyBvuDB5uUQLEU**
- Rober Cialdini (The Guru of Influencing skills): **https://youtu.be/1_urunjhCsw?si=2fpIQzAhh8_KYstE**
- Blogs on Personality and EI: **https://youtube.com/@thecoachprashant?si=30m-k90QLJLOuUiCm**

Get ready for the real world!

***Figure 2.10**: From village roads to global goals; that's the Vembu blueprint*

Zoho's Rise from 0 Funding: Sridhar Vembu's Journey of Making 8700 cr Company

Zoho's Rise from 0 funding to a billion-dollar company. Sridhar Vembu was born in 1968 in a small village in the Thanjavur district of Tamil Nadu. Despite his modest beginnings, Vembu always thought differently and had an inquisitive mind. In 1994, Vembu joined Qualcomm as a wireless systems engineer in San Diego, California. Despite his promising career and high-paying job, he felt he was missing something in his life. He wanted to start something of his own; It was a calling towards entrepreneurship. This drive led him to leave Qualcomm. Along with his brothers, he started AdventNet in 1996. The dot-com crash in 2001 dramatically reduced AdventNet's customer base from 150 to just 3. Despite these setbacks, Sridhar Vembu remained resilient. He turned down offers to sell the company and believed firmly in its potential. Shridhar had saved cash from his earlier profits. Instead of selling, he used the company's cash reserves to pay his employees, forgoing his four-year salary. He had not even fired any employee. Despite multiple acquisition offers from giants like Salesforce, Vembu chose to keep Zoho independent, focusing on long-term growth and self-sufficiency, which made it a successful

company. By 2021, Zoho had become a billion-dollar company in revenue and had achieved a huge customer base. The company continued to thrive during the COVID-19 pandemic, with revenues soaring to 6711 crores INR and profits of 1918 crores INR. Despite his monumental success, Sridhar Vembu remains grounded. He lives in a village in Thanjavur and is often seen riding his bicycle. His commitment to social entrepreneurship and rural development is evident through initiatives like the Zoho Schools of Learning and the Zoho Rural Schools Program. These projects aim to bridge the digital divide and provide education and job opportunities to underprivileged communities. Sridhar Vembu's contributions to technology and society have earned him numerous accolades, including the Padma Shri (2021).

Build your vocabulary

Learn and use the Words and Business phrases used in this chapter to improve your Spoken English Skills:

1. **Networking:** Mutually beneficial, reciprocal relationships with others.
2. **Tenacity:** Never-say-die attitude. The ability to be constantly after something till you achieve it.
3. **Uni-dimensional:** One-sided. Not having another angle to it.
4. **Soul searching:** Introspection or looking at one's own strengths and weaknesses.
5. **Off-guard:** When someone is caught doing something, or something happens without you being prepared for it.
6. **Hierarchy:** The placement of job titles and positions within a group or family system. This is how one recognizes the seniority or people of power in an organization.

Chapter 3 Self-image Management

Your Personal Branding from First Impression to Lasting Impact

LEARNING MILESTONES

This chapter will enable you to:

- Make the best First Impression on others.
- Boost your self-esteem and self-confidence.
- Build your personal brand.
- Do a personal SWOT analysis.
- Understand 'Executive Presence' and Gravitas.
- Develop a commanding social media presence.
- Learn new business phrases and increase your vocabulary.

Expert Quotes

Leave an Impression.... Not a Stain!

– Prashant Sharma

3.1 What is the First Impression?

First impression can be defined as the effect one has on others due to the impact of one's personality. This first impression is formed within 40 seconds of your first meeting. And lasts a lifetime! While you continue to make impressions upon people that you meet, the impact that you make in those 40 seconds in the first meeting with another person is called the First Impression.

This first impression process occurs in every new situation. Within the first few moments, people pass judgment on you. This judgment may be fair or unfair. You can never know exactly what others think about you, or how they would describe you when you aren't in the room. You can, however, draw inferences about the impression you made based on your interactions with them.

If you are lucky, people will give you direct feedback about your personality that tells you what they think about you and your persona. Other times, you may receive indirect signals about your impression, through ratings, job offers, recommendations, testimonials, or promotions. Taken together, this direct and indirect feedback shapes your perceived first impression.

***Figure 3.1**: Your Vibe says "Professional" & your Aura says "Power"*

While we don't have full control over how others perceive us, what we can do is influence them to make the most powerful and impactful first impression. This is because once the first impression is made, it is virtually irreversible. First Impressions are extremely difficult to change.

Sometimes it can take a lifetime to alter an impression once made.

Your looks and mannerisms are just a small part of your impression. First impression means the overall projection of your personality by the way you conduct yourself in different situations, your grooming and dressing, mannerisms, habits, behavior, and attitude.

3.2 Creating a great First Impression

Creating a good First Impression largely involves:

- Personal brand and charisma
- Image impact and self-management
- Interpersonal and relationship skills
- Executive Presence
- Developing Gravitas: Inculcating a magnetic, commanding personality

3.3 Types of First Impression

1. **Planned First Impression**

It is planned when you are aware of it.

Example:

- Job interview or scheduled interaction
- Meeting with the client or at work
- Intimate occasions
- Social occasions and family commitments

2. **Unplanned First Impression**

It can be unplanned when you are not prepared for it.

For example, people looking at you when you are walking to the office, when you are traveling, when you are shopping or eating at a restaurant, in fact, any place where people around you are strangers to you.

3.4 Self-Image and First Impression

First Impression is a function of Self-Image. In other words, how you perceive yourself largely influences how the world perceives you. Being well dressed, well-mannered, and well-groomed will have no effect if inside that person is feeling low or suffering from low self-esteem. A Positive self-image puts the wind in your sails! The enthusiasm and the energy that spreads create the best First Impression. Thus, Self-Image and First Impressions are closely related.

Self-image is how you view yourself, your self-worth, and your abilities. It is the value you place on yourself and how you feel about life. Self-image is influenced by your self-esteem and your body image. Self-image is so strong that you can spend your entire life validating it.

Self-image is what YOU think YOU are

It is a combination of many factors: how others have behaved with you and treated you, and how you felt when you compared yourself to others.

3.5 Factors that affect one's self-image

- Colleagues & Peers
- Friends
- Mentors & coaches
- Parents
- Teachers
- Social Media & Television
- Movies
- Magazines
- Successes & Failures

Case in Point

Ria has grown up as a slightly overweight child. Ever since she was young, she has been used to people calling her `fat'. She has tried various diets and exercises, but does not seem to be able to alter her body shape. She is envious of the other people in her office who are able to fit into smaller-sized, tight-fitting clothes. She is acutely embarrassed by her body, and thus her self-image has suffered. She has started second-guessing herself, her work, in fact, everything she does. This results in a dip in her work performance, and her appraisals also suffer. While she is obsessed with becoming thin, she has lost sight of the big picture, i.e., her relationship with her superiors and her attitude towards her job.

She finally sees a therapist who helps her and suggests ways to boost her self-esteem. Ria is now comfortable in her own skin and has stopped making comparisons with others. Instead, she is focusing on excelling at her job, and her manager and colleagues are very happy with her. In fact, for the first time, she has been invited to the CEO's house for a get-together.

3.6 Beautiful on the inside

"Inner Beauty is as important as outer beauty."

For the exterior to shine, it is very important for the product to be perfect on the inside as well. It is not enough to spend billions on the exterior of a building if the roof leaks at the slightest rain. When a customer buys an expensive designer product, they are expecting not only the product to be luxurious, but the overall buying experience to be luxurious as well. Apple products are a testament to that fact.

Great designers spend an equal amount of time on designing how products look on the inside as much as the outside. Irrespective of whether the customer will notice or not. Great design does not let irregularity in manufacturing or design defects slide.

Case in Point

Steve Jobs, as quoted in Walter Isaacson's biography titled `Steve Jobs'

On Jobs' father, who rebuilt cars and held design and craftsmanship in high regard:

"One of the most important things he taught Steve was that it is important to be a great craftsman, even for the parts unseen. When they were building a fence, he said, 'You have to make the back of the fence that people won't see look just as beautiful as the front, just like a great carpenter would make the back of a chest of drawers ... Even though others won't see it, you will know it's there, and that will make you more proud of your design."

Steve Jobs reportedly made Apple spend millions to change the design of the motherboard of the Apple II because the lines were not straight!

As a customer, you and I rarely see the inside of an Apple product, but the attention to detail is what makes great products.

Comparison then can be made between First Impressions and Self-Image. Whereas First Impressions are largely made on the exterior of a person, the Self-Image deals with what the person is feeling internally. Both need to go hand in hand for a dynamic personality.

3.7 Ways to make the best First Impression

1. **Positive Body Language:** Body language is perhaps the first thing people see while forming their first impression of you. Dress, voice, gesture, courtesy and etiquette, listening skills, posture, grooming and hygiene, eye contact, etc., all form a package that can either prove to be a wonderful present for others or a deadly combination that can undo your best intentions. Powerful and Positive Body language is the first but most important step towards getting people to accept you.

2. A bright smile & handshake: As the saying goes, "Smile and the world smiles with you." As a part of your body language, a warm and confident smile will put both you and the other person at ease. It makes you look friendly and approachable. However, keep in mind the cultural differences. In Western countries, it is customary to smile at strangers in public places like elevators or public transport. But don't go overboard with this, as your smile can be misconstrued as an invitation to make contact. But don't let that stop you from genuinely smiling.

The handshake is an internationally accepted form of greeting. Shake hands for 2-3 seconds firmly but not in a crushing grip. Never shake with wet hands, and make sure you shake hands with both men and women in a group.

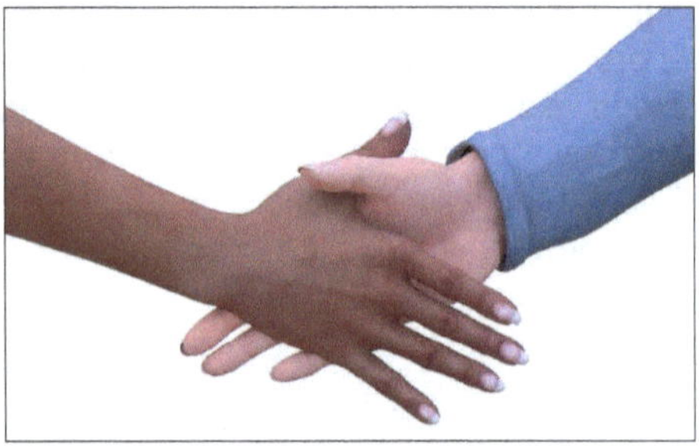

***Figure 3.2**: A good handshake is where confidence meets connection*

Case in Point

Neil was coming out of the washroom just before his job interview when he saw the interview panel signal to him to come in. He quickly collected his portfolio folder and ran his hands over his hair. As soon as he entered, the main interviewer extended his hand. Neil gave him the 'fish'! In other words, he shook hands with his wet hand. Immediately, a look of disgust was seen on the interviewer's face. He took out his handkerchief and wiped his hand dry. Neil had shaken his hand immediately after coming out of the washroom, with wet hands! The interviewer was not happy at all. Once the question and answer session was concluded, Neil again held out his hand, which the interviewer did not take. It was a very awkward moment for everyone, and Neil did not clear the interview round.

***Figure 3.3**: Bro shook my hand like a soggy noodle!*

3. **Be yourself:** Authenticity always shines. If you are trying to behave like someone else or put on an act, it will soon become clear to everyone that you are trying to fool them. People are smart, and your artificiality will soon be exposed. Instead, be yourself. Explore your personality and play to your strengths. Be genuinely interested in other people. One would like to be in the company of other people.

Remember the 4 Cs when interacting with others:

- Calm
- Cool
- Comfortable
- Confident

This will make the others feel at ease and comfortable around you.

4. **Blend in:** Make the effort to fit into your environment. While it is good to be different and stand out, it is not always appropriate to be the odd person out from the crowd. Dress professionally in a workplace setting and casually outside. Appropriate behavior and mannerisms must be exhibited depending upon the situation and your company. Doing a little research before you actually set out for the occasion will go a long way in making you feel and appear prepared and relaxed. Show your individuality in your time and own space. Don't let it adversely affect your relationships with others.

Case in Point

Rocky is a part-time musician, looking to build a full-time career in advertising. He gets his first break in an ad agency in Mumbai and soon rises up the ladder in his company. After 6 years, his company was acquired by a Korean Company, known for its traditional values. His office shifts to the Korean company's Delhi headquarters. Rocky soon finds himself in the company of others dressed in formal attire in the office. He feels totally out of place in his coloured hair, torn jeans, and tattoos, which were barely noticed by anyone in his old office. Others laugh at him and talk about him behind his back. He insists on dressing in his usual manner, but finds that he is not getting any recognition at work. His colleagues and superiors don't take him seriously. But he refuses to change. Soon, he is forced to leave his job and look for another, but it's not easy to find another job in the recession. He feels that maybe he should have tried to learn the new company's culture.

5. **Punctuality:** Your time management is your responsibility, not that of others. Being on time shows respect and seriousness for the occasion. The same standards of good punctuality have to be exhibited on the job and outside the job as well. You should be known for your adherence to time schedules. Once this happens, you will start getting more favorable responses and create better relationships in all areas of your life. There is no room for excuses in the real world. Whether it is a job interview or work, a social occasion, or a personal appointment, do your research about the location, weather, traffic, etc., in advance. In this era of Google Maps, there is no excuse for being late. Remember, if the others can reach on time, so can you.

I am late....Because I started late – Winston Churchill

6. **Talk to convince:** Speaking with strangers or meeting people for the first time, especially public speaking, makes most people a little nervous. This is perfectly normal. Stranger anxiety shows itself in nervous tics of the face, trembling, sweaty palms, weak voice, racing heartbeat, etc. This makes you look unsure, hesitant, and ruins your first impression. Practice speaking in front of the mirror and take public speaking classes to gain speaking confidence. Learn the art of small talk in professional and personal situations to break the ice and get along better with others.

Speaking to make the best first impression

1. Before a job interview, do some research on the company. Compliment the interviewer on some positive development in that company, like record profits or a takeover, to show off your knowledge.
2. While attending a party as a guest in a work colleague's house, take a small gift. Make some positive comments on the area or location, and compliment the host for the arrangement and the food.
3. Before making an impromptu presentation: Talk about a previous presentation or something that has just happened around everyone in the company. Involve everyone in the opening words and then plunge into your main talk.
4. Before attending a social occasion: Make sure your general awareness levels are high. When meeting a stranger, ask neutral questions like `what do you do', or `do you live close by'. Avoid controversial topics like race, religion, salary, or politics. Do not get into arguments or loud discussions with anyone.
5. If anyone is sharing a personal anecdote or experience, listen and speak only once they have finished. Completing others' sentences or sharing your own experiences over theirs is rude and can sound offensive.

Remember, good speakers are perceived to be more knowledgeable than others.

7. A Positive mental attitude: A Positive attitude shows your face, your body language, and your actions. Life becomes happier and sunnier, and Monday Mornings appear to be events that cause excitement rather than pain. Face the challenges of life head-on rather than procrastinating. Look for opportunities in areas where others fear to go. Remember that bad times never last. Good People do. So, whenever you feel down or low, reach out to someone you can talk to or take professional help.

Your attitude defines your altitude.

***Figure 3.4**: Perspective turns problems into possibilities*

3.8 Developing your personal brand

Personal branding is the practice of promoting yourself and your career as a brand. It is the constant process of establishing your image or impression in the minds of others about yourself. Everyone has a personal brand, whether they are aware of it or not.

Your Personal Brand is what you stand for. It is the sum total of the combined experiences and impressions that you leave on anyone who comes into contact with you, either physically or digitally.

Developing a powerful personal brand is extremely important, as it is the gateway to making your place in society. When you develop a strong personal brand, it becomes easy for people to remember you when promotions or awards are handed out. Always remember that being low profile all the time can be detrimental to your career.

Out of sight is out of mind.

Personal branding enables you to remain visible and in your key stakeholders' minds at all times. In a competitive professional environment and crowded personal space, it is very difficult to stand out from the crowd. Your personal brand helps you to emerge as a First Among Equals.

If your personal brand is strong, people remember you positively in your absence and emulate your characteristics.

Most people want to be described as technically sound, socially skilled, of honest character and values, and committed to their work, friends, company, and family. Research shows that the most wanted traits are trustworthiness, caring, humility, and capability.

3.8.1 Power questions towards a powerful personal brand

? Ask yourself the question: *What do I want my key stakeholders to say about me when I'm not in the room*? This description is your desired professional brand.

? Likewise, you might also ask yourself in another way: *What would I care about that my key stakeholders might say about me when I'm not in the room*? The answer to this question is your undesired professional image.

3.8.2 Steps to manage your professional brand

1. **Accept** that if you aren't managing your own professional image, someone else is. In other words, your Personal branding is done by others in the way they respond to you. So, it is in your best interest to be in control of your personal brand.
2. **Observe** the fact that people are observing your behavior and actions and are forming opinions about your competence, character, and commitment. They then translate these opinions into action and spread the word around about you accordingly.
3. **Work at it** constantly. Personal branding does not happen in a day. It takes effort, time, and commitment to spread the right impression about yourself. Through social media and physical contact, your actions over a period of time spread the word about you, and people begin to form the right impression of you. That's the beginning of your personal brand.
4. **SWOT:** Do a Personal SWOT analysis

3.9 How to do a personal SWOT

SWOT stands for Strengths, Weaknesses, Opportunities, and Threats

A SWOT analysis on oneself is an objective and sharp look inwards. Once you honestly prepare a list of your strengths and weaknesses and identify potential opportunities and obstacles in your life, you can make informed decisions. These decisions help in creating the best impression and creating your personal brand.

Ways to do a Personal SWOT:

- Take a strategic and proactive approach to your accomplishments.
- Identify your ideal state of mind.
- What are the core competencies and characteristics that you want people to associate with you?
- What part of your personality would you like to highlight, and what part would you like to minimize?
- Assess your current image, socioeconomic status, and immediate environment.
- View the environment around you from a micro and macro perspective. In other words, things that immediately affect you and things that can have an effect, both positive or negative, in the short and medium term.
- How equipped are you to handle those potential situations: economically, financially, education-wise, and exposure-wise?
- How do others currently perceive you?
- Conduct a cost-benefit analysis for your self-image change. For example, if you had to change yourself from being a very casual and free-spirited person to a very conservative and traditional person, is it worth it? Is the

time, money, and effort justified? Would you be compromising on your authenticity?

- Do you care about others' perceptions of you?
- Are you capable of changing your image?
- Are the benefits worth the Physiological, psychological, emotional, and financial costs?

Sample SWOT analysis

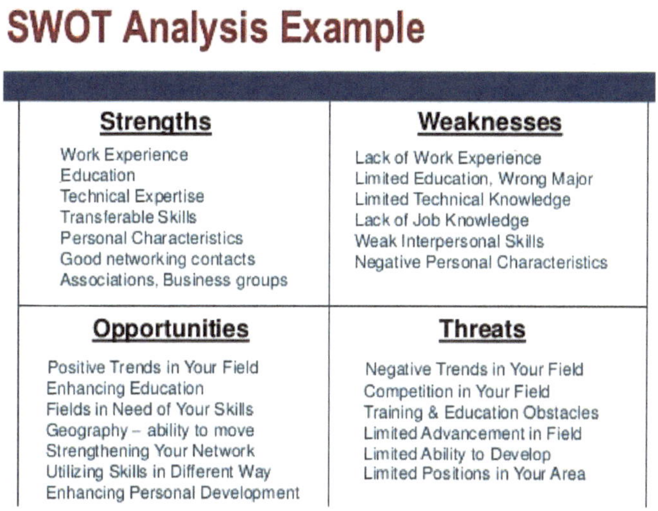

SWOT Analysis Example

Strengths	Weaknesses
Work Experience Education Technical Expertise Transferable Skills Personal Characteristics Good networking contacts Associations, Business groups	Lack of Work Experience Limited Education, Wrong Major Limited Technical Knowledge Lack of Job Knowledge Weak Interpersonal Skills Negative Personal Characteristics
Opportunities	**Threats**
Positive Trends in Your Field Enhancing Education Fields in Need of Your Skills Geography – ability to move Strengthening Your Network Utilizing Skills in Different Way Enhancing Personal Development	Negative Trends in Your Field Competition in Your Field Training & Education Obstacles Limited Advancement in Field Limited Ability to Develop Limited Positions in Your Area

***Figure 3.5**: SWOT helps you plan with purpose*

3.10 Correlation between Self-Esteem and Self-Image

- **SELF-IMAGE:**

  The way we see ourselves
- **SELF-ESTEEM:**

  The way we feel about ourselves
- **SELF-CONFIDENCE:**

  Belief about our ability, capability, and potential

***Figure 3.6**: When you believe, you begin*

Benefits of Positive Self-Esteem and Self-Confidence:

1. When you accept yourself, you can live comfortably with your personal strengths and weaknesses, without undue self-criticism.
2. When you respect yourself, you acknowledge your own dignity and value as a unique human being.
3. You treat yourself well, in much the same way that you would treat others.
4. We feel good about ourselves, and we make others feel good as well.
5. We feel in control of our lives and are flexible and resourceful.
6. We are able to make choices about how we run our lives.
7. We enjoy the challenges that life throws at us and are ready to take life head-on.
8. We can realize our own potential by combining all our abilities in a balanced and harmonious way.

3.11 How to build Self-Esteem & Confidence

"Life is a numbers game; the more times you try something, the better the odds of achieving it."

1. **Acknowledge your insecurity:** Whatever is making you feel low, depressed, shy, or inferior, first acknowledge its presence. Write down the situations when you feel this way. Learn to accept yourself with your strengths and weaknesses. And then focus on making your strengths work for you. Everyone is good at something. Find your USP.
2. **Don't give depression permission:** No one can make you feel bad without your permission. So, don't let negative thoughts enter your mind.

***Figure 3.7**: Believe in yourself before you expect others to*

3. **Talk it out**: To friends, to family, to a counsellor, to anyone you trust. Talking and sharing the pain is a huge start to developing self-esteem.
4. **Learn from your mistakes**: No one is perfect. Everyone started out somewhere in life. Make mistakes. Fail surely, but only a fool makes the same mistake twice. Look out for negative patterns or past behaviours that might have held you back before.

5. **An attitude of gratitude**: Be thankful for what you have. Focusing on what you don't leads to a sense of insecurity, inadequacy, and loss of self-confidence. By appreciating what you have, you can fight the feeling of being incomplete and unsatisfied. Achieving that inner peace will do wonders for your confidence. Maintain a `Gratitude Journal'.

6. **Avoid self-pity**: Don't let anyone pity you, and don't keep looking for sympathy. Shallow words may make you feel good temporarily, but have no effect in removing the root cause of your unhappiness. Never allow others to make you feel inferior; they can only do so if you let them. Your happiness lies in your own hands. Take control of your life and your happiness.

   Don't give anyone the key to your happiness.

7. **Do something new**: The thrill of learning a new sport, a new hobby, reading a new book, or a new language energizes the mind. A Learning mindset creates a sense of excitement and achievement. Do something that you have been meaning to do and putting off. The start is the hard part, but it becomes easier from then on. The feeling of elation and accomplishment from having done it will fill your life with positivity. You will be ready to take on greater challenges that the world has to throw at you.

   When was the last time you did something for the first time?

8. **Fake it till you make it:** Act confident. Look confident even if you are feeling scared from the inside. Displaying a little vulnerability is Ok, but don't show others your weaknesses. Walk with an erect posture and a smile on your face. Pretend you're a completely confident version of yourself. After a while, you will begin to internalize it. In other words, to look positive will become part of your basic nature.

3.12 Executive Presence

"You are present even when you are not present. In the minds of the people who make decisions about you."

Executive Presence is both your physical and non-physical presence. Your Executive Presence is the set of qualities and characteristics that represent perceptions of your competence and character as judged by your key stakeholders: (i.e., clients, managers, reportees, colleagues).

Leaders are appreciated for the first impression they make. Leaders that we admire have a quality that can't often be seen; it can only be felt. It is called 'Executive Presence'.

Whether it is presenting their results, making decisions, interacting with their peers or teams, or appearing for meetings, all leaders are expected to be the pillars of their organization. The right combination of correctly managing the body and mind makes an average leader grow exponentially. Research has shown that a powerful first impression is a major factor in establishing executive presence.

The higher one rises, the greater the need to make the best First Impression.

Good leaders with executive presence are also great communicators. They are generally perceived to be more aware and well-informed than others. They develop better inter-personal skills, which has a positive effect on their personality. They make faster decisions and implement these more efficiently, set creative targets and personal goals that can be achieved on time. An increase in their self-confidence and morale leads to the development of Gravitas.

Do only leaders need to work on their Executive Presence? No! All professionals must be conscious of their Executive Presence because their presence is what creates a perception about their skills and capabilities.

Reflect on your own Executive Presence by asking these questions:

1. What do People think about me, talk about me, whether I am physically present or not?
2. What is my reputation? Do people take me or my commitments seriously? Or do others doubt my motives and actions all the time?
3. Am I the `Go-To Person' for my stakeholders? Someone that they can reply upon?

A yes answer to all three above will give you an idea about your Executive Presence.

3.12.1 Gravitas

Gravitas is that magic quality that inspires people to follow you. That ensures that the boundaries are not crossed. People maintain a respectable and appropriate distance from you without having to tell them. That gives you credibility and an `executive presence'. You either have it or don't. It can't be faked.

What is Gravitas?

- Gravitas is your personal brand. It is what separates you from the pack. People with Gravitas command respect. Others demand it by virtue of their job titles. Gravitas has nothing to do with age. It is your mileage! It comes with experience.
- Gravitas helps you to choose carefully between confidence and arrogance. Your Gravitas lifts you up as a leader, where you are able to make objective, fair decisions.
- People look up to you because you have Gravitas. You know when to speak and when to remain silent.
- Gravitas is the ability to remain calm, composed, and handle bad situations with grace and courage. Leaders with Gravitas don't often show extreme emotions.

***Figure 3.8**: Be the energy you want to experience*

3.13 Managing your Social Media Image

Social media is an integral part of our lives. In the day-to-day hustle and bustle, we use various forms of digital media for communication. However, since this communication is not face-to-face, many times we forget basic etiquette that would have applied if we were communicating physically. We start using short forms, abbreviations, excessive punctuation, misspellings, and wrong tone of communication due to excessive use of social media. It then becomes more important to realize that digital communication on social media is no different from face-to-face.

The same rules apply on social media as would apply in normal one-to-one communication.

Your digital footprint is the mark that you leave on different social media and websites. Comments, posts, shares, likes, upvotes, and blogs are all examples of your online presence. In this SM influencers era, where friendships and popularity are measured in `likes', it is essential to have a clean and professional digital footprint.

Most of the hiring now takes place online. Whether it is Facebook or LinkedIn, Snapchat or Instagram, irrespective of the app or social media platform, recruiters and stakeholders are watching and observing you. The kind of posts and material you post, your comments, your images, and your responses are all being noted and filed away by someone. That someone may be your next boss, your next employer, your next partner, or your next investor.

And the important part is that they are forming an impression of you just based on your digital presence. In many cases, without ever even meeting you! And you may never even come to know about it. Hence, it is prudent and wise to have a good digital presence.

Figure 3.9: Your online presence speaks before you do

3.14 Ways to ensure a professional and clean digital presence

Different rules must apply when interacting on different social media platforms. Social media platforms can be categorized into:

1. Professional platforms
2. Social Platforms

Leveraging LinkedIn for Professional Growth

Figure 3.10: Use professional social media wisely

- LinkedIn is not a friendship, dating, or personal details sharing site. Remember to avoid any personal comments, images, or inappropriate contact whatsoever. Please keep it professional.
- Use a Professional photo on professional sites like LinkedIn. Get a proper image clicked in a studio or by a professional with a pleasant expression. Your image is the first form of contact for a person who visits your profile.
- Your profile must be complete in all respects. Complete as much information as possible.
- The information given must be correct and verifiable. This gives you credibility and makes you appear reliable and honest.
- Use keywords and power words that can help you to come up in searches by recruiters and influential people.

- In the work experience or summary sections: While it is good to be honest, avoid excessive mention of failures or setbacks. Instead, mention the failure and what you learnt from it.

Use a storytelling format to describe yourself and your life's journey so far.

- No spelling mistakes, typos. Spend as much time as you can on proofreading and spell-checking as you would on making your CV.
- If you want to add someone to your network, do your research on that person and then approach them. Address them properly while sending a contact request or asking for a recommendation. Send a small note along with your request and thank them once they have added you to their network.
- Do not ask for a favor or sell something immediately upon being added. Relationships take time to mature. Cultivate the person, like their posts, engage with them, and then at the right time, approach them with your offer.
- Try to help others if you have information or a skill that you can share. This is one of the best ways to get noticed.
- Add to others' knowledge. Add value in your posts rather than simply repeating or retweeting. Engage in constructive information that makes you look good.
- Pay it forward. Help others without expecting anything in return.
- Spend time on writing original posts and blogs. AI-generated posts or content do not get much traction as the LinkedIn algorithm suppresses such content.
- Appreciate others' writings and posts, and you will be similarly rewarded.
- Give credit where it is due. Don't share or use others' posts or blogs without giving them credit.

Best practices for other social networking platforms

- Post things that other people can share.
- Don't post photos or material that you will regret later.
- Don't be childish and immature.
- Remember that your posts will be seen or shared by people who are not in your network. Someone is always watching. So be careful about what you post. If your profile is open, others will visit it and form their perceptions. If you wish to restrict who visits your profile, then lock it.
- Don't keep sending friend requests. If someone does not accept for a considerable amount of time, do not contact them again.
- Work on remembering people's names and interests.

- Find your common ground (interests, life experiences, occupations, etc.) and build upon it.
- Avoid sharing information of an extremely personal nature, as it can be misused.
- Beware of stalking, phishing, and fake news. Get familiar with and use the privacy settings to your advantage.
- Some situations need a personal contact. Here, a meeting, call, or message will be appropriate. Don't blindly use social media for all occasions.

***Figure 3.11**: Digital conversations, diminished human touch*

3.15 Summary

Your first impression is very important, and you get only one chance to make a powerful impact. It is very important to be prepared and know the type of people you are going to meet or the situations you will encounter. This is life, and in life, there are no retakes. The same is with First Impressions.

Low self-esteem results from you having a poor self-image caused by your attitude. If you have high self-esteem, you will be confident, happy, and sure of yourself. Your self-image will go up, and your personal brand will become more powerful. Self-esteem is therefore crucial to you and is a cornerstone of a positive attitude towards living. You can develop the courage and self-confidence to overcome any adversity in life.

Whether you are trying to build your network, grow your business, find a job, get noticed by the media, impress powerful people, or make friends, an impactful, attractive, and visible personal brand is the key to success. It helps in building your reputation, integrity, and credibility.

Social media is a double-edged sword. If used correctly. It can greatly enhance our self-image and personal brand. And if not, it can cause permanent damage in relationships.

Knowledge Check:

1. What is the meaning of First Impression?
2. Why is it important to form a good First Impression?
3. What are the ways of creating a great First Impression?
4. What is self-image? What is its correlation with First Impression?
5. List the ways of developing your personal brand.
6. What role does self-esteem play in developing a good self-image?
7. How does one develop executive presence and gravitas?
8. What is a digital footprint? List the ways in which you can create a clean online presence.

Get ready for the real world!

"Wow, what a Personality Rahil has, man! I wish I could speak English like him", said Sam! "Every time he speaks in class, I just feel like looking at him only. He is so popular in college. Member of the dramatic society, so in demand with the `in' crowd. The teachers also love him. "

"Yes", said Ahmed, "I wish my parents had a lot of money. Then he could put me in the English medium. I could also speak like these people in our class."

Sam said: "I studied in English medium, but it was in name only. All the teachers spoke in Hindi, and the one who could speak decent English was a Yoga teacher! I feel so inferior with this high-class college crowd. Ahmed said; I feel so depressed and angry that I can't match up to these people."

Just then, there was a voice behind them: Rahil said, "Guys, I heard you. Do you think I always spoke like this? I, too, am from a similar background to yours."

"That's not true," said Sam. "You seem to come from such a privileged background."

"You think so?" said Rahil. "Do you know my parents divorced when I was 8 years old? My mother brought me up in my village. But that's another story I will tell you. Tell me why you guys are so sad and underconfident."

Sam told him. Rahil heard him out and then said, "You know what? I think you guys suffer from low self-esteem?"

"Self-esteem? Low? What's that?" they asked.

Rahil said: "Self-confidence means being personally assured of one's abilities, capabilities, and potential. A talented person without confidence is like a car without a battery. Confidence is the psychological steroid that boosts our power. Self-esteem is a way of being, thinking, feeling, and acting that implies that you accept, trust, and believe in yourself.

Self-confident people trust their own abilities, have a general sense of control in their lives, and believe that, within reason, they will be able to do what they wish, plan, and expect. Having self-confidence does not mean that individuals will be able to do everything. Self-confident people have expectations that are realistic.

Even when some of their expectations are not met, they continue to be positive and to accept themselves. For many years, I've been fortunate to experience and work with people who've learned the SECRET!

"But what's the point of all this?" said Sam. "We can never become as popular as you. You speak English so well! You know how to dress, how to talk to the opposite sex. I feel I will forever be stuck like this!"

Rahil said: "No! That's not true! Sam and Ahmed listen to me:

I will tell you the benefits of having high self-esteem. When I was studying in the village, one day my uncle came and asked me some questions. I answered very boldly. He was impressed and told my mother about a scholarship that was available to village students to study in a public school in Delhi. My mother was very shy and underconfident, and she wouldn't go and enquire on my behalf. I went to the village Head Panchayat about 3 km away by myself and found the details. I coaxed the headman to fill out the forms for me, and immediately, I got the scholarship. That's how I got admission into Delhi's finest school!

(illustration 19a)

Improving your Self-Esteem

Ahmed said, "Rahil, all that is fine, but it's too late now to think of all this. We have exams and projects. So much work! We will have to start thinking of placements as well. How do we even think about our self-esteem?"

"But that's exactly my point," said Rahil: "Unless you raise your self-esteem and confidence, you will not attain success. You will remain on the fringes of success. Let me tell you about the Affirmations.

Rahil said: "Every day that I felt angry, bitter, or depressed or inferior to others, I used to talk to myself. I used to tell myself that I am the best. Nothing can come in my way. Gradually, I started believing in myself. That is called Positive affirmation.

Positive affirmations are carefully worded positive statements that are designed to establish new thinking patterns in your mind. Using affirmations is a very effective way to build self-confidence.

1. The way to use affirmations is to repeat the statements to yourself (out loud).
2. When you repeat an affirmation, feel it, believe it, and know it!
3. Put some positive emotion into it.
4. Allow yourself to experience feelings of joy, satisfaction, power, and self-confidence as you recite each affirmation.

5. Another great way to use affirmations is to say them while looking in a mirror.
6. Use words like I CAN! I WILL!

Sam and Ahmed said, "Thanks, Rahil. From today, we promise that we will not feel inferior to anyone. We will focus on my strengths and try to think positive.

Applied Knowledge:

1. Imagine yourself in Rahil's place. How would you react when faced with life's challenges?
2. How can you practice what Rahil has suggested in real life?
3. What can we learn from Sam & Ahmed? How can we avoid developing this attitude?
4. What are some affirmations that you can use in your daily life?

Additional resources for self-development:

1. Amy Cuddy: A masterclass in developing self-esteem and self-confidence, and Powerful Body Language: **https://www.ted.com/talks/amy_cuddy_your_body_language_may_shape_who_you_are?utm_campaign=tedspread&utm_medium=referral&utm_source=tedcomshare**
2. Coach Prashant: Build your Presence & other Videos on Increasing your Visibility

   https://youtu.be/BUyU0TE1Phc?si=Kjprvgne4tclony8

Build your vocabulary

Learn and use the Words and Business phrases used in this chapter to improve your Spoken English Skills:

1. **Inculcate:** To learn or gain knowledge or values or adopt new ideas by repetition.
2. **Wind in your sails:** Encouraged or pumped up to perform better.
3. **Stakeholder:** Someone who has the capacity to help or hurt you, who can provide growth or advice.
4. **Second guess:** To have a doubt, to have some suspicion on oneself or someone else's motivations.
5. **Misconstrued:** Miscommunication, to understand the meaning of something wrongly
6. **USP:** Unique Selling Proposition. It is what sets you or a product apart from the others. USP is something that you have that your competition does not. One should spend lots of time and effort in developing a USP.

Chapter 4 Building High-performance Teams

Teamwork, Conflict Management and negotiation Skills

LEARNING MILESTONES

This chapter will enable you to:

- Understand team building and its importance.
- Recognize the difference between Group v/s Team.
- Apply the stages of team building.
- Become part of a high profile and winning team.
- Have meaningful relationships with your family & friends.
- Make conflict work in your advantage.
- Manage conflict, disagreements and fights.
- Master negotiation to get the beast deal of yourself.
- Learn new business phrases and build your vocabulary.

Expert Quotes

"Coming Together is a beginning.

Keeping together is progress.

Working together is success."

-Henry Ford

"T.E.A.M = Together Everyone Achieves More! "

TEAM BUILDING

Team Definition: Two or more people plan and work interdependently towards a common mission.

Short Story

NOBODY DID IT

There is a story about four people named Everybody, Somebody, Anybody, and Nobody.

There was an important job to be done, and Everybody was asked to do it. Anybody could have done it. Nobody did it.

Somebody got angry about that because it was Everybody's job.

Everybody thought Anybody could do it, but Nobody realized that Everybody

wouldn't do it.

Consequently, it resulted in Nobody told Anybody,

So, Everybody blamed Somebody.

But still NOBODY DID IT!!!

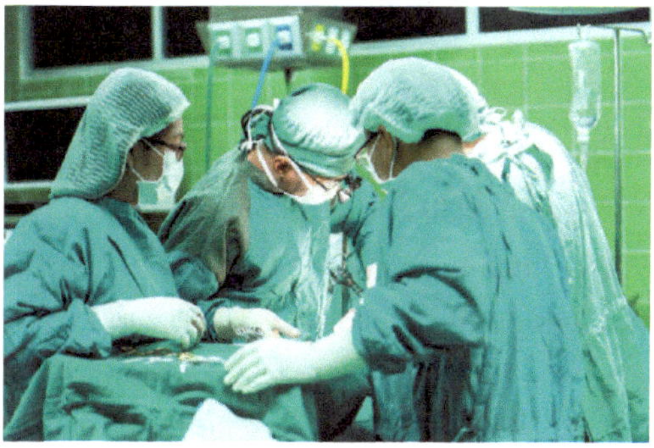

***Figure 4.1**: Where trust meets talent, even miracles feel routine.*

4.1 Team Building –The Key to Working Together

A person is introduced to the concept of Teams at a very early stage in Life. In schools, students are placed in different `Houses', sports teams, extra-curricular activities, etc. Every Team has its unique mission, its unique goal. However, the team members are all aligned with the same mission and with the same goal. They wear the same uniform. They have the same team song. They have similar activities. They have the same zeal to win. They are all part of the same Team. In Higher education and professional life, teams are a fact of life.

In professional life, whether you are a people manager or an Individual Contributor SME, no person can function alone. No one person can claim sole credit for the performance of the company or profits. This is the reason there is no `I' in the word `Team'. The result of individual effort is in the Team's effort.

- Neeraj Chopra is one of the best athletes in the world, possessing multiple records. The viewer only sees his performance on the track & field when he throws the Javelin spear. But behind those few seconds of effort is the effort and work of a huge team comprising a coach, physiotherapist, nutritionist, sports scientists, sports agents, etc.
- We only know of Neil Armstrong, the first man on the moon. But it wouldn't have been possible without the efforts of thousands of people at NASA.
- Similarly, group sports teams consist of individually brilliant members. But each player is dependent upon others to attack individually when it's necessary, but at the same time help or pass to others when the moment comes.

***Figure 4.2**: Teamwork makes the dream work*

MBA Perspective

Manoj Sharma, COO of a Top 10 Insurance Brokerage Company, USA, remembers his MBA days at Wharton Business School:

"Professional Colleges, especially Top MBA schools on Day 1 immediately place their students in small teams. We too were placed in a similar team. Whether one likes it or not, you are stuck with the same team for the duration of your MBA. We had to complete assignments and projects together. Every team member's performance and grades were dependent on the others' performance and contribution. This is done to prepare the student for what lies ahead in professional life. Teams are a basic reality. When we move ahead to our professional life, we are immediately placed in a team with other people. Teamwork is inevitable."

In Corporate, teams are aligned with the mission and the vision of the company. When the entire team performs and acts in alignment, that's when goals are achieved and careers are made.

Individual performance in a company can only be noticed and enhanced when the team performs as a whole.

If you want to go fast, go alone.... But if you want to go far...Go together!

- African Proverb

The ability to work cohesively in a team is a very important soft skill. Most Leaders look for people who can work and shine in teams. A good professional is expected to work along with the teams and realize common goals. Professional success is all about going the complete distance, showcasing your skills, and performing as expected. In such a scenario, it is very important to be a good team player.

- While it is true that teams create synergy, the fact is that Teams also create conflict. Fights and disagreements are part and parcel of every

team. But that does not mean that we should be wary of teams. Instead, we have to embrace teamwork and become valuable team players who are the first pick of every team leader.

Case in Point

Scene from Chak De India, Yashraj films, 2007

The coach tries to integrate players from various provinces in India. However, the players who have been conditioned to think only about their self-interest while playing for their home provinces find it hard to play as a team. Passing on the field so crucial to hockey success is a trait that is simply absent in them. The coach is frustrated and develops strategies to force the players to not just build a team but also to integrate as a team to achieve the heights of success.

***Figure 4.3**: When the 'We' becomes stronger than the 'Me'*

4.1.1 Group v/s Team

A Team starts out as a Group, but every group is not a team. In college or even at work, we talk of a particular person belonging to a `group'. But in Professional life, the word Team is used. The reason for this is that while group members are experts or skilled in a particular task, similar to team members, they don't always work towards a common objective. The group could consist of a bunch of people who are performing individually to complete a task. But the moment they align themselves to a common goal, mission, and vision, agreed by the rest of the group, they become a team.

For example, a Music band could have individually brilliant musicians, but they may not be able to perform together brilliantly. On the other hand, an orchestra is led by a music conductor who ensures that all the superb musicians play according to their own strengths, but the end result is that the composition is played as a team, as a perfect union of instruments and vocals.

Case in Point

The Brazilian football team has individually brilliant players who play for the top clubs around the world, scoring hundreds of goals and earning millions.

But when they play together as a team, the results are not always favorable. In the FIFA 2014 World Cup, Brazil, despite their superstar players, crashed out of the tournament, losing 7-1 to Germany in a humiliating defeat.

***Figure 4.4**: Great teams think 'You' before 'Me.'*

In a group, the participants are individually accountable for performance, but in a team, everyone is mutually accountable. The Group focus is on individual contribution, while the Team focus is on Synergy.

Synergy is the magic that happens when the whole is greater than the sum of the different parts. Each of the fingers of the hand is valuable and strong, but when they come together, nothing can beat the power of a fist. That is the magic of a team.

While the group has its own advantages, the benefits of teamwork are far greater. When a bunch of friends start up a company, it results in a group of people performing various roles. When it becomes bigger in size and numbers, it becomes a team.

Beware: Individual egos and agendas can bring the company into a dire situation where it becomes a collection of `groups' or silos.

Case in Point

The case of the `Anti-Corruption Party' started up out of New Delhi: A group of socially charged and idealistic individuals came together for a common cause: Fight Against Corruption. Gradually, the team increases in size, strength, and aspirations. Different personalities bring in different thoughts, ideas, and values. There is a clash of cultures. Some leave, some stay. However, the team has now become ambitious, and lofty targets are set for the team. Whenever the targets are not met, there is dissent and disarray. The common public who spent their time, money, and effort in bringing the party to power feels

disillusioned. It is up to the leader, then, to ensure unity in the flock and to make sure all adhere to the same vision and mission.

4.1.2 Stages in Team Development

A Team doesn't form just by chance or accident. A team is an entity that has a life of its own. It also goes through various stages of development, first proposed by Bruce Tuckman in 1965, who said that these phases are essential and inevitable in order for the team to grow, face challenges, solve problems, find solutions, plan work, and deliver results.

The 5 Stages of Team development are:

1. **Forming:** This is getting to know each other, a period when the team is just formed. The team members are assigned various roles, and they showcase their skills and get acquainted with the other team members. This is when they start thinking of themselves as part of the same group.
2. **Storming:** In this phase, the team begins its work, and the project gets underway. Meetings take place, and views, ideas, and concerns are exchanged. This is when escalations and delays are debated, blame is assigned, and conflict takes place.
3. **Norming:** In this phase, team members now see themselves as part of the same team and largely align themselves with the team's mission. Ideas are exchanged to solve problems as well as to fix accountability.
4. **Performing:** In this phase, the team has begun to work cohesively as a group, roles and expectations are firmly established, relationships and partnerships have been formed, and the team has started producing results. The focus is now on the achievement of the goals and the removal of obstacles.
5. **Dissolving:** The project has now come to an end, and the team gets dissolved and reassigned to the next task or project.

4.1.3 How to become part of a winning team?

The process of getting people with different skill sets together to perform a common task within agreed-upon variables is called Team Building.

In most companies, the moment one joins the company, they are placed in a team. But how do managers decide who should be in which team? It's not enough to look for the most brilliant performers and place them together.

Each member has supported the others, even at the cost of personal glory. Every team member has to perform their tasks to the best of their ability, but at the right time, at the right place, at the right speed, within the right budget. All of which have been agreed upon at the beginning of the project. How does one become part of a winning team? Many times, we feel envious of other teams who seem to be performing so well. Those teams get praise, credit, and recognition while the others are constantly criticized.

This is what makes a winning team. What then are the attributes that winning team members have? What does it take to become a member of a high-profile team that gets the success, glory, and praise that leads to professional success?

The following are some attributes of winning team members:

1. **Trusting your Leader:**

Whether it is your Manager or Academic Mentor, it is very important to trust the person who has included you in the team. Keep an open mind about their decisions and be aware of your immediate and macro environment. Be sensitive to a toxic team culture that can have an adverse effect on your future prospects. At the same time, be close to the team leader to gain access to opportunities. Align yourself with the team leader and trust their decisions and timing.

Case in Point

People who are shrewd investors, like Warren Buffett, or those like Elon Musk who can foresee disruptive technologies, are leaders in their fields. One may not always agree with their style of functioning, but these are the kind of people that we should align ourselves with and try to be on their teams so that we can learn from them. People who took a bet on Mark Zuckerberg, Jeff Bezos, Sam Altman, or Bill Gates' vision are billionaires today.

***Figure 4.5**: Real leaders mirror the trust you give them*

Place your faith in the Leader, and it will be reciprocated.

2. **Aligning with the team vision & mission:**

It is essential to be aware of the culture, norms, and rules that the team will follow. If the leader has not made it clear what the mission, goals, and targets of the team are, the team members should request that a common charter be made and followed.

This is a very important step for showing initiative and getting you noticed in the eyes of your seniors.

3. **Adding value to the team:**

Remember that no one wants to carry another person's weight. If you are not adding any value to the team, then you are as good as deadwood. You have to pull your own weight and, in many situations, carry double that weight. Whatever the project or circumstances demand, a good team member is always valuable

and adds something that is missing or lacking in the team. If your team is like a crossword puzzle, be the missing piece. This ability is invaluable for corporate success. Find out what the team lacks or wants, and align your talents and skills to that need.

Once there is a perfect fit in what you have and what the team wants, you will find yourself thrust into leadership.

***Figure 4.6**: Don't just fit in: be the one who completes the picture*

4. **Taking ownership:**

Taking ownership means owning up to your responsibility when the need arises. Mediocre professionals pass the buck and do not want to take any responsibility. This `not-my-job' attitude is not appreciated by leadership. A good team player not only takes ownership but also makes themselves accountable for the outcome of that task. Whether success or failure, good team players make sure that they feel responsible for the realization of the team's success.

Ownership ensures that the Team leader knows they can rely upon you in times of trouble and will always remember and appreciate this about you.

5. **Communication & interpersonal skills:**

The ability to communicate is probably one of the top attributes of every team member and is on the wish list of every team leader. Giving and receiving timely feedback with grace and politeness is a key skill in management. Respecting others' opinions, especially in meetings, active listening, and empathy skills are invaluable to pick up signs of potential conflict. There is a classic quote by Steven Covey in his book 7 Habits: *"Seek first to understand others before you seek to be understood."* Communication helps a good team member to do that.

Communication skills help you in being proactive rather than reactive.

***Figure 4.7**: Choose effort over ego, teamwork over toxicity*

6. A Positive Attitude

Once you are part of a team, channelize all your efforts into being the best team player. Don't get involved or caught in politics or toxic negativity. Approach each day and each task as if it were the day that you will get evaluated and assessed on. Don't waste valuable time and energy in complaining and indulging in backbiting. Every team leader wants a positive personality in their team who helps in coming up with solutions rather than being part of the problem.

There are three options for every team member:

Accept the situation as it is, improve the situation, or leave the situation.

- Be willing to make things better for all.

4.2 Have meaningful relationships with your family & friends

When we speak of Teams, we normally think of teams at work. However, teams should not be viewed simply through a professional lens. Relationships with our friends and family are also examples of teamwork. A family set up of parents, grandparents, relatives, and children is all part of a family team. Friends and acquaintances come together to foster lifelong networks, which are also teams.

Figure 4.8: *Family is the OG team built on love, not KPIs*

However, in this hyper-social media age, where `likes' are taken as signs of popularity, it is essential to lose sight of who actually constitutes a true team member. Who will be there with you in your times of need? Likewise, if one points the needle inwards, are we model team players for our friends and family? Are we working with them on a common ground: be it friendship or a relationship?

Once we understand this, working in teams at work becomes easier and more enjoyable. The same principles of cooperation and companionship apply at work and beyond. Success results for those who are able to be dependable team players in whatever situation: challenging or happy, professional or personal.

It is essential to foster teamwork in all aspects of one's everyday life.

Here are some ways in which we can become super team players with our friends and family:

1. **Don't get Personal:** Learn to accept the actions of others at face value without always looking for a hidden agenda. Similarly, sometimes our loved ones need an outlet for their frustration. If they have an emotional moment in front of you, be a good listener. Remember, you too might be in a similar situation someday.

2. **Don't let emotion overwhelm you:** Anger and Stress are easy to exhibit. But like an arrow, words that are said in anger cannot be taken back and often lead to feelings of regret.

   Pro Tip: When you feel yourself getting angry, lie down. It is almost impossible to remain angry while horizontal. Or if you can't lie down, then lean back on your chair.

3. **Do activities together:** Involve your friends and family in your life, your routines. Whether it is work or a workout, talk and share your experiences and encourage others to do the same. Shared experiences can lead to bonding. Family outings perform the same task as a company offsite. In a peaceful and informal environment, up close with nature, people become more introspective and uninhibited, paving the way for a complete and effective learning process.

4. **Stop texting and start talking:** Gen-Z is known to text more than they talk. However, there are many situations when emails or messaging just don't work. Whenever emotions are running high or there is a conflict or miscommunication, it is best to just meet or talk. There is almost nothing that can't be resolved by speaking. Phones and digital media are a good way to evade confrontation, but sometimes direct contact is the best way to resolve issues and differences. Face-to-face or calls are also appropriate to express empathy or sorrow. The `personal touch' can't be replicated in email. And your friends and family will reciprocate when you need that personal touch yourself.

***Figure 4.9**: Put the phone down. Pick the person up*

5. **Wishing and greeting:** Birthdays and anniversaries are excellent occasions to be in touch with your contacts. Most people love to be remembered on their special days. Surprise people by actually calling rather than sending a text. This again is a great way to show someone that you care.

6. **Show integrity:** Integrity is defined as doing the right thing...when no one is watching. Do good things for others or help others in any way that you can. The good karma will come back to you in unimaginable ways. Integrity is a soft skill that gives you credibility and makes you appear more responsible and dependable in others' eyes. Pay it forward. If anyone has helped you in any way or you have a skill that can be imparted to someone else, teach them, mentor them. Young people who lack exposure especially need guidance, and you can inspire others in ways that you never thought possible.

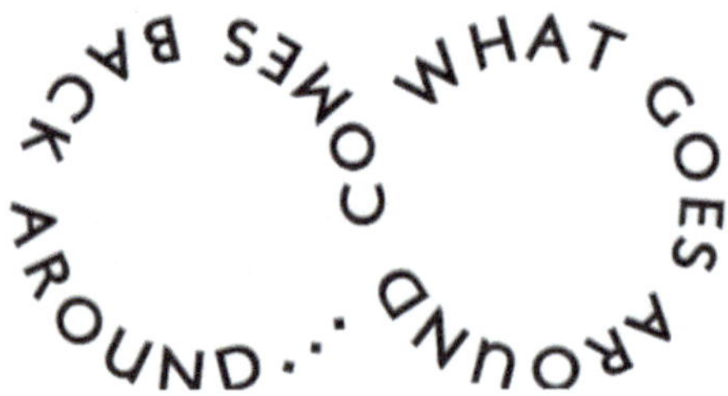

***Figure 4.10**: Every ending is a new beginning*

4.3 Managing Conflict

Making conflict work for you

Personal or Professional teams are often a source of conflict. When different personalities come together, there are clashes and confrontations. Fights, escalations, and disagreements are all part of teamwork.

Conflict should not be confused with anger, fighting, or hostility. Conflict is a difference of opinion. It happens when there are divergent views on the same situation and when two or more people cannot agree on a common solution. The same people who are best friends and ideal members now appear like enemies. That's due to our past experience with conflict, most of which has been negative.

It is a fact that conflict cannot be avoided. But conflict can certainly be managed and resolved. But is all conflict bad? Should conflict be avoided? Or can we learn from conflict and use it to our advantage? While many of us do not do very well in conflict or even avoid it, the fact is that conflict has many positives:

***Figure 4.11**: Respect differences. preserve relationships*

The following are the key benefits of managing conflicts:

1. **New ideas emerge out of conflict:**

Conflict can act as a stimulus for new thought, new ideas, and a new point of view. Conflict can open up new possibilities that otherwise could have been overlooked or not even been considered.

2. **Conflict brings about a change:**

Change is the only constant in life. Change is essential for personal, professional, and organizational growth. Differences of opinion can often result in a status quo, meaning nothing changes. Things continue as usual since no solution can be found. Conflict can force people to ask difficult questions: Questions that have answers that can break deadlocks. Conflict presents an opportunity to bring about change, which is most often resisted.

3. **Conflict builds relationships:**

Sometimes people stop communicating due to conflict. Or on the other hand, people just act nice to each other to avoid conflict. Either situation is very damaging to relationships. In the absence of communication or mutual respect, work is conducted on a superficial basis. This is a cause for escalations and slip-ups. Conflict forces people to communicate, listen to each other, and respect each other's point of view. This creates more channels for conversation and creates a more productive environment. Settlements arising out of conflict often bring people closer: at work or even in their personal lives.

4. **Conflict opens minds:**

Team Members are constantly being told to think out of the box. To think creatively. But this is often not possible due to work constraints. Conflict can foster innovation and broaden people's perspectives to fresh, new, and

unexplored ideas. It can make them realize that they are thinking differently, and this can result in different outcomes.

5. **Conflicts beat competition:**

Organizations or people who avoid conflict lose a chance to see how they can improve their service or products. Competition is unyielding, and in a tough environment, unless tough decisions are taken, the bottom line can be impacted very adversely. Avoiding conflicts prevents stagnation and keeps the product and ideas fresh and always ready to fight the competition.

4.3.1 Ways to resolve conflict

While the author does not suggest that we should seek conflict, it is not a good idea to avoid or hide from it altogether. Whenever one is faced with a conflict situation, the following steps can help in getting the most out of the conflict:

1. **Acknowledge conflict:**

Don't be in denial. Let's not look the other way or always avoid conflict or confrontation. Instead, acknowledge disagreements and deal with them. The `Ostrich Attitude, ' i.e., burying your head in the sand hoping that the problem will go away, does not work in the real world. Problems will happen. But these have to be tackled head-on. Recognize the fact that you yourself could be responsible as well. The blame doesn't always lie with the other party. Silence is not a response to conflict. Action is.

2. **Look for win-win:**

Win-win results in both parties gaining something. Win-lose is the kind of fight that we are most used to. When a person exerts power over another and emerges victorious, there is only 1 winner. The loser feels rejected, angry, and humiliated. This is a source of tension. Win-win is a school of thought that focuses on something to be gained, some benefit to be achieved by both parties. Even if they lose something, they should still end up gaining something.

***Figure 4.12**: Win together, grow together*

3. **Communicate:**

Dialogue, Conversation, and Listening are the three pillars of good conflict resolution. There is nothing that can't be resolved by taking support from these three pillars. Put yourself in another person's shoes, feel their pain, and empathize with them. That's when the real magic happens, and barriers come crumbling down. When we open our minds to different thoughts, ideas, and viewpoints, we create a more stable and peaceful state of mind.

4. **Negotiate to resolve conflict:**

Conflict can be resolved through a successful negotiation process. If all parties approach the conflict with a mindset towards achieving a win-win, then conflicts are successfully resolved. This can be better understood in the next section.

"Everything is Negotiable. Just Try! You don't get anything unless you ask for it."

4.4 Importance of negotiation skills

Research shows that managers/leaders spend 25% of their time negotiating and resolving conflicts in the workplace. Therefore, the success of employees and organizations rests heavily on developing practical negotiation skills.

***Figure 4.13**: The best agreements benefit everyone*

Normally, we assume that negotiation happens only when we have to buy or sell something. However, we negotiate in all walks of life. Negotiating a promotion or salary hike, negotiating with your friends, trying to influence them somehow, and so on.

The assumption is that the price must be kept very high as the seller or very low as the buyer. But that's not always true. What happens after a successful negotiation? The buyer and seller both achieve their objectives. The seller gets their price, and the buyer receives the product at the price they are willing to pay

Negotiation involves discussion. It involves give and take whereby both parties reach a `win-win'. Negotiation is a very important tool for conflict resolution.

***Figure 4.14**: Choose contribution over self-interest.*

However, it is not easy. Negotiation is something that has to be learnt, and hence it is important to understand the key aspects of negotiation as a soft skill.

Firstly, it is essential to understand that Negotiation is different from bargaining and compromising:

1. **Compromise** means giving a concession or settling upon a middle path. It is *not* a means of getting what you want. Whenever anyone says let's compromise, they are actually prepared to lose something.
2. **Bargaining** is generally haggling or arguing your point. Here, there is one winner and one loser, which in other words is called a `zero-sum game'.

Bargaining is a small subset of negotiation. Negotiation is a much broader concept. All bargaining is negotiation, but not all negotiation is bargaining.

Case in Point

Mr Mathur wants to go to Goa for a holiday. But his wife, Mrs Mathur, wants to go to Shimla. Neither can agree on a destination, so they arrive at a compromise. They end up going to Corbett! In this case, neither party got what they wanted.

The next year, before the vacations start, they sit and have a discussion. They share their preferences with each other. Finally, in the summer, they decided to go to Shimla, and in the winter, they decided to go to Goa. In this way, they negotiated a win-win agreement.

4.4.1 BATNA & WATNA

In the Negotiation, it is critical to know your BATNA. Not just your own, but also your opponent's as well.

Fisher and Ury coined the term BATNA in their book "Getting to Yes".

BATNA = Best Alternative to a Negotiated Agreement

Your BATNA is what is waiting for you if the negotiation is not successful. If what you are being offered is more than your BATNA, then the deal should be

accepted. If the BATNA is less than what is being offered, then go ahead and do the settlement. Before entering into a negotiation, one must keep in mind all the alternatives. Adequate research and homework must be done to find out what other choices and alternatives are available in the market. This helps you in making informed decisions while buying. We should always look to improve our BATNA

Case in Point

Mr. Bala wants to buy an LED TV for his house. He checks online and sees the price as INR 40000. He goes to the market, to his friend's shop, who offers him the same model for INR 42500. Mr. Bala's BATNA is now INR 40000. However, he wants to maintain a good relationship with his friend and help him in his business. His last experience of buying an electronic item online was not very good.

Thus, Mr. Bala offers INR 39500 to his friend with an offer of paying cash. He knows the price of INR 39500 is acceptable to his friend, as his friend will not lose money on the deal; in fact, he will still make a modest profit. His friend accepts the offer. Both parties emerge happy.

Case in Point

Reshma earns INR 35000 per month in her current job. Her company now wants to transfer her to another city by giving her an INR 5000 raise in salary. However, Reshma calculates the cost of moving and relocating to be much higher than INR 40000.

She starts looking for another job. Registers herself on some online job portals and knows a few recruiters. Immediately, she starts getting job offers and is offered INR 45000 in the same city. Her BATNA is now INR 45000. She now goes to her current employer, with whom she is keen to continue. She asks for a raise of 25%. She gets the raise and is happy to move and work in the same company.

Fisher & Ury have outlined a simple process for determining BATNA:

1. Develop a list of actions you might conceivably take if no agreement is reached
2. Improve some of the more promising ideas and convert them into practical options.
3. Select, tentatively, the one option that seems best.

WATNA is the Worst Alternative to a Negotiated Agreement

Whereas BATNA is the best-case scenario, WATNA is the worst-case scenario. What's worse can happen if you don't reach a settlement, take the offer, or negotiate? WATNA is the Exact opposite of BATNA.

Both BATNA and WATNA are necessary before trying to resolve a conflict-related negotiation.

Steps to becoming a skilled negotiator:

1. Prepare! Analyze! Research!
2. Try to find out the other party's needs.
3. Try to get to the core of the problem objectively. In other words, don't get biased or influenced. Think like a neutral party.
4. Don't assume that your position is weaker or the other is stronger. Be confident. Back yourself.
5. Observe others when they negotiate and then develop your own negotiating style.
6. Don't smile or show any emotion while negotiating. Don't appear happy or sad at any offer.
7. Identify your BATNA, WATNA, and **WAP** (**Walk Away Price**)
8. Don't reduce your offer or make any concession once you have made your initial offer. Wait for the other party to make their offer first.

4.5 Summary

Without Teamwork, it is virtually impossible for any person to succeed. Team building is a process of aligning the strengths of different personalities and combining these strengths into an unstoppable force.

A Team has synergy and momentum, which is simply not possible for a single person. Yes, isolated success can result from going solo, but sustained success will result only from being part of a great team and integrating perfectly with your Team.

Teamwork does not always result in conflict, but without conflict, the Team can slip into a comfort zone. No new ideas come forth, and team members are lulled into a sense of false security.

Negotiation is a very important and necessary tool to resolve all kinds of conflicts. Professional conflicts to personal dilemmas like: Which course or certification should you do to upskill yourself, making job and salary-related decisions, and making personal decisions concerning your friends and family. A good negotiator makes good decisions, which stand in good stead for a lifetime!

Knowledge Check:

1. What is the difference between a Team and a Group?
2. What is the advantage of working in a Team?
3. How does one become a part of a high-profile and winning team?
4. Is all Conflict a negative thing? List your reasons.
5. What are some ways to resolve conflicts?
6. What are WATNA and BATNA? Give two examples of each.
7. What are the ways to become a skillful negotiator?

Case in Point

Salil Kumar is a salesperson in a small medical store. The company has five employees operating in 1 shop. Every employee has a lot of work, but the owner, Mr. Zaveri, is a tough but fair Boss. Every sales target is celebrated with an impromptu party in the office consisting of snacks and tea. Gradually, the business grows into a large pharmaceutical company based in Mumbai. There are multiple offices and hundreds of employees.

Salil is now a sales manager. He has been working overtime to crack a deal with a group of hospitals. Day and night become one, and it is sometimes days before Salil even sees his son. He even misses his wedding anniversary. Finally, he achieves success. The order is his! The big day arrives, and Sail gives the good news to his boss, who quickly pats him on the back and leaves for London. Salil transfers the order to the suppliers, who put it into the pipeline of orders. Salil, who has worked day and night for the order, now runs from pillar to pillar in the company trying to expedite the order, but the bureaucracy of a big organization is too much. Mr. Zaveri tries to expedite things on the phone, but to no avail.

The clients are getting very restless, and the order is in danger of getting delayed. Salil is very frustrated. He has to send a small batch to the client for their approval, but the dispatch department packs the courier box and forgets to send it for 5 days!

The initial group of committed individuals, which became a team, is now again in danger of becoming a group working in silos.

No one is willing to take ownership or accountability. The team is not working together; rather, it is a bunch of individual groups just focused on their own domains.

Applied Knowledge

1. What is the problem related to teamwork that Salil is facing?
2. How could his boss have supported him better?
3. What can Salil do to ensure better teamwork?
4. How can we make sure this problem does not occur again?

Additional resources for self-development

1. **Patrick Lencioni:** The Five Dysfunctions of a Team

   https://www.tablegroup.com/topics-and-resources/teamwork-5-dysfunctions/

2. Steve Jobs speaking about why conflict is necessary in teams: **https://youtu.be/1zybuzVgGsA?si=k_8-RuR4DMOD47g9**

Build your vocabulary

Learn and use the Words and Business phrases used in this chapter to improve your Spoken English Skills:

1. **To align yourself:** To become part of, to recognize opportunity, and join together.
2. **Cohesive:** Combined, something or someone who can work as a team.
3. **Accountable:** be responsible for.
4. **Escalation:** To increase in level, usually used to show a problem that is going beyond control.
5. **Hidden agenda:**_Hide something, facts that are not visible openly.
6. **Domain:** Area of expertise.
7. **Silo:** Groups of individuals working on their own interests, not as a team.

Chapter 5 Time Management and Goal Setting

Turning Effort into Results through productivity and focus

LEARNING MILESTONES

This chapter will enable you to:

- Get more out of your 24 hours.
- Understand the true nature of time.
- Beat the bad habit of Procrastination.
- Practice easy ways to manage your time.
- Ensure results from your hard work.
- Set SMART goals and realize your dreams
- Have an optimal work-life balance.

Expert Quotes

Make time for yourself to be yourself

You will never find time for anything if you want time, you must make it

Think about what you want out of life ... not how much you can get done

"If you do what you've always done, you'll get what you've always gotten". (Anthony Robbins)

The best time to plant a seed and grow a tree was

20 years ago, the second-best time is now.

The greatest pat we can give to ourselves is to say "I had enough time for everything that I believed was important".

5.1 What is Time Management?

Time Management is the art of managing time effectively so that the right time is allocated to the right activity. It enables you to provide specific time to activities as per their importance. It refers to making the best use of time, as time is short and scarce!

- Time management is not clock management.
- Time Management is essentially self-management

Managing time means leading the life you want with resources in hand and achieving your goals. Time management consists of managing, self-planning & goal setting for getting the desired results.

***Figure 5.1**: Run your schedule before it outruns you*

Case in Point

Time for a Reality Check from a thought experiment:

Do you know how an average 70-year-old's life is generally spent?

- 25 years of sleeping
- 8 years of studying
- 6 years in rest and illness
- 7 years in holiday and recreation
- 5 years in commuting
- 4 years in eating
- 3 years in travel or commuting
- 12 years of working

Now, can you see the large amount of time we spend on sleeping and leisure activities?

5.2 Can time be managed?

The reality is that you can't manage time; you can only manage activities. Managing activities involves applying common sense and self-discipline to produce the desired results and saying `NO' to those activities that either waste time or produce negative results.

Case in Point

Have you ever watched a Circus where a lion trainer carries a stool into a cage of lions? And wondered what he was trying to do? Get himself killed!!? Even though the lion tamer has a whip in his hand, he knows the stool is his

most important tool. He holds the stool by its legs and shoves it towards the animal's face, attracting his attention. The audience waits for the lion to jump on the tamer and eat him. But nothing of that sort happens.

Instead, the poor lion tries to focus on all four stool legs at once, and in so doing, gets paralyzed, and this paralysis overwhelms him. His attention gets diverted to the stool, and he gets confused. He loses focus. He becomes weak, and thus the tamer gets control over him.

In a similar fashion, disorganized people who can't manage time are those who lose focus. They cannot concentrate on their efforts when they face lots of tasks. So they end up focusing on all the wrong things. They put their time into time-wasters and lose sight of their goals.

5.3 The need to manage time

Many people, especially students, get discouraged from trying to learn new knowledge or skills because of a lack of time. They feel that their lives are already too busy, and they don't see how it is possible to fit more into their already packed lives. Between academics and social media, professional and personal commitments, most seem to be rushing from one moment to the next.

Online courses taught by the world's best faculty have a completion rate of less than 5%! Participants of these courses sign themselves up for both paid and free classes, but are not serious about completing them. They come late to class or study in a haphazard manner. They procrastinate when it comes to submitting projects and assignments. And then at the end of the semester or completion of the courses, they wonder why their grades are so low!

Figure 5.2*: No time to learn? Then it's time to manage*

For Professionals and other people, acquiring knowledge is not a priority when work-life balance is a huge problem. This is the reason why Time management is necessary for everyone.

5.3.1 The nature of time

To practice the art of Time management, you first need to understand the nature of time.

Figure 5.3: *Time doesn't show up. It slips away. Spend it wisely.*

1. Time is an intangible resource.
2. Time is a personal resource
3. Time is tricky by nature

Time is an intangible resource

You can't buy time, rent it, borrow or steal it, store or save it, renew it, or multiply it. All you can do is spend it.

The reality is that you cannot save time. When people say they are "saving" time, it simply implies that they're spending less time on a task. They're not saving it for the future because all time must be spent immediately.

> We may have similar education, money, or talent to many people. But unlike other resources, we all have the exact same amount of time. Time is the only aspect in our lives where we are all truly equal.

TIME is a personal resource

Your time Is your own. Only you have the ability to spend your own time.

What kind of person, or a student, or a professional, you are is revealed by your usage of time.

For example, for an unhealthy person, a fitness plan is the most important thing in life. But that person does not spend any time or waste time on other things instead of fitness, then it reveals their true character. Similarly, at work, to-do lists, calendars, reminders, and plans are irrelevant if the professional doesn't have any time to even look at them! It shows a lack of seriousness and a careless attitude about their careers. James Clear, in his book *Atomic Habits*, says that your habits are how you show your identity: So your goal should not be to just save time. Your goal should be to become an efficient person.

***Figure 5.4**: Don't just save time: become the person who owns it*

How you spend your time reveals the person you want to become.

Time is tricky by nature

You can be busy all day and accomplish very little. No one ever seems to have enough time, yet everyone has all the time to waste! It seems we are spinning our wheels while being stationary in one place, like the experiment, where mice are placed inside a stationary wheel that moves on its own axis vertically. The mice keep running, sometimes for distances up to 9 km! They feel that they have been running while the wheel has not moved.

The demands of the 21st century have created a lot of work for us. However, for effective time management, we need to work smarter, not necessarily harder.

Working Smart does not mean working less. It means spending time on what truly matters.

5.4 Hard work v/s smart work

The combination of hard work and smart work is the formula for success. Think about what needs to be done, and then think again about the best way to accomplish it - not necessarily the way you've always done it, or the fastest way, and certainly not the hardest way.

Case in Point

Consider the story of two students preparing for their final presentation. Both were ambitious and determined, hopeful of coming out first. But one was hardworking and ambitious, skipping meals, researching every presentation online, referencing books, interviewing others, memorizing the text by rote without understanding the basic concepts, working day and night on the look and feel of the presentation.

The other appeared to be a little more laid back, working for just a few hours daily, and focusing on a few key resource materials. The go-getter worked all day, expecting that he would be awarded and his hard work would pay off. His opponent, however, took an hour-long lunch and then resumed her steady pace.

Finally, when the results were announced, the eager beaver was disappointed to lose to his lazier opponent. Angry because he felt he deserved the prize after working 24 x 7, he finally confronted his opponent and said, "How can you win? I just don't understand it. I worked for longer hours and much harder than you. You took so many breaks, and yet you still won. It's not fair! Where did I go wrong?"

She responded, "I focused on the audience, their needs, and what they wanted out of my presentation. And made my presentation accordingly. And since they got what they wanted, I got what I wanted.

Hard work will always pay off. Smart work pays better.

We often confuse the activity with accomplishment. Just because we are busy does not mean we are productive.

5.5 Skills to become a better time manager

Time Management can be easy if we just know where to focus. If we are able to decide on what to act upon and what to ignore. Which facets of our lives demand more attention? And which can be parked for later.

These are decisions that can be made by applying a few simple tools and techniques, which are discussed below. These have been developed after years of discussion, debate, and research, and countless interviews with experts. What has worked earlier for successful people can definitely work for you.

However, keep in mind that time management is not a theoretical concept. It involves self-discipline and commitment, which give lifelong success.

1. **Planning & prioritizing:** Identifying time stealers and knowing what to focus on, what to postpone, and what to avoid. Learn to say No.
2. **Avoid procrastination:** Don't do later what you can do immediately.
3. **Set goals & deadlines:** Setting realistic timelines for achieving written goals.
4. **Focus on task completion:** Concentrate on and complete one task at a Time.

Let us discuss each in more depth.

1. **Planning & prioritizing: Where does time go?**

Steven Covey, the author of *'The Seven Habits of Highly Effective People,'* conceptualized the Time Management Matrix. This matrix can be used to divide your time into four quadrants:

- *Quadrant 1 (Q1)*: Urgent & Important: These are tasks that require immediate and urgent attention. These cannot be postponed. Not doing these tasks leads to tension and escalation.
- **Quadrant 2 (Q2)**: Not-Urgent but Important: These are critical tasks whose completion matters in the medium to long term, but have no immediate effect or consequences if not done immediately. While we

should focus on being in Q2, these are the things that get neglected the most. These lead to procrastination.

- **Quadrant 3 (Q3)**: Urgent but Not-Important: These tasks are the reason why we are unproductive. We perform these tasks with a high degree of urgency only to realize that these were a complete waste of time.
- **Quadrant 4 (Q4)**: Not Urgent and Not Important: These tasks are like guilty pleasures. We perform these because we need a break or just want some instant gratification. However, these take up a substantial portion of our time.

To judge importance v/s urgency, good time managers view the tasks in terms of:

- Impact of doing them
- Effect of not doing them

Good time managers generally aim to be in Q2. While Q1 is unavoidable, constantly being in Q1 leads to negative consequences for the mind and body. Hence, the effort should be to move from Q1, Q3, and Q4 to Q2.

The Time Management Matrix is shown below with some examples:

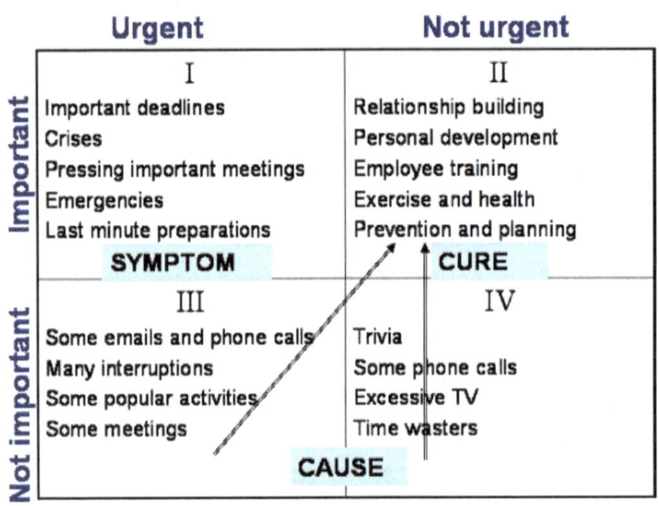

***Figure 5.5**: Busy is not the same as productive*

Case in Point

The 4 Quadrants can also be used to identify your time-spending personality type. Shown below are some examples of the traits of the different personalities. Can you identify yourself? Remember, the objective is to finally be in Q2.

Can you identify yourself?

Q1 **THE BUSY PERSON**	Q2 **THE PRIORITIZER**
• Last-minute preparation for tomorrow's presentation or exam. • Paying bills and taxes on the absolutely last day. • Senior demanding overdue report. • Visit a friend or family member hurt in an accident.	• Get an annual Health Checkup. • Work incrementally on a project or presentation due in 21 days. • Visiting parents, calling a friend • Split the current project into small bits daily. • Spending quality time with family and friends. • One-to-One with the team..
Q3 **THE YES PERSON**	Q4 **THE WASTER**
• Going away from the desk or studies for frequent breaks. • Idle gossip. • Constantly sorting out others' problems and issues. • Respond instantly to all posts, emails, and social media messages. • Inability to say NO.	• Compromising on sleep and health to binge-watch • Addictions and Escapism • Distractions • Procrastinating on projects or tasks. • Negative attitude and poor health.

The basic requirements to reach Quadrant 2 are:

- Clear definition of organizational roles and specifically your own role.
- Selection of and focus on SMART goals.
- Development and utilization of schedules.
- The practice of daily adapting in the work role.
- Learning to say NO!

***Figure 5.6**: No more burnout. Just better boundaries*

2. Prioritizing

Prioritizing means deciding what is important and what's not. Which tasks to take on and which to leave. Sachin Tendulkar, the great Indian batter, has the ability to decide which balls to play and which ones to leave, which is proof of

his greatness. A true professional does not jump to take on every assignment. Prioritization prevents your life from becoming overloaded and ensures peace of mind.

To help you prioritize, you will need to differentiate between:

- Effectiveness: doing the right things
- Efficiency: doing the right things correctly

The difference between the efficient and effective use of time:

- **Effectiveness** refers to doing the right things. When you are efficient, you do the job facing you in the best possible manner.
- **Efficiency** refers to doing things right. When you're effective, you may or may not do the job in front of you. You do what most needs to be done at that particular point in time.

And when you're a good time manager, you use both approaches. You look at all the possible tasks in front of you; select the most important task, and do it in the best possible way. When you learn how to do that and do it consistently, your work will be more productive, and your life will be more peaceful. You will have successfully avoided wasting time.

Case in Point

Your `to-do' or `activity log' list shows that you need to submit your project a week later by next Thursday. It would normally take 4 days to make the presentation, but when you suddenly have to go out of town and cannot work on it for the next 3 days, you have only 1 day to complete it. And you don't know how, but you drop everything else and manage to complete it and submit it. You are amazed at how a job you thought would take you 4 days took only 1 day to finish. This is Parkinson's law.

Parkinson's Law: "Work expands to fill the time."

***Figure 5.7**: Plan your time, protect your goals*

3. **Procrastination: The enemy of time**

How many times have we felt, Oh, I don't feel like doing it now, I'll do it later. But that later never comes! It is nothing but procrastination- the habit of putting things off to a point where you have no choice but to do it.

Procrastination is the action of delaying or postponing something. It is a voluntary activity where, intentionally, the task at hand is given another time or another date for completion. And then again and again till it goes into a hopeless loop of delaying and self-justification.

Procrastination is often a result of two main causes:

1. The task in hand is **overwhelming.**
2. The task in hand is **unpleasant.**

The attitude of "set it and forget it" looks easy, but this procrastination habit is a productivity killer. Continuing to put off daily tasks will lead to weekly tasks, which will lead to monthly tasks, and before you know it, you have a mountain of tasks with no time to complete them.

Mark Twain, the famous author, and subsequently the noted author Brian Tracy, have given possibly the best solution for beating procrastination:

Figure 5.8: *Tackle the beast task early. Peace unlocked*

Eat the Frog, as the name suggests, has nothing to do with eating Frogs! Rather, it is very simple and easy to apply; it states, "If the first thing you do in the morning is eating a frog, anything else you do during the course of that day will be better than that!"

In other words, if you accomplish the most difficult tasks first, then whatever you do after that will appear to be easier and thus more enjoyable and rewarding. Therefore, always try to do the most difficult things first! Everything else that follows will be easier in comparison.

The Eat the Frog principle has three steps:

1. Eat the Ugliest frog first! Do the most difficult task first.
2. Eat it now! Not after 5 minutes. Not later. You have to do it now!
3. Doesn't help to just look at it! You actually need to eat it.

Case in Point

Whenever you feel overwhelmed by work or studies, remember to BOOM!

BOOM :

- Be Aware
- Organize your thoughts- write it down
- Overcome: temporary pain for getting permanent pleasure
- Move (Do it now!)

5.6 The 4D Principle to Beat Procrastination

***Figure 5.9**: How to create time*

When you face a task, decide to deal with it according to one of the following 4D principles:

- **Do it:** Attend that meeting, answer that mail or message only if it cannot wait till later.
- **Delegate it:** Get someone else to do the task and supervise them.
- **Dump it:** Reject the task or delete it from your inbox if it's a waste of time.
- **Deadline:** If not urgent, schedule a later time in your calendar when you will tackle the task.

Case in Point

Sangram works in a private limited company. He is a Field sales manager who is required to file the sales reports with his head office on a weekly basis. Every Friday, the field salespersons from remote locations email their figures to him, and he makes the presentation. His report needs to be emailed with detailed data and analysis on the sales performance. The presentation takes him 10-12 hours to make. It is very stressful, and his entire Wednesday and Thursday are spent chasing his salespeople to email the reports. They are

busy with sales, so they sometimes send the reports with mistakes and inconsistencies that cause him great stress and anxiety. He usually starts working on the presentation on Thursday and emails the report on Friday night. A full 20 hours. Of effort! He is doing 80% of the work in 20% of the remaining time.

Sangram has a heart attack, and his doctor tells him he cannot take any more stress. He reevaluates his life. And working style.

He goes back to work. He organizes webinars on how to use CoPilot, ChatGPT, Gemini, Preplexity, and other AI to prepare their reports. He organizes data writing workshops conducted by experts for his staff. He creates an MS Teams group for his salespeople. Now, he tells them to send him images and photos of their sales invoices on a daily basis. They are freed from manual data entry and instead focus on sales. His presentation and figures are now online and up to date on a daily basis, and his Friday report is now prepared in 3 hours. He is now doing 20% of the work in the remaining 80% of the time.

He emails the weekly report on Friday evening at 3 pm and goes home to spend time with his family.

5.7 Goal Setting

"A goal is a dream with a deadline." -Charles Henry Parkhurst, D.D.

A Goal: The purpose toward which an activity is directed; an end; an objective.

We all have some goals in our lives. We achieve some and are not able to realize others. But how exciting it would be if we could realize all the goals we set out to achieve for ourselves. Even though planning for achieving goals is a time-consuming exercise, it is one that can end in fulfillment and joy. Joy at having saved time that can be used for personal gain.

***Figure 5.10**: Know the target, trust the journey, hit the mark*

Goal setting is the process of deciding what you want to accomplish and making a plan of action to achieve the desired results.

Benefits of Goal Setting

- You manage time efficiently and effectively.
- You get a feeling of achievement, which fills your mind with positive thoughts.

- Positive thoughts help you to take control of your life.
- People take you more seriously because you `walk the talk'.
- You are able to focus on more meaningful things in life.
- You are successful in your own eyes, regardless of what that means to other people.
- Your job becomes more meaningful and fun.
- You are able to form better relationships with people.

5.7.1 How to Set Achievable Goals

We can realize our goals by following these two simple ways:

1. Commit to your goals in writing
2. Make SMART Goals

Goals are just dreams till you write them down.

1. **WRITE your goal down**. Whether it is a calendar entry, a to-do list, or putting goals done in writing, it creates a sense of commitment.
   a. Once it goes into writing, you develop a sense of urgency, and the goal gets etched into your subconscious permanently.
   b. Words convey images, pictures, feelings, and emotions to the brain. We can plan `something' without realizing fully what that something is. It is intangible, i.e., it is not something that we can touch or feel. It is simply in our mind.
   c. By putting those thoughts into words, magic happens! A commitment is made between action and intention. By putting it down in words, which now takes on a physical body or shape? It is a constant physical reminder to take action. It becomes something that motivates us.
2. **Make SMART Goals:** Anyone, whether it is a person or an organization, can use the SMART criteria to set goals and objectives that can be realized.

   SMART =
   - Specific
   - Measurable
   - Attainable
   - Relevant
   - Time-bound

S: Specific and well-defined objectives. Define exactly what you want. Set goals that are ambitious but achievable.

M: Measurable outputs and inputs. Figure out how you're going to measure your goals. Set a clear timeline for the achievement of your goals.

A: Achievable in terms of resources & expectations. Commit to being personally responsible for achieving your goals. If part of a team, be sure that accountability is clear, who is responsible for what.

R: Relevant to the overall business and personal strategy.

T: Time-bound with an operational and written schedule.

In addition to *SPECIFIC*, the goals should include:

- No stretching
- Systematic
- Synergistic
- Significant
- Shifting around frequently

In addition to *MEASUREABLE*, the goals should be:

- Meaningful
- Memorable
- Motivating
- Magical

In addition to *ACHIEVABLE*, the goals should be:

- Action plans
- Accountability
- Acumen
- Agreed-upon

R means *RELEVANT*, but it also stands for:

- Realistic,
- Reasonable,
- Resonating,
- Results-oriented,
- Rewarding,
- Responsible,
- Reliable,
- Rooted In Facts And
- Remarkable.

T means *TIME-BASED*, and it represents:

- Timely,
- Tangible And
- Thoughtful.

5.8 Work-life balance

In this hectic world, work-life balance has taken a backseat. Most students find themselves bombarded with information. Friends, family, social media, studies, academic performance, competitive exams and interviews, and job hunting all put pressure on them. Professionals and entrepreneurs have performance and business pressure. All these pressures take a toll on personal relationships and cut family time. Even on vacations and holidays, people are glued to their cellphones doing business and work or just scrolling.

In such a high-pressure and dynamic environment, how does one find time to do what one desires? Achieve goals? Or spend quality time with friends and family? How about personal fulfilment? The answer lies in striking a perfect work-life balance. But to run after perfect balance is perhaps an illusion. The answer, then, may lie in Work-life integration.

5.9 Work-life integration

It is the realization that whether we like it or not, our work, academic, and personal lives are forever joined together. So the secret then lies in integrating various areas of life together. For example, avoiding elevators and taking the stairs

to work or college if you don't get time to exercise. Taking calls while walking or putting life events and milestones in your work calendar.

There is no such thing as Work-Life Balance. It is all Life! The balance has to be within you.- Sadhguru

5.10 Summary

Whoever said that Time = Money is right.

Every day and every minute of every day is worth money and must be treated with respect. So often, we hear people say: Let's do Time pass. But they fight for every bit of money that is due to them. Will they ever do Money-pass? Of course not! Just as we handle money responsibly, the same respect should be given to time.

Time Management is Self-Management. If you want to enjoy one of the greatest luxuries in life, i.e., the luxury of having enough time, remember there is only one way. Time Management

Take enough time to think, plan, and prioritize things. You will add years to your life, and more life to your years. Setting SMART goals and knowing how to execute an action plan will put you ahead of the competition in the long run.

Knowledge Check:

1. What are the ways in which you can practice Time Management?
2. How well can you differentiate between Urgent and Important tasks?
3. Analyze your day using the Time Management Matrix. Plot your actions and tasks in each Quadrant. See how much time is spent on urgent issues compared to that spent on important and non-urgent issues.
4. Define SMART goals.
5. Exercise: Set 1 1-goal that can be achieved within 60 days, for yourself, using the SMART criteria. Prepare a SMART plan and track the progress of this goal plan. At the end of 60 days, analyse your success or lack of it with reasons.

Additional resources for self-development

1. Brian Tracy: Eat the Frog: **https://www.briantracy.com/blog/time-management/the-truth-about-frogs/?srsltid=AfmBOoozWkVZ3CQZ7H13t0LGpKl_ujaJ8S_YljQ9fww5IljNeFXnBgDW**
2. Steven Covey: **https://www.franklincovey.com/courses/the-5-choices/choice-1/**
3. Coach Prashant: **https://youtube.com/shorts/oUM9Pgv86XU?si=h9b-SHrO8HBLRSuRO**

Get ready for the real world!

Case in Point

Rhea, a working professional, wants to become physically fit. Her goal is to lose weight and become physically fit. She has tried various diets but has been unable to lose any weight so far. Her boss, herself a fitness enthusiast at work, sits down with her and suggests to her the SMART system of goal setting. Rhea now makes a health plan that is structured and that she feels is achievable.

Specific: She first puts down on paper exactly how much weight she wants to reduce and what her fitness ideal looks like.

Measurable: She ensures that her fitness plan has goals that can be measured over a period of time. Weight reduction, BMR, and treadmill analysis are all analytics that will help her in measuring her performance.

Achievable: Are her goals achievable and accountable? What is the role of diet in her plan? How much will the trainer contribute towards ensuring that she sticks to her plan? What about her self-discipline and self-control, i.e., Personal accountability

Relevant: Are the fitness targets achievable within the constraints of professional and personal commitments? With her job and family commitments, will she be able to follow her diet and exercise plan? When, what time, how much in a day?

Time-bound: Has she set a time frame and defined timelines within which the goals have to be achieved? How flexible are these timelines? How frequently will she monitor the same?

Rhea starts her fitness goal, and at the end of her pre-defined fitness plan period, she not only achieves her weight loss goal but also beats it by 5 kgs! She is thrilled!

Applied knowledge

1. Identify any good habits you have regarding time management that you can learn from Rhea
2. Why wasn't Rhea successful initially in her efforts?

Build your vocabulary

Learn and use the Words and Business phrases used in this chapter to Improve your Spoken English Skills:

1. **Circle back:** To come back to something after trying something else
2. **Laid back:** Lazy or suffering from a lack of initiative.
3. **Eager beaver:** A person who always volunteers and is always willing to do a task first.
4. **Optimal:** Something that is used or applied to its full potential. Working at a capacity that is conducive to positive change.
5. **Hit the ground running:** To get started on something without much training or preparation.

Chapter 6 High-Impact Communication Skills

Building Professional Excellence, Credibility and Reputation

LEARNING MILESTONES

This chapter will enable you to:

- Learn the essentials of communication
- Appreciate the applications of communication
- Understand the communication process
- Find out why miscommunication takes place
- Develop ways to increase our communication skills
- Practice the 7Cs of communication
- Master the Dos and Don'ts of communication
- Enhance your cross-cultural communication
- Explore Indian-isms and ways to avoid them

Expert Quotes

The most important thing in communication is to hear what isn't being said –

Peter Drucker

The Art of Communication is the language of Leadership

-James Humes

"A wise man reflects before he speaks; a fool speaks, and then reflects on what he has uttered."

- French Proverb.

6.1 The true meaning of Communication

The word Communication is derived from the Latin word "communicare" = make common, share, participate, impart.

Communication is a part of our lives from the moment we are born. It is the basis of all interaction. We communicate with everyone that we come across. Even without speaking! We are communicating all the time. However, often we are told to become better communicators. In times of failure, conflict, or anger, we experience miscommunication. We realize the problem was not the lack of communication but rather in the manner in which the communication was

done. Good communication skills remove miscommunication. Communicating effectively is much more than just saying or writing the correct words."

Most of us aspire to be leaders. We want to be at the top of our game. We want approval and acceptance in society. Good communication helps us to impress and convince others of our point of view. Good communication is the basic quality of Management and Leadership.

What then is Good Communication? And why is it that despite communicating all our lives, there is still so much room for improvement? We will try to answer these questions and also learn tools and techniques to become master communicators in all aspects of our lives.

Communication is a process that involves the transfer of meaningful ideas, information, feelings, and messages from one person to another through the use of shared language or symbols.

Communication does not happen by magic! It is a voluntary process. It takes place when your ideas are transferred to another's and arrive without distortion, complete, and clear. Communication is successful only when the meaning and intent of the sender is understood and acted upon.

Importance of Communication

For students

Our academic system encourages excellence mainly through good marks and grades. However, connection to the real world happens only once a person graduates into professional life. And gets a rude jolt when faced with the fact that those marks and technical skills account for very little. People get praised and promoted, end up with plum postings and assignments solely on the basis of their ability to connect well with their bosses and clients. Thus, it becomes very essential to gain mastery over communication skills at the earliest possible time in one's life.

Communication is your crucial link between the external world and yourself. It is the bridge that enables the smooth traffic of messages to pass between you and those you want to influence. Communication skills are tested in your job interview, group discussions, and your interaction with your prospective employers in order to make the best first impression.

One look at listings on job portals and recruitment postings reveals that most companies, irrespective of their domain, look for candidates with good communication skills.

***Figure 6.1**: Reset. Refocus. Rise*

For professionals

It is a well-known fact that communication skills are the single most important decisive factor in choosing managers. In the author's long experience as a corporate soft skills trainer, the majority of the training conducted is related to communication skills. The author has found, through working with thousands of corporations and other professionals, that communication skills, including both written and oral presentations, are the main factors contributing to professional and personal success.

Technical skills are the first step towards entry into professional life. But good communication skills are the stepping stones on which the path to your success will be paved.

For organizations

Organizations also want to project the best possible image of themselves to their stakeholders. This could be for product promotion, lobbying, fundraising, or to highlight achievements. Corporate Communication managers have the responsibility to ensure that the corporate messages are transmitted with the best possible public relations activity. They have to make their company look good!

Inadequate or incomplete communication is the source of conflict and misunderstanding. It interferes with productivity and profitability. Virtually everyone in business has experienced times when they were frustrated because they just couldn't "get through" to someone. They felt as if they were speaking a strange language or were on a different "wavelength."

For teams

Often, teambuilding and team integration are brought into focus as conflicts occur. Synergy is what makes a great team. Communication is essential to achieve this synergy between team members. The ability to communicate effectively is a basic requirement for each team member.

For inter-personal relationships

Managing relationships is an art that involves meeting of minds. Compromise and agreement are the basis of good human bonds. However, the reality is that our minds and others are not necessarily in sync. You may think differently, and the others may perceive our message differently. There are different realities for different people. This is why conflicts, disagreements, fights, and divorces happen. Communication is the bridge between our separate realities. Communication is what joins us to others. To communicate is to relate. To be one in thought with the receiver of our communication enables optimal human relations. And this is the ultimate benefit of communication.

6.2 Communication made simple

Communication is not just thinking, speaking, or expressing yourself. It's not just delivering a message; it is much more than that. It is a complex art and technique of getting others to understand you. It is an active process, which involves encoding, transmitting, and decoding the intended message.

Encoding: *Changing the message from mental form into words, gestures, and language.*

Decoding: *Interpreting those words, gestures, or language together with context, tone, and voice.*

In an ideal situation, good communication results in the sender and the receiver thinking about exactly the same thing. The sender has succeeded in transmitting an idea from their mind to the mind of the receiver.

Case in Point

Karanpreet, on his first day of work, stood outside the main entrance building at Cyber City, Gurugram. He had arrived from his native Punjab the previous day, his first day outside his small town, where he also did his Engineering and got placed on campus. He stood hesitatingly in the main lobby of the building. Kalpana was watching this from a distance. She recognized Karanpreet as she had interviewed him on campus. At first, she thought he didn't want to go inside to begin work. She kept watching him and saw as he struggled with the doors, the revolving turnstile barriers, using his access card, etc. She went up to him, smiled, and without saying anything, used her card to let him in. She stood in the doorway, not allowing the elevator doors to shut. Karanpreet jumped after her, and then he turned back, looked at her, and without saying anything, smiled back in gratitude. Their communication was complete.

6.2.1 Avoiding Miscommunication

"Between what is said and not meant, and what is meant and not said, most of love is lost." – Kahlil Gibran

When the sender's message is misinterpreted, or any misunderstanding or misconception takes place, it is called miscommunication. 70% of all communication

effort is misunderstood, misinterpreted, twisted, rejected, disliked, distorted, or simply ignored- even if it is within the same society, group, or culture! The purpose of good communication is to eliminate miscommunication at any cost.

Case in Point

An English professor wrote the words: "A woman without her man is nothing" on the board and asked his students to correctly punctuate the sentence.

All of the males in the class wrote: "A woman, without her man, is nothing."

All the females in the class wrote: "A woman, without her, man is nothing."

Case in Point

A prisoner was about to be hanged and had put in a mercy petition. However, his petition was rejected by the Governor many times, and on the day of his hanging, a message arrived that left the jail warden scratching his head. He couldn't decide what to do. He gave the message to his subordinate, who was also confused. The message said:

'Hang him not, release'. They understood that they needed to release the prisoner, which they did.

A few days later, the Governor visited and asked about the report of the hanging, which was to have taken place the previous week.

When the jailor showed him the message, the Governor was aghast. You idiot! You let him go?!! He shouted, I wanted you to: 'Hang him, not release'!

One comma in the wrong place made such a difference!

6.3 Learning high-impact communication

The good news is that anyone can learn to communicate better. Communication is a skill. And like all skills, you can learn to be a master communicator with organized training coupled with practice. The reality is that good communication requires practice. If you have the desire and are willing to work hard, you can be the master communicator you always wanted to be.

The 7Cs is a master tool that ensures that communication is of the highest quality.

6.4 The 7c's of communication: Checklist for excellent communication

Importance of the 7 C's

In this digital age, where messages are being composed and received on the go, in a hurry, in travel, in complicated and volatile situations, the chances of miscommunication and conflict are very high. How then does a person ensure that their message is correct and complete in all respects unless they get feedback, which is not always possible?

The answer is the 7Cs of communication that help busy people ensure that any message going out from their systems is of the highest quality and standard.

The 7Cs is a master checklist to ensure perfect communication. Its purpose is to ensure that the message is sent and received without any miscommunication, and feedback is given, and the necessary action is taken. In short, the communication process becomes complete once the 7Cs are applied to any message, be it verbal or non-verbal. However, the 7Cs are most effective in written communication, where the chances of miscommunication are very high. This is because the sender does not have the luxury of using body language. Where the words have to perform the job of replacing the physical person, the 7Cs can be an invaluable tool.

Those aspiring to be good communicators must understand the basics of the 7Cs and apply them immediately in their daily communication.

The 7Cs are named thus because every criterion of this checklist begins with the letter C, and they are seven in number. Although they are just seven small words beginning with the letter "C", they are invaluable in the world of communication. They can be truly called the 7 Wonders of Communication Skills.

A message is said to be effective when the receiver understands the same meaning that the sender intended to convey. For any communication to be effective, it must have these seven criteria:

1. **Complete**: Your message should be able to answer the 5W+1H principle. Podcasters, investigators, and lawyers all use it. This is the 'Socratic Questioning' method that states that good communication must be able to answer the following:
    - ✓ Who?
    - ✓ What?
    - ✓ Where?
    - ✓ When?
    - ✓ Why?
    - ✓ & How?

***Figure 6.2**: Socratic Questioning*

2. **Compact:** The Communication must follow the KISS framework. KISS stands for KISS:

   - Keep
   - It
   - Short
   - Simple

   Ideally, most communication should be concise, to the point, and not waste the receiver's time. Details when asked, not as a default, especially in executive communication.

3. **Considerate:** The ability to think like the receiver is being considerate. What are their likes, dislikes, background, state of mind, and seniority? Good communication must answer these questions about the receiver.

4. **Concrete:** Say What you Mean and Mean What you Say.

5. **Clear:** There is no room for assumptions in Business Communication. What you mean to say and what the receiver interprets can sometimes be two different things altogether. Good Business Communication removes all communication.

***Figure 6.3**: Own the Gap. Close the Gap*

6. **Courteous:** The rules of courtesy and politeness apply to all Communication. One must always be polite and kind in communicating with others. Communicate with others how you would like to be treated.

7. **Correct:** Check the message for grammar, syntax, tone, and other errors.

Case in Point

Abhay, a Team Lead at an IT company, was always getting scolded by his boss for sending poor-quality messages. His boss was irritated when Abhay's emails had wrong spellings, unclear meanings, or were simply too long. Some of Abhay's clients also complained to his boss that Abhay's emails were sometimes too direct or even rude.

A client showed his boss an offensive and rude email that Abhay had sent. It said: "Make sure that you send me the figures by tomorrow. ' How can he order me like this?" the client asked Abhay's manager. "Doesn't he have any sense of respect?"

Abhay had a very heavy workload and was unable to give every email of his the same attention. He was always in a hurry. Even though he wanted to act on this feedback, he was unsure how to proceed.

Then his Boss told him about the 7Cs and how they could be applied. Abhay understood the concept, and his entire communication changed 180 degrees for the better. He started getting compliments from clients and developed better relationships with his colleagues.

Abhay also started using AI tools like ChatGPT and the Grammarly App to check his messages for the 7Cs before sending. Before pressing `send', Abhay would ensure that his message was complete in all respects, was to the point, and backed his figures with concrete facts.

To that same client, now whenever he wanted some information, he would use the right tone. words 'please', can you send', 'thank you', etc. He was polite and courteous to the receiver and made sure that he used spell check and proofread his messages before sending. All this took not more than 30 seconds, but the positive effect on his professional and personal life was phenomenal!

7Cs checklist for your Business Communication	Points to check if your communication contains all the following:
Complete	Contains all the information to get your desired response.
Compact	Short & Sweet message. Only has relevant information.
Considerate	`You' attitude. Put yourself in the place of the receiver.
Concrete	Definite facts and specifics rather than vague and general.
Clear	Use of simple language and easy sentence structure.
Courteous	Polite and correct tone of language. Convert orders into requests.
Correct	Correct spellings, grammar, and language. Spell Check!

6.5 The DO's of communication

How does one become a master communicator? There is simply no magic pill. However busy you may be, irrespective of your social and educational background, the fact remains that these same tools and techniques are available to all of us.

It is up to us to use these techniques to become good communicators.

The author has observed, by training thousands of professionals and people from diverse fields, that people who communicate well show some similarities. These great communicators advise:

1. **Pay attention** to the 7Cs of Communication: Think about what you are going to say, rather than simply saying what you think.

2. **Observe:** A simple and easy-to-practice method is to observe good communicators around us. What makes them so good at communication? Pick up the best from those people and apply the same to your own lives. And immediately you'll see the difference. Magic can happen. Sometimes overnight.
3. **Determine the outcome** that you wish from your communication. The outcome or result will help you to choose the timing, medium, tone, etc.
4. **Use the STOP principle**: Pause before you send. Think to yourself: Should I really send this now?
   - STOP
   - THINK
   - ORGANIZE
   - PROCEED
5. **Be Aware of your immediate environment.** Increase your knowledge of diverse subjects. It will help you to become more confident, a dynamic speaker, and a very interesting person.
6. **Work on your voice** pitch, volume, and intonation. Bring variety to your speech. Use the voice recorder on your smartphone to listen to your own voice and take feedback from others. Speak clearly and audibly.
7. **Don't interrupt!** Learn to let others finish their sentence. If you have been interrupted, always do a little recap of what has already been said.
8. **Tone**: Use the correct tone. Ask yourself how you would have said this to the person if they were face-to-face? Especially in writing, pay attention to the tone by converting statements and orders into questions or requests. Make that extra little bit of effort to sound polite, especially to clients and superiors. You may think they don't notice, but it's a fact that your correct tone can improve the effectiveness of your message and chances of getting a positive result by almost 50%!

   Tone is body language in words. Tone is a reflection of your personality, so use it wisely!
9. **Ask questions:** The more you ask, the more clarity and knowledge you will obtain. Don't be shy. Raise your hand!
10. **Learn to customize** your speech depending on the audience or the other party. The same message can be said in many ways, depending upon who you are speaking to. Speak in a language that another person can best understand.
11. **Use the KISS principle:** Keep it short and simple. Long-winded message tends to bore others, and boring is a sin in communication. Keep your messages vibrant, concise, and interesting.

Case in Point

Abhishek has to communicate the plan for the annual company picnic to his team. Below in the left column, you will see the dialogue or messages between the two parties. In the right column is an explanation of how the

communication principles of effective communication and the 7Cs have been ignored and then subsequently applied:

Communication	Principle
"Dear Team: as informed earlier, we are going to our company event.	**Lack of 7Cs:** Abhishek is communicating with his team verbally. This can be a cause of confusion, especially when communicating with a group. The communication should be in writing.
"The details are the same as last year."	Wrong Assumption made. He assumes that all team members are aware or still remember last year's event. The reality is that there may be additions to the team who were not present the previous year. Or people may have forgotten. **Correct**: "The following people will be going, the dress code is, the agenda is.... "Along with all other specific details to help the team come up to speed.
"You all have to attend. I will not allow any dropouts".	The tone here is wrong. It can offend people as they may feel that Abhishek is throwing his weight around or trying to act superior. **Correct:** "100% attendance is required, and sorry, but no request for cancellations will be accepted."
Be there at 5 o'clock, near the clock tower. The vehicle will wait for 15 minutes.	Essential details are missing: for example, 5 am or 5 pm? Also, where exactly is the Clock Tower? Which locality/ town? Fifteen minutes is a very vague time frame, as there is no starting time. **Correct**: The correct format is always: Day/Date/Time/ Place. E.g, "We will meet on Sunday, June 3rd, at 5 am, next to Metro pillar number 96, clock tower, Patel Chowk, New Delhi. The company transport will arrive at 5.15 am and will wait for all participants till 5.30 am".
Reply from a team member: "Abhishek sir: can I come myself?"	Here, the team member is not clear what they want to know: Come where? Does " myself mean by myself? Or will I be able to reach by myself? **Correct**: Abhishek Sir, is it ok if I reach the picnic venue on my own, as I live very close to It? What time should I reach there?"

6.6 Communication mistakes to avoid

Professional communicators avoid some commonly committed errors. They have the skill and practice to avoid these traps and hence ensure error-free communication. Students of communication would do well to observe the communication sent by others and check for errors and faults. Professional communicators advise the following:

1. Do not use big words straight out of a dictionary, heavy technical terms, and jargon that are not understood by others. If you have to be technical, please say it in the simplest manner that one can understand, even by a layperson.

2. Do not speak too fast or even too slow. Don't speak in a boring monotone, as it can get very boring for the others to listen or maintain concentration. Use the voice recorder on your phone to listen to areas of improvement in your own voice.

3. Do not speak when there is noise or external sounds that can make you inaudible. Don't speak on the cellphone while driving or in traffic. Important calls must not be made while travelling due to call drops and disturbances. Instead, these should be done in a quiet environment.

4. Do not assume that the others can understand your message. Ensure clarity. Assumptions can cause huge miscommunication. Don't assume, as it can make you appear underprepared or foolish in the eyes of others.

***Figure 6.4**: Say it clearly. Hear it carefully.*

5. Maintain neutral emotions and only communicate when you are in a neutral state of mind.

6. Do not interrupt the speaker, and don't allow yourself to be interrupted often. Be assertive but not aggressive while speaking. Set the rules for communication before you begin.

7. Don't jump to conclusions. Do not hesitate to ask questions. Don't get intimidated by people who speak loudly. Instead, focus on the message and communicate your message assertively by gathering all information.

Never make a promise when you are happy. Never make a decision when you are angry.

Cross-Cultural Communication

Communication is one of the most basic methods of getting your idea across.

But when it comes down to communicating with someone outside your comfort zone or from another culture or country, things can become complicated. Generally, in communication, we seek to reduce uncertainty and misunderstanding. Good cross-cultural communication can ensure that.

Cross-cultural Communication involves relatively greater degrees of uncertainty due to the difficulty in predicting a stranger's responses.

As we grow up, we see around us or even experience at times: racial, caste, religious, color, gender, sexual preference bias, prejudice, and other forms of discrimination. Jokes and memes on social media only reinforce these beliefs and stereotypes. It's only when we actually come across people from other cultures that our false beliefs that have influenced our thinking all these years come crashing down!

Communicating better with people of other Cultures

While interacting with people from other countries or cultures, some things need to be observed to ensure the best communication. Good communication skills can also overcome language and cultural barriers by keeping in mind the following:

1. Training programs, reading, talking to people from different cultures, and learning from past experiences.
2. Avoid voicing your personal opinion regarding race, religion, sexual orientation, and other controversial issues, and these should also not affect your behavior.
3. Be informed about politically correct language and customs in international cultures. E.g., use of Ma'am v/s Madam in the USA. (Madam is not used in the US; instead, Ma'am is preferred.)
4. Embrace Diversity: Recognize, accept, and learn to co-exist with differences. Diversity is not a negative, and your own views are not always positive. Be open to change. Use gender-neutral and politically correct language.
5. Don't encourage discrimination of any sort by accepting or forwarding racist or insensitive jokes.

Case in Point

Aastha is a new joinee at her company. She comes from a small-town conservative family, and her family has been involved in the Indian freedom struggle and politically active. She has grown up hearing that her religion is the best and that others are inferior. Her circle of friends has also been from similar backgrounds.

Aastha gets a job in a large company in Gurgaon. On the first day of her job, she sees that her team leader is from another religion, which has been criticized in her family all her life. Her co-workers are from very different regions. They have different beliefs and eat different types of foods.

She is not able to fit into her new environment, so it is alien to her. She gets angry and defensive at others and appears aloof, and does not mingle easily.

Her team lead senses her hostility towards him and, in turn, gives her poor appraisals.

This cycle kept getting repeated till one day she decided to quit her job.

Her HR Head calls her and asks her what the problem is. After much cajoling, she tells him. The HR head is very understanding, having been through a similar situation himself when he was new. He counsels her and organizes a series of **(DEIB) Diversity, Equity, Inclusion & Belonging** trainings for the entire team. There is henceforth a strong focus on cross-cultural alignment in the organization from that point onwards. After this training, she emerges as a changed person. She is more accepting of her beliefs. She recognizes and accepts differences in others and works with them. She does not encourage racial or political jokes from her friends and family and asks them not to forward the same to others as well.

Aastha is soon popular with her foreign clients and coworkers. She is soon due for a promotion.

6.7 Indian-isms: Wrong usage of Indian English and its funny interpretations:

Indian-isms are certain errors committed by Indian speakers while speaking in English. These words have common acceptance in India, but in other countries and cultures, they have different meanings. Thus, Indian-isms create confusion and miscommunication. These can also cause ridicule and unintentional humour, and thus should be avoided. It is important in business communication to know about common Indian-isms.

Some common Indian-isms and their correct Business English usage are:

Indian-ism	Correct International Business English
Luggage is in the Dickey	Luggage is in the Boot
Radhika this side	This is Radhika speaking
Myself Ramesh	My name is Ramesh
I am **living** in Mumbai/ I put up in New York	I live/stay in Mumbai (both are ok)
Order a Pizza	Order a Pizza

Indian-ism	Correct International Business English
Please **revert** to me	Please get back to me (revert actually means to return to the former state)
Where is your **better half?**	Where is your partner/spouse?
My cousin has **passed away**	My cousin has died
I **passed out** last year	I graduated last year
Prepone the meeting	Bring the meeting forward
I am **out of the station**	I am not in town/city, or I am travelling at the moment
What is your **good name**?	What is your name?

6.8 Summary

Communication is a process of ensuring that the correct message reaches the correct receiver, at the correct time, in the correct manner, and results in the desired outcome in the manner intended by the sender.

Good Communication has the power to make or destroy relationships. Communication can be formal or informal, upwards or downward, verbal or non-verbal in the hierarchy.

The master communicator keeps in mind the 7Cs and uses these tools to their advantage. Communication should not be confused with English language skills. While good Spoken English is essential for professional success, good communication skills can help to hide defects or gaps in one's English. Good communication is a tool that can help people in every situation: whether it is in an organization or at home with the family. An increase in communication removes misunderstandings, avoids conflict, and helps a person to make lifelong relationships and networks.

Knowledge Check:

1. Define communication. How is it useful?
2. Explain the communication process. Give one example of the communication process from your own life.
3. What are the 7Cs of communication? Explain their applicability in Business Communication.
4. Name each of the 7Cs and give two examples of each from your daily communication.
5. Explain five ways to develop masterful communication skills.
6. Give five examples of things to avoid as explained by the experts.
7. List and explain briefly five ways to develop optimal communication when communicating with people from a different culture.
8. List five common Indian-isms that you commonly hear and their correct usage.

Get ready for the real world!

Jay, a software engineer from a small town, graduated and was placed on campus. His first job was with Infosoft, India's leading software company in Bengaluru. First day on the job, he arrived eager and happy, and it turned out to be the worst day of his life.

By the time he went home, he was sad, dejected, and very miserable. Instead of going home, he went to a local pub and proceeded to get absolutely drunk.

The next morning, he barely made it in time for the office. Another bad day, and he was ready to quit. He went to the canteen and sat there with a coffee. Just then, his Training Manager, Amrik, came in and saw Jay sitting there, a forlorn and demoralized figure.

"Hi", he said, "How's the job?" he asked.

"Horrible," said Jay. "My colleagues are not taking to me, one of the first customers I spoke to on the phone got so angry that he complained to the manager about me. A client told me I was very rude on the call. I don't think I can do this."

Amrik said, "Hey, you have such sound technical knowledge, but from what you have just told me, you suffer from a lack of communication skills. It's a common problem among graduates who are straight out of college. Our education system does not encourage soft skills, and the majority of students lack good quality communication skills training."

Jay said, "But why? How? What did I do wrong?"

Amrik said, "You lack soft skills, especially communication skills. If you master these skills, then I am sure you will have a great career in this company:

Jay said, "I never thought about it this way. Yesterday morning, I simply went to my desk on my first day of the job and started working. I didn't shake hands or introduce myself to anyone. I felt the people in the office were angry with me. But why should I go around meeting people? My job requires me to be on the system all the time. What's the point of talking and speaking unnecessarily?"

Amrik said, "Those are the reasons for your lack of communication skills. These are called barriers to Effective Communication. Your inability to break these barriers has caused miscommunication. Some of these barriers are emotional barriers and biases, lack of attention and interest, and distractions. Irrelevance of your message to the receiver, expectations, and prejudices leads to false assumptions or stereotyping. Your attitude shows all that.

Jay said, "Wow! I actually did all those things. I am such a fool. No one will take me seriously now.

Amrik smiled and said, "No, that's not true. Surely, if you follow my advice, you will become a great communicator. Get trained on communication skills.

Don't make assumptions about others. Respect others' opinions. Don't keep questioning others all the time. Learn to listen and then put forward your viewpoint assertively, without shouting. Recognize that others are under stress as well and try to make others' lives easier. Your own will become a pleasure!

Applied knowledge

1. What are the major communication mistakes that Jay made on his first day?
2. Notice these mistakes in yourself or others and take steps to correct them.
3. What advice from Amrik can you follow in your daily life?

Additional resources for self-development

1. First Personality: The 7Cs of communication

   https://youtu.be/RqdsrtPRJ7g?si=ZE2OKudKPh1CjSdg

2. Coach Prashant

   Managing your Boss or Clients

   https://youtu.be/bxK1I3I4BGE?si=KvQjrLuLVCrWIM4F

Build your vocabulary

Learn and use the Words and Business phrases used in this chapter to improve your Spoken English Skills:

1. **Top of the game:** Master of something, expert.
2. **Stepping stone:** A necessary step in achieving the goal.
3. **Different wavelength:** Having different points of view.
4. **DEIB:** Diversity (celebrating differences), Equity (treat everyone as equal), inclusion (make people feel they are part of your life), & Belonging
5. **Voila:** French word that means: 'There', it has happened!
6. **Culture Shock:** The feeling that the situation is totally different from previous experience, and finding nothing in common with a strange culture.

Chapter 7 Communication in the AI Age

Leveraging AI as your personal coach, mentor and guide

LEARNING MILESTONES

This chapter will enable you to:

- Use AI in your daily communication
- Practice high-impact writing using AI
- Use AI ethically
- Using AI to boost your inter-personal skills
- Have enriching conversations using AI
- Learn new business phrases and increase your vocabulary.

7.1 Using AI in your everyday communication

Case in Point

Laima hails from a culture where English is her first language. She also speaks in her native tongue quite fluently. Due to cultural nuances, Laima speaks English with an accent. She goes to work in a GCC in another province where the work and cultural norms are very different from hers.

She speaks in meetings but feels that she is not communicating well. Her messages to clients are also getting negative feedback. The organization organizes communication skills and voice & accent training sessions by external facilitators, but these are in large groups. Moreover, these sessions are held during the day shift while she works the evening US shift.

Laima starts to hear about AI tools and is intrigued. While she sees her colleagues use AI only to compose emails and reports, she starts to research deeper. She finds an array of AI tools that can help her with her Communication Skills.

For example, she uploads some of her own voice recordings to AI and asks for feedback. The feedback is detailed and personalized. And available 24 x 7 , something that is missing in physical trainings. In another tool, she uploads a large mail report that she had sent to the client, which created a lot of escalation due to its poor content and tone. The AI tool converts her mail

into a podcast where two seemingly human bots talk about her report and areas of improvement. She is able to interrupt the podcast in real time and ask specific questions about her feedback that the tool answers. On another tool, she gives the tool a situation and context of an upcoming presentation and asks it to simplify her graphs and visuals in a storytelling format.

She uses other AI tools to make her language better and improve her vocabulary, as well as her storytelling skills.

AI has numerous applications in the real world. But improving Communication skills is perhaps one of its best use cases. AI tools have the capacity to be your personal Communication coach and guide. It's just a matter of knowing how to use the AI to your advantage. AI is not replacing our ability to communicate. Rather, it is enhancing it. Whether you are a native English speaker or not, AI has the ability to help you communicate like a Pro. Let us also harness the power of AI to amplify and enhance our own Communication skills.

As with a human coach, receiving and giving feedback is also required for a more value-added interaction. Supposing you needed help with creating a presentation. AI can create a beautiful presentation for you; that's the easy part. But to have it done by AI, the same way that you would have made it, requires constant interaction. Once the AI starts understanding your queries, it gets a sense of your personality, and you will find the AI-generated content to be more and more in sync with you. Whereas your coach's availability is limited or an online training program has a finite duration and limited availability, the AI can be your constant companion. AI can warn you about the consequences of sending a message if it spots deficiencies in your tone and choice of words. Whenever you make a communication error or receive critical feedback about your communication, AI becomes a learning opportunity.

7.2 Getting better at using AI for communication

Using AI requires patience and the ability to question, challenge, and debate. Rarely will the first response generated be the ideal response. The ability to give various follow-up prompts is essential. The AI tool also suggests follow-up prompts; however, it is better to have a vision of what you would like the ideal solution to be. Imagine paying someone to teach you something. In real life, you would ask questions, express doubts and frustrations, and share successes with that person, in order to get the maximum out of the relationship. Well, AI is just like that, the bonus being that it is mostly free unless you move to the pro versions.

Keep in mind that AI should not replace your own thinking. AI is a collaboration tool, not a substitute. AI is not Lazy learning. It is a tool to enhance your productivity by taking away the effort and time that you would have spent composing something yourself. It can be a devil's advocate giving you a contrary view or exposing some blind spots in your thinking. But never should it replace your capacity to be creative, to express emotion, and to infuse your personality in your communication.

AI can generate the solution for you, but the practice of the solution has to be done by you only. Hence, critical thinking skills are required to get the most out of our AI tool. The AI-generated response might be correct in its approach, but it might not work in your situation, given your culture or taste. Hence, AI needs to be used to save time and effort, but your input is still required to make it your own.

7.3 Easy steps to incorporate AI as your communication coach

1. Draft, write, make notes, speak, annotate. Repeat:

Whatever your language skills, start communicating with the AI without any assistance. Don't ask AI for help on inputting a prompt into the AI, as that defeats the purpose of training the AI for yourself. As a habit, first write it down yourself without any help. If it's your resume, write it in your own style, highlighting your achievements in your own words. If it's a presentation pitch, then create it with the same words with the passion that you would have displayed. Then, the next step would be to input it into the AI tool, see its response, and ask it for improvements. This will help you to compare the AI responses to your own and see the difference, if it is indeed for the better or not. You might just realize that your own draft was better. So be it!

2. Incorporate AI in your daily life situations

Supposing you are going to appear for a job interview. Before the interview, ask the AI to play the role of the recruiter and ask you a variety of questions. Record your voice. Ask the AI about your voice, how is your tone, do you use filler words like umm.. or like....? Ask the AI direct questions like: 'How do I sound?' Practice answering the same. When it's done, input the conversation you had with the recruiter into the AI. Ask it to play the role of the recruiter when you provide the answers. This before-and-after simulation can help you in preparation and improvement.

3. Replicate emotions in AI

Emotion in communication is the essence of being human. This is a key differentiator between the human and the machine. There are more than a thousand ways to say: "Great to see you!" The amount of emotion that you can infuse into a simple statement like that is incredible. Why not use AI to infuse emotion into your words? Practice everyday phrases and words using different emotions and tones with the AI. For example, take a message that you are planning to send to a senior stakeholder: " I would like to have more time to complete this project." Ask the AI to re-compose this in different styles: assertive, humble, pleasant, aggressive, urgent, relaxed, friendly, etc. This will help you in understanding different emotions in communication and also help you to flex to those different styles.

***Figure 7.1**: AI won't feel your emotions, but it'll help you express them*

7.4 Practice High-Impact writing with AI

There are several LMs like ChatGPT, Grok, CoPilot, Claude, Gemini, Deepseek, Preplexity, etc. that one can use to compose messages. The AI landscape is rapidly changing, and newer tools and models will keep evolving. Irrespective of the tool, AI should not be used to simply copy and paste its responses. Rather, AI tools can be used to help you sound real, authentic, and original. No one likes a copy, and since everyone has access to the same tools, how then do you sound like yourself?

1. Start with the most comprehensive and appropriate prompt. Remember, you need to control the AI tool. It cannot give you the right solution without your prompt. The AI waits for your command or direction (your prompt) and then generates the response. The direction that you give to the tool will determine the output. The art of giving the right directions to AI is called Prompt Engineering. You might need to give more than one prompt. Multiple prompts will help the AI get trained on you and develop an understanding of the kind of questions you want and the information you seek. Some AI tools enable you to add `Custom instructions' that are additional prompts to further refine your query.

2. Start by telling the AI tool how you usually communicate. Give it as much detail as possible. Don't be focused too much on your English grammar, vocabulary, or language skills as long as you can communicate at a basic level. So start by sharing some of your writings. Upload to the AI some emails, reports, or assignments that you have written or submitted in the past. This enables the AI tool to understand that you normally don't use certain words that AI tools often use. Like Nevertheless, Delve, Unveil, etc. If you do use these words in your everyday conversation, you can add that as well. Do you like to use emojis? Or punctuation? Do you use paragraphs or do you prefer long texts? Do you use short forms like Rgds (regards), Tks (Thanks), etc? This is helpful to get the AI tool to understand your personality.

3. Determine the tone of your message.

Case in Point

Aayush and Ridhima work together. They are not just colleagues but also good friends outside of work, having attended the same college. At work, they interact with each other on MS Teams and email. While they are extremely formal when communicating with clients and leadership, their tone is generally casual and easy-going when they communicate with each other. Recently. Aayush sent some important information with some errors he had overlooked to Ridhima, who presented it to her client without checking. There was a huge escalation. Aayush wants to send Ridhima a message of apology. He uses AI to compose the message. The message is perfect in its grammar and wording, but extremely formal in its tone. It sounds as if a stranger is writing to another for the first time. Ridhima reads the message and gets even more annoyed.

AI tools need context. Determine who you are writing to? What kind of communication do they prefer or would they like to receive? And what is the tone that would be appropriate for them? Is it formal? Informal. Friendly. Distant? Do you want to sound in control? Or cooperative? Concise or wordy? Warm or cold? Do you want to ensure that the message uses words that you would use normally? Do you want the grammar to be correct? Again, the more detail the better. In case you are not able to think of the right words to describe your tone, an online dictionary can help. Remember, humans at times tend to state opinions that might end up inflaming emotions in others. AI writing is generally polite, inoffensive, and neutral in tone. If what the AI generates does not reflect who you are, your readers who normally correspond with you will immediately get to know that your text is completely AI-generated. So your tone and personality are important for the AI to understand.

Pro Tip: **Upload the LinkedIn profile of the person with whom you are communicating. Tell the AI to frame the message for a person with that personality. You can also save this as a template for future use.**

4. Determine the outcome or result that you would like. Do you want more time to complete the assignment? Are you submitting a report? Are you apologizing to the client? Are you sending a status update to your manager? Are you sending a pitch for more money? More business? Whatever your goal, the prompt must be framed accordingly. The AI tool needs to be told what the exact answer is that you are seeking. The more the detail, the more the context, the better the response. For example, if you give a general prompt:" help me create an email to my client because I am late in sending them some information", the AI will give you a generic, cookie-cutter template. This same template might have already been used by millions of others. Maybe already sent before to the same client!

So, supposing your client is really furious at the delay. But this is an old client, and through your past interactions, you know they might give you another chance,

provided you assure them of the reasons and timely resolution. So the prompt should include this extensive detail about the client. The AI response will be different and sound like it's genuinely coming from your heart. However, it is important to fact-check the response to determine whether it is appropriate and if it aligns with the 7Cs checklist mentioned in the previous chapter.

Case in Point

Use AI to shift your mindset from a reactive approach to a proactive approach. For e.g., instead of telling the AI: "I want to reply to an appraisal email received from my manager where they gave me a bad rating." Instead, a different prompt can shift the mindset: "I wish to reply to my manager (give some context about the manager's persona) that will help me to project my personal brand and accomplishments better and instill in the manager a sense of trust in my abilities."

7.5 Using AI Ethically

***Figure 7.2**: AI is the tool. Integrity is the skill. Use it ethically*

AI has democratized access to information. Now, almost everyone has AI tools available to them for communication, education, and in their professions. Reduction of effort, saving of time, and the ability to provide solutions that till now took a large amount of time are drivers of the adoption of AI. However, in this pursuit of shortcuts, ethics need not be compromised. It is important to understand that AI models are being trained on existing content, often the **Intellectual Property Rights** (**IPR**) of others. While a mechanism of giving credit and royalty to the source is still being developed, information is being pulled up through AI and passed on. It is our collective responsibility to ensure that AI is used ethically.

7.6 Students using AI

College assignments, homework, information, and textbooks. Everything has been disrupted by AI tools. Educators and Institutions are reporting a vast amount of work being turned in by students as having been AI-generated. This kind of cheating then gives rise to the fundamental question: How to ensure that students develop their critical thinking, problem-solving, and creativity skills, given the temptation to generate immediate solutions via AI. Is AI the lazy way

of learning? Has AI become the shortcut to learning? It need not be so. Students need to demonstrate academic integrity, as this is a foundation for a long and fulfilling professional life.

Ways to leverage AI ethically as a student:

1. **AI is a research assistant:** It should be used to research topics that provide the basis for perspectives and insights that students come up with on their own. Just by copying AI-generated content, the students' perspective is not highlighted. Going forward, educators will reward insight more than information.
2. **Transparency is the key in using AI:** To give credit to the AI component in the submission creates an environment of trust between the educator and student. Suppose educators are informed which part of the submission is AI-generated and the reasons for the same. In that case, they can then focus on the overall merit of the submission rather than viewing the entire student's work with suspicion.

Figure 7.3: *Create your work. Credit the AI assistance. Everyone wins*

3. **AI content can be a basis for bias, discrimination, and a lack of privacy**. Generative AI models have been trained on content that could be anti-diversity or have a bias towards one line of thought. Whereas students would do well to adopt a 360-degree perspective to any idea or thought, and not get influenced by only the thought that the AI pushes. An all-rounder viewpoint is appreciated by educators and recruiters alike. AI can also impersonate people, and hence, students need to be careful about sharing sensitive and personal information with AI.

7.7 Professionals using AI

Whether you are a working professional or a self-employed entrepreneur, the use of AI can be a force multiplier for your business. From making pitches to drafting critical cross-cultural communication, AI can be the differentiator between business success for those who use AI and those who don't. AI tools can result in higher efficiency, greater productivity, and faster solutions. Professionals need

to move beyond using ChatGPT and other Gen AI simply to draft communication. And instead take advantage of the multi-sensory speech-to-speech, speech-to-text, and vice-versa capabilities of AI.

***Figure 7.4**: AI doesn't replace you : It accelerates you*

Ways to leverage AI as a working professional:

1. **AI can be a sounding board or a coach**; However, it is not a substitute for a real coach or physical mentorship. This is because the AI models cannot accurately discern the need for prescribing help, especially in mental health cases or suicide prevention. On the other hand, AI tools can be used to get a different viewpoint on a work situation. Professionals, often working in isolation, need counsel and advice that AI can provide to come out of seemingly difficult situations. Asking AI for help if one is stuck in a professional problem or dilemma can throw up multiple solutions to try. This sparks action and a propensity to make faster decisions rather than get stuck waiting for a solution.

2. **Access to knowledge or insights** that have been inspired by others facing similar issues is a good way to learn. However, not knowing the source of information generated by AI is not an excuse for using that information for personal gain. AI can save valuable time in routine, physically demanding work. This time can be best used for innovative and original thinking, traits that are vital for career success. However, not disclosing the use of AI when providing solutions to paying clients can have serious legal and moral implications. Remember, professionals should use AI to add value to themselves, rather than train AI to replace them eventually due to its inappropriate usage!

3. **Help in data generation and analysis:** As discussed earlier, AI is an excellent Communication Skills coach. Making visually appealing charts or infographics, helping with data analysis and storytelling, breaking down complex datasets, documents, and PDFs into podcasts and videos, and speech-to-text are all communication enablers. From writing complex pitches to simple thank-you notes, AI can generate

the appropriate content. At the same time, AI-generated content can appear generic and obviously copied to the trained eye. And this erodes client trust. Hence, professionals and organizations must maintain fair practices and hold themselves accountable by complying with industry standards rather than simply boosting their own bottom line.

7.8 Using AI to boost your Inter-personal skills

Learning interpersonal-human skills from AI! It might sound like a contradiction at first. AI is a digital tool. An inanimate object. Then how can it help me become better at getting along with others? The key here is to understand that AI by itself cannot help you develop people skills. Rather, AI acts as a Gym Trainer: someone who suggests exercises and prepares an exercise plan. And then provides guidance on how to repeat and practice those moves so that they become part of your basic nature. AI cannot do the push-ups for you. It can only be the guide. But even as a guide, it is extremely powerful because the AI suggestions and feedback can be just the motivation that one needs to up their people skills game. The main thing to keep in mind is that AI is like a mirror. It cannot replace you or your personality, but instead provides valuable feedback about your strengths and areas of improvement.

Figure 7.5: *AI doesn't talk for you : It just helps you talk better*

1. **AI as an accountability partner:** In the quest for self-improvement, AI can be your friend, philosopher, and guide. It can prod you, poke you, push you towards action. If you are someone who procrastinates or needs help in getting started, AI can be a constant reminder that you need to work on your interpersonal skills. AI can remind you that you need to reach out and engage more. When you find your engagement levels dipping or the willingness to network reducing, AI can provide critical feedback or suggest easy ways, baby steps, and incremental steps to help you break the inertia. Whether you are an introvert or an extrovert, AI can be an aide to your personality. It should not be your replacement. Rather, AI is the perfect companion and ally who constantly reminds you that relationships need nurturing. Get started!

2. **AI as a warning sign:** Ever received an email that made you hot under the collar? Have you ever sent a message to someone in extreme anger or high emotion? And regretted it later. Well, AI can help avert such disasters. Often, when emotions are high, the rational brain gets hijacked by the emotional brain (called an Amygdala Hijack). At such times, it becomes difficult to make correct decisions about what is right and what is wrong. What is appropriate, what is not. AI can be the voice of reason for you at such times. Using AI to help you respond rather than react to emotional situations. AI can help in addressing your feelings and emotions, and at the same time, provide an outsider's perspective on how your communication might have a negative impact on others and adversely affect your relationships. Using AI to reframe and redraft responses in a polite and measured way can help in avoiding relationship problems.

3. **AI for expanding your horizons:** Often, we operate in isolation with just a handful of friends, family, or colleagues to guide or support us. These stakeholders, while being important in life, often have a limited view of life itself. People that you have grown up with or worked with have similar experiences to you. They might not have the experience or exposure to be able to provide another point of view. And having multiple perspectives is a core foundation of good interpersonal skills. A one-sided view of life leads to limited interaction and missed opportunities. AI can help you expand and stretch your thinking by throwing up multiple scenarios to develop better relationships. AI can play the devil's advocate, debating against your chosen plan of action. AI can help you become aware of any bias that might be clouding your judgment. You might find holes in your thinking or blind spots, negative perceptions that people have about you that you had not considered. AI can play the role of multiple coaches.

7.9 Using AI to have enriching conversations

While we have become masters at texting and messaging, many of us struggle with having hard or crucial conversations, whether in our personal or professional lives. We try not to offend others and thus avoid having these kinds of tough conversations. There are numerous situations when we have to act against our basic nature: Saying No to a friend, giving tough feedback to a reportee, addressing tension with a colleague, talking to parents or seniors at work can feel uncomfortable and awkward. These are the situations where one requires courage and the ability to silence the doubts that the subconscious mind throws up: What if the other person feels offended? What if they never speak with me again? What if I lose my job? And so on.

In such situations, AI can provide templates, scripts, and words that can make it easy to start the conversations. AI can guide you if your tone or words are offensive or inadequate. AI can help you break the fear mindset and get you to think empathetically, from another's point of view. AI can help in creating a safe environment so that the conversations can feel honest and don't create hard feelings.

1. **Using AI to find the words:** Often, the subconscious mind generates doubt about the need or outcome of the hard conversation. This creates inertia and procrastination. In this situation, having the right words to start the conversation can really help. And that's where AI adds real value. AI can help in striking the right balance of words depending on the context. It can suggest different ways to convey the same thought or emotion. Having a clear plan to open the conversation reduces mental stress and enables real and respectful conversation. Before having a conversation, if you are experiencing extreme emotions, share your thoughts with the AI tool first. AI can help in highlighting the usage of words that might be prejudiced and inflammatory. It will help you plan better for the upcoming hard conversation.

2. **AI can help plan for different scenarios:** What if things go wrong during the conversation? Let's assume you are giving feedback to another person, and all of a sudden, that person has an emotional breakdown. If this were something you did not foresee, it could escalate the entire situation. AI can help you in planning multiple scenarios for the same situation by simulating likely reactions. By being prepared for things to change rapidly, the conversation stays on track, and one can regain emotional control over the situation. AI can suggest appropriate timing and settings for different personalities based on the context and prompt that it has been provided. This can help you to customize your communication and be ready for VUCA situations.

3. **AI can be an excellent reflection tool:** Real Improvement and growth happen when one reflects upon what went well. And what didn't? What did you say that caused a reaction? Or didn't say? Did the other person actually respond to your words the way you wanted? All these thoughts can help in gaining clarity on best practices for the future. AI can help you recognize patterns in your words and behavior. These self-limiting patterns can be an obstacle to having enriching conversations. For e.g., AI can make you aware of your talking-listening ratio, wherein your active listening skills need improvement. AI can help you learn from the past and give suggestions to be better prepared for the future

7.10 Summary

There is more to AI than simply using it to compose messages and visuals. AI has the capacity to become a constant communication coaching aide. While it cannot replace human intervention completely, AI, if used wisely with guardrails, can provide timely advice, feedback, and suggestions to enhance your communication. Usage of AI in daily communication, such as emails, messaging, speaking, and listening, can help make it a habit. New technologies are constantly being launched, and eventually smartphones will get replaced by AI Personal Agents that will provide communication advice in real time.

AI has the ability to improve your relationships and help create lasting networks. Care must be taken to ensure that AI does not cross the boundaries of Privacy and Diversity, Equity, and Inclusion. While AI can provide counsel and mentoring, one must be mindful of exercising personal judgment in sharing thoughts with AI and following its advice without adequate thought. AI is simply an ally. It is an aide. It is not a replacement for human judgment. Use AI to enhance your Communication for personal growth and professional career. Together with your personal experience and advice from your trusted stakeholders, AI can elevate your communication from good to great!

Knowledge Check:

1. How can AI enhance Communication Skills?
2. Can AI be a substitute for a physical Communication Coach?
3. Explain how AI can be a force multiplier in improving Writing skills?
4. What are the ethical issues to keep in mind whilst using AI for Communication?
5. Is AI suitable only for improving Students' communication?
6. How can working professionals benefit from using AI for Communication?
7. AI can provide the words and courage to have crucial conversations. Explain.

Additional resources for self-development

AI Tools are constantly evolving, and the reader would do well to be updated on the latest tools. While this is not an exhaustive list, at the time of printing, these were the tools used by the author for many communication-related tasks:

- **AI assistants:** ChatGPT, Grok, Claude, Gemini, Deepseek, Copilot, Preplexity
- **Video generation:** Synthesia, Google Veo, OpusClip, Daal-e
- **Image generation:** GPT-5o, Midjourney,napkin.ai
- **Meeting assistants:** Fathom, Nyota
- **Automation:** n8n, Manus
- **Study Plans & Research:** Deep Research, NotebookLM, Diffit
- **Writing:** Rytr, Sudowrite
- **Search engines:** Google AI Mode, Perplexity, ChatGPT search
- **Graphic design:** Canva Magic Studio, Looka
- **App builders & coding tools:** Lovable, Cursor
- **Knowledge management:** Notion Q&A, Guru
- **Email:** Hubspot Email Writer, Fyxer, Shortwave
- **Scheduling:** Reclaim, Clockwise
- **Presentations:** Gamma, Copilot for PowerPoint
- **Resume builders:** Teal, Kickresume
- **Voice generation:** ElevenLabs, Murf
- **Music generation:** Suno, Udio
- **Marketing:** AdCreative, AirOps

Chapter 8 Presentation Skills and Public Speaking

Speaking and Presenting with Clarity, Confidence and Presence

LEARNING MILESTONES

This chapter will enable you to:

- Understand the Essentials of Public Speaking.
- Learn keys to overcome fear of speaking.
- Understand how to Write and Deliver High Impact presentations.
- Master the Speech Organization Formula.
- Transform into a charismatic speaker.
- Plan and deliver impactful Presentations.
- Develop a powerful platform presence and personality.

Expert Quotes

If you can't explain it to a 6-yr. old, you've not understood it yourself

– Albert Einstein

Speak only when you are sure that your words are better than silence

-Unknown

"Better Speakers made Better leaders"

- Author

8.1 Overview

Public Speaking & Presentation skills are perhaps the most essential of all verbal communication. This is because if you can't explain it, you can't sell it. Right from show-and-tell in schools to in-office presentations to sophisticated product launches, leaders have used public speaking opportunities to showcase themselves and their talent. Steve Jobs' launch of the Apple products was a global event, still remembered and respected. Good speakers have an `aura' around them. They are generally perceived to be more knowledgeable and intelligent than other students. One normally associates a good speaker with a great personality! An effective speaker will have a much greater influence on the world than a stammering bundle of nerves.

Irrespective of what you do or what you want to achieve, public speaking and presentation are always a necessary part of your path to leadership. Hence, it

becomes all the more essential to overcome all apprehensions and anxieties and instead embrace any opportunity to do so.

8.2 Public speaking is private speaking

Public speaking is not just about standing on a stage and making presentations or speeches. In fact, we are all constantly public speaking. How? Private speaking is what we do all the time. Answering phone calls, making requests, sending out emails, looking at instant messaging, speaking with our family, appearing for interviews, announcing our achievements, and so on. Speaking in everyday life is private speaking. It's what you do anyway without realizing it! Thus, every speaking opportunity is an opportunity to become a better public speaker.

8.3 Student's perspective

Like it or not, every student has to speak in public at some point or another. Whether it is presenting their project work, interacting with their peers or teachers, appearing for group discussions or job interviews, or excelling in the real world, students from all streams need the all-important public speaking skills.

***Figure 8.1**: Inappropriate communication damages credibility*

8.4 Professional perspective

Public Speaking makes professionals in an organization stand out over their peers. Great visibility often results in greater growth. Shy or reticent people often get overlooked for promotions or good projects. People are generally put off by professionals who don't speak well. Corporate professionals, doctors, lawyers, architects, and self-employed entrepreneurs have to constantly interact with their clients and employees, vendors, and teams in order to manage them and sell their services. This is possible in today's world only with good speaking skills.

8.5 Glossophobia

Glossophobia is the fear of public speaking. A recent study showed that Glossophobia is the Number 1 fear in the world. Most people in the world prefer death over speaking to a crowd!

That's why only five percent of people are capable and willing to speak to an audience. The question is: Why are those five percent ready, willing, and able to take the platform, while the others shrink with the fear of speaking? Statistics show that the fear of speaking is greater than the fear of death.

- Due to this fear, valuable opportunities to organize, to debate and speak, to display leadership qualities are lost.
- Lack of communication skills creates negative emotions, which invariably hinder academic and personal growth.

To the average person, if you go to a funeral, you're better off in the casket than doing the eulogy- Jerry Seinfeld

***Figure 8.2**: Your fear is temporary. Your voice is powerful.*

This fear of Public Speaking affects 90% of all people. This means that you are not alone. If you feel butterflies in your stomach or have sweaty hands or racing breath before a presentation, you are not alone! Others feel the same as you. That's why it is a golden opportunity to train yourself to become a better speaker and thus attain an edge over others

8.5.1 Keys to overcoming the fear of public speaking

Have you ever felt shy or nervous before a presentation? Do you feel uncomfortable while speaking in front of an audience, even if they are your colleagues and friends?

Fear of speaking generally emanates from fear of being judged by others. Often, being in the limelight or the center of attraction makes people uncomfortable

while making presentations. This reflects in their lack of confidence. One feels that any small mistake will get highlighted and reflect on their future relationships.

But it need not be so. Stage fear and anxiety can be conquered. The ability to speak in public with ease, confidence, and poise is not inborn. Public speaking is a skill, and like all skills, it can be obtained with organized training coupled with practice.

While it's true that speaking comes naturally and confidence, eloquence comes through practice; great speaking skills are rarely due to talent; great speaking skills are taught. Here are some easy and practical ways to overcome fear of speaking, be it in a social setting or professional presentations

1. Practice! Practice! Practice!

Practice is the best of all instruction.

To be prepared for a speech, you should calm your anxiousness and nervousness. Planning and preparation are the start of good public speaking and involve extensive practice. The old saying that `practice makes perfect' is most true in public speaking. A survey on Olympic Gold medalists showed that the single most important factor in winning a gold medal is practicing longer than one's competitors. Practicing speaking can be done in the following ways:

a. Rehearse your presentation or speech alone at first. Do not attempt to memorize your speech. PowerPoint and other softwares allow you to time yourself. You can also use the AI function in PowerPoint to ask the AI to give feedback on your practice.

b. Practice it in front of the mirror and in your phone's voice recorder. Speak out loudly. Pay attention to your posture, body language, and gestures. Hear yourself speak on the voice recorder to see the flaws in pitch and pace of your voice.

***Figure 8.3**: Mirror practice today = Killer presentation tomorrow*

c. Rehearse in front of a friend and family member and take advice and feedback. Request them to ask you questions and interrupt you to simulate the actual presentation. Test your visual aids and slides' duration, etc.

d. Speak whenever you get an opportunity: at work, at a nearby club, volunteering, just anywhere where you get an audience.

"There are always three speeches for every one you actually gave. The one you practiced, the one you gave, and the one you wish you gave." - Dale Carnegie.

2. Convert Negative Energy into Positive Energy:

Due to anxiety, the body goes through psychological stress. This stress can be positive or negative. Yes, Stress can be positive as well. This is called Eu-Stress. The negative stress is called Distress. Athletes and top performers convert their negative energy into positive energy. Everyone admits to feeling a bit nervous. But by self-talk and self-belief, they feel Eustress. The body triggers a fight-or-flight response. Ensure that you will fight yourself!

Amy Cuddy, the leading authority on Body Language, recommends using the `Superman pose' to make yourself feel 'taller and stronger' and hence more confident.

***Figure 8.4**: The Superman Pose*

Tell yourself: this will be a good presentation! You will encounter success!

F.E.A.R. gives you two choices:

Feel Eager And Ready

OR

Forget Everything And Run

Leaders take stressful situations head-on. They don't run away, they fight. And emerge as winners.

3. Recognize that fear is normal for public speakers:

Mark Twain said, "There are two types of speakers: Those who are nervous and those who lie!"

This is very true. Almost all leaders, from Robin Sharma to Mahatma Gandhi, spoke about their fears when they started public speaking. But with practice, they gained confidence. One can see top athletes like Sachin Tendulkar and Tiger Woods' interviews from their initial days when they started playing. And can you see the difference in confidence when they speak now! Fear is normal for almost all speakers. It is normal to experience some tension and anxiety in the first 10-15 seconds of the presentation. But this will eventually go away, leaving you to enjoy yourself as a confident speaker.

The audience admires a person who speaks despite being nervous. But you lose their respect by apologizing for not being prepared or for being nervous. Don't use words like: "I'm sorry, I'm not good at speaking", OR "I didn't get time to prepare...." Just get on the stage and start speaking.

Tip: Arrive early at the venue. Give yourself time to settle down and get familiar with the surroundings. Talk to some of the participants prior to the presentation. For job interviews, especially make sure that you arrive at least 30 minutes prior to the interview. This will give your body some time to settle down.

4. Visualize yourself as a powerful speaker:

Creative visualization is a technique used by elite athletes, the super-rich, powerful leaders, and speakers from all walks of life. Basically, it involves imagining yourself in a place where you have succeeded, and the world is applauding you. That place is called the `sweet spot'.

The Visualization technique basically implies that you have an incredible power within you that you have never been taught to use. The daily practice of visualizing your dreams as already achieved can significantly accelerate your realization of those dreams. Visualization activates the law of attraction, thereby attracting into your life the people, resources, and circumstances you will need to achieve your goals.

***Figure 8.5**: The mind visualizes before reality delivers*

Tip: Sit in a comfortable position, close your eyes, and imagine looking at your goal as if you already reached it. Imagine being inside your mind, looking out through your eyes at the ideal result. The best time to visualize is when you first wake up, and right before you go to bed. These are the times you are most relaxed. Do this for at least 7-10 days before an important speech or event.

5. Know your audience:

According to Leeds, every audience has a **DSIM** – a **Dominant Self-Interest Motive**. It is the speaker's duty to identify the DSIM of their audience and use it to their advantage. DSIM is basically the need in every person that is waiting to be fulfilled. Every person in the audience is expecting to gain something from your speech. It could be knowledge, monetary gain, or inner peace. Whatever it is, if your speech is tailored to your audience's expectations, they become friendlier and respond positively. This alleviates fear and makes the speaker most confident.

***Figure 8.6**: Understand the audience before you deliver*

6. Practice storytelling: Show passion

"Don't just make Eye contact. Make Heart contact" -Coach Prashant

Speak about something you believe in. When you are passionate about a subject, your sincerity shows in your speech. The audience responds very favorably to personal stories and experiences, and this again helps the speaker to become more confident. When you speak about a subject that you care about, your body language becomes more positive.

7. Devise tricks to overcome your fear:

Different speakers have devised their own unique ways to overcome stage fright. Winston Churchill, the famous politician, used to imagine his audience as naked! This made them seem less serious in his mind. Others imagine the audience sitting on a commode. Yet others think of some loved one or think of a funny video prior to their speech. Find whatever works for you and use it to your advantage.

Tip: Remember that your audience is just as human as you. Don't make them into something bigger in your mind than they are.

8. Think positive:

Think of the audience as your friends. Often, we tend to think of public speaking as a high-stakes event where we will lose our reputation and get a bad name if we give a bad speech. This, however, is not true. The truth is that your colleagues, who are your audience, will continue to remain your colleagues and friends. They will be in a similar position when it's their turn to speak. Hence, people are generally sympathetic and rooting for your success. Think that your audience wants you to succeed, and your relationship with them will not change after your speech, irrespective of the outcome.

9. Breathe:

Focus on your breath. Inhale and exhale 10 times with your eyes closed. Work on your voice. You are born with the voice you have, but you can always improve its quality by working on pitch, intonation, and volume. Bring variety to your voice. Learn to breathe deeply before every speech. It not only helps your voice but also helps you relax and calm your nerves. Breathing, in fact, is a very good way to bring pauses into your speech if you speak too fast out of nervousness. Do some **loosen-up** exercises before it's your turn to speak. Look side to side. Touch your head on either shoulder. Work out your arms in half-circles and roll your shoulders back. Loosen your lips. Stretch your jaw wide.

Figure 8.7: *Say it clearly. Say it confidently*

8.6 Delivering the presentations

Successful presentations are nothing but ways of presenting information to influence and convince others into believing what you want them to believe.

A good presentation is much more than a bunch of slides thrown together. Often, presentations fail because of the presenter's lack of preparation or ability to connect with the audience. The lack of effort and commitment shows in a hurriedly made presentation, and this can adversely affect careers and relationships.

Effective public speaking and presentation skills require ensuring that your message actually appeals to your audience and that they are motivated enough after listening to you actually to do something about it.

8.6.1 COPTA-The powerful presentation method

A presentation is generally the most effective mode of communication with a group of people, as it allows the 'presenter' to interact personally with the 'audience'. Even if it is through the medium of video rather than face-to-face, presentations are still personal events. The audience, in turn, has the opportunity to interact with the presenter on their topic. This makes it essential for individuals to make that presentation count, to be passionate and motivating to get the desired results.

A good presentation is result-oriented as it focuses on the outcome as much as the actual delivery.

COPTA is a very impactful and powerful technique to ensure that the presentation is made and delivered effectively. A good presentation needs to be a COPTA presentation. Use the COPTA method as a checklist to ensure that the presentation is complete and delivers the message in the most exciting and imaginative manner. COPTA stands for:

- C= Connect
- O= Organize
- P= Prepare
- T = Time
- A = Appearance

1. **Connect:**

Connecting with the audience is the rapport that you share with them. That personal connection that makes your audience feel that you are one of them and you want to better their lives in some way by informing, educating, displaying, launching, or whatever the purpose of the presentation is.

Connection with the audience is very important. Different people need to be handled in different ways. The following are some fundamentals that need to be kept in mind, irrespective of the audience we address.

a. Audiences and their expectations vary widely. Knowing this will help in making the presentation more personal.

b. Knowing the number of people in the audience, their background, seniority level, and cultural and economic makeup.

c. The level of expertise of the audience ensures that the information is neither too detailed nor too basic.

d. What are the inter-group politics or dynamics?

e. Who are the key decision makers?

Throughout the presentation, try to put yourself in the audience's shoes. Ask not 'What do I want to say?' Rather, 'what do I want them to hear?' A client does not want to hear the obvious features of your product. They want to hear the benefits of your product. Once you make the connection between the product and their lives, the sale is made.

Convince your listeners

Don't talk to Inform...Talk to Convince

Your goal in any presentation is actually very simple: you must convince your audience to act upon your message or adopt your point of view. The four rules of reaching that goal are:

- Grab their attention
- Make it easy for them to understand you
- Establish common ground for agreement
- Show them how your message benefits them

Case in Point

If you want your audience to quit smoking, you have to give them good reasons. And just by saying that Smoking is bad, no one will be convinced. Instead, by showing graphic visuals of people with cancer due to smoking, alarming statistics, and giving some personal examples, the audience realizes how close they are to premature death if they don't quit. Scare them into quitting! Use that as a technique rather than giving information and figures that don't resonate with them.

Your Presentation must be Personal, but the benefits must be universal.

We must define the aim and objectives accurately and write them down. The outcome that we desire from the presentation will determine our ability to relate to the audience. Our audience will have some objectives too. It is our duty as speakers to fulfill those objectives.

Handling difficult questions from the audience who are still not convinced:

Most speakers like to present and sit down without having to face the audience again. However, your audience will need more convincing, especially if they have questions and queries. It is the duty of every speaker to answer their audience's queries to their satisfaction.

The three biggest fears of a speaker regarding questions are:

A. Having to answer every question

B. Not knowing the correct answer

C. Losing Your Control

What to do when someone asks you a question?

A. Welcome questions – Don't be apprehensive. Be ready for the fact that you will be asked questions, so be prepared accordingly.

B. E.A.R = Remember this: EMPATHIZE * ACKNOWLEDGE * RESPOND

C. Set the Ground rules: Don't allow yourself to be interrupted in your main presentation. Inform the audience at the beginning that you will take questions and answer them after the end of your presentation.

D. Repeat the Question: to give yourself time to think of a reply.

E. Analyze the question for: Content □ Intent □ The actual person asking.

F. If you don't know the answer, don't lie. Instead, tell them you will find out later and let them know. And make sure to do that once the presentation is over.

2. **Organizing your Presentation**

Every presentation must have three parts:

- Introduction
- The Middle
- The Conclusion

While this may sound very obvious or basic, it is surprising how often presentations get spoiled due to a lack of proper organization.

The solution lies in using the talk organization formula (TOF):

Highly recommended by the author for over 25 years, also known as the Magic Formula, it is an excellent guide for speech organization. This is very helpful due to the fact that, as the speaker, you are the driver who has to take the audience on a journey. The driver cannot be lost or take the long route, as this will make the audience bored or negative. Instead, the speaker must show that the speech or presentation is a logical flow of ideas. This gets the speaker credibility and respect.

The Talk organization formula enables you to:

A. Organize your thoughts in a logical manner.

B. Present those thoughts in a persuasive and entertaining manner.

C. Speak without having to worry about what to say next.

D. Successfully sell the benefits of any idea or product.

E. Ensure that you don't have to struggle with your subconscious mind as to what to say next. By following a logical sequence, your mind is free of tension, and the words come more easily.

THE FOUR PARTS OF THE FORMULA

PART 1	ATTENTION
PART 2	PROPOSITION
PART 3	SOLUTION
PART 4	BENEFITS

1. **ATTENTION**

Begin with a joke, example, story, anecdote, or poem. Grab the audience's attention. Put your audience at ease and generally break the ice.

Remember the Introduction:

- Tell a relevant story.
- Follow a logical chain of events.
- Always be easy to understand.
- Relate to the subject of the talk that will follow.
- Always be short and sweet.

The introduction

- Don't jump straight into the presentation. Start with an example. Preferably from the speaker's personal experience. The example should be related to the main body of the speech that is to follow.
- Even technical presentations should start on a lighter note with reference to a recent occurrence within the company (like a Hackathon, or Sports day), or some event that has just taken place (like a placement week), or some general comments.
- The purpose of a good introduction is to grab the audience's attention and to hold it.
- It also enables the speaker to relax and calm their nerves.
- It acts as an ice-breaker with the audience and establishes rapport.

Different ways to start a presentation

1. Finding something in common with the Audience.
2. Reference to recent situations or events of common interest.
3. Challenge the audience!
4. Use an exhibit or visual aid.
5. Surprise Audience with Claim or Statistic.
6. Ask a Rhetorical or Open-ended Question.
7. Quotation or a Humorous anecdote: We may have a story which may or may not be funny, but It grabs attention in many ways. It may be a human interest, preferably personal and based on real-life events, and ideally, which happened to you.

2. **PROPOSITION**

- Tell your audience the purpose of your speech.
- Demonstrate your technical knowledge of the subject
- Share the features of your idea or product with them.
- Tell them what you intend to tell them.
- State the general situation, topic, or problem that you wish to discuss.

Answer the following questions:

- How did that state of affairs come about?
- How does such a problem, event, or situation occur?

In the first part, you grabbed the audience's attention. In this part, hold their interest.

3. **SOLUTION**

- Give the solutions to that particular problem.
- How can the particular situation that you are talking about be changed?
- What can be done to bring about positive changes in that particular situation?
- Show the audience that you are a master of your subject.

Your conviction and commitment to your topic should become apparent by the fact that you have concrete solutions, which you should articulate and explain.

4. **BENEFITS**

Every person thinks about their own self-interest. A good speaker recognizes this and appeals to the audience's Dominant Self Interest Motive-DSIM. Once the audience sees the benefit of the proposition, they start getting convinced.

Answer the following questions that your audience has in their minds, irrespective of the topic:

- How will the solutions you have outlined help us in any way?
- Why should we listen to you and your point of view?

✓ This is the most important part of public speaking because here you put your entire speech in context.

✓ You have taken up your audience's time. Justify yourself by telling them WHY they should act upon what you are suggesting. Always leave people wanting and asking for more.

Case in Point

Sample Speech based on the Talk Organization Formula

TOPIC: SPORTS IN INDIA

EXAMPLE: Talk about famous Sportspeople of India, Sania Mirza, PV Sindhu, Virat Kohli, Abhinav Bindra, etc.

PROPOSITION: Why does India not produce a large number of sportspeople? We are responsible. We are not a sporting nation; we don't run or play. no sports culture in the country, poor facilities, and no money in sports. Youth have different aspirations from previous generations.

SOLUTION: Be active- love your body, involve youth, like other countries have talent nurturing programs starting in schools, more exposure, love your country.

BENEFITS: A Healthy, happy nation, alternative careers, more opportunities for retired sportspeople, more money, Laurels for the country.

3. **Preparation**

Good Preparation shows in the ease with which the audience can relate to your presentation and consequently the ease with which the speaker can present.

A presentation without struggle, strain, or stress is an ideal presentation that the speaker has prepared well.

Tips for Using PowerPoint and Similar Software

1. **Font**: Use a large, legible font. Preferably 20 pt. Calibri or Helvetica.
2. **Heading**: Every slide to have a Heading in a bigger font, separated from the main body.
3. **Images**: Use illustrations on all slides. But too much artwork will distract rather than attract.
4. **Background**: white with a dark color font, preferably dark navy blue.
5. **Organization:** One idea only per slide.
6. **The 6 x 7 rule**
    a. No more than six lines per slide.
    b. No more than seven words per line.
7. **Animations**: use `fly in' to have the text appear one at a time.
8. **Consistency**: Be consistent in using bullets and numbering. Use the same type of fonts, colors, bullets, and numbers across the presentation
9. **Typefaces:** Avoid full caps, italics, and bold
10. **Walk around,** making eye contact rather than looking at the screen.
11. **Use visual aids** or objects to highlight points being shown on the slides.
12. **Others:**
    a. Use a slide changer with a laser pointer
    b. Don't Just read from the slides.
    c. Use the Presenter view option with a timer.
13. Remember, PowerPoint or the software is just another tool for your presentation. It is not your presentation.

Tip: Your audience can read faster than you can speak. Putting a lot of information on the slides will divert the audience's attention, and they will begin to tune out of your speech and instead start reading. So, always have just a few keywords on the slide and then proceed to explain and elaborate on those keywords.

4. **Timing**

Have you ever sat through a speech or presentation wondering when the presenter will sit down? Presentations that are too long tend to drag on forever and bore the audience.

In presentations, being boring is a sin.

1. Time yourself while practicing to ensure that all the material has been given importance. Also, prepare yourself for the duration you will be speaking. Ask the organizers how much time you have to make your presentation
2. Practice all the visual aids and other tools beforehand, not during the presentation. Do not use any untested tool or technique that you are not familiar with, as it wastes time
3. The point of satiation is reached at the peak of popularity. Every audience has a threshold beyond which they will lose patience. Attention spans are limited. Hence, end while you are getting a good response, not when people start yawning or looking restless!
4. Always have a watch or software clock in view.
5. You'll never have enough time to say everything. So, decide what is important and end with that.

Adherence to time shows respect for the audience, and nothing can impress an audience more than being shown respect.

5. **Appearance**

First Impressions matter a lot in effective public speaking. Your audience will often assume how you will be presenting based on the way you look. Hence, it is very important to look your best. However, looking your best is not just about paying attention to your clothes. It is the overall package of your body and mind. The following need to be kept in mind:

"Dress maketh a man"- Shakespeare

1. **Your voice**: How you say it is as important as what you say. Your voice needs to be strong, varying in pitch and volume.
2. **Posture**: Have a confident, erect posture, no slouching or drooping shoulders.
3. **Smile:** Use the power of a smile to make others feel at ease. Your smile can diffuse the most serious of situations. So, make sure you smile at appropriate times, even if you are feeling nervous. Keep smiling!
4. **Dress appropriately:** For the occasion. Find out the dress code of the people you are addressing and blend in. A rule of thumb is to dress one level above the audience. For males, wear a tie if the audience wears pants/shirt to work; Wear a suit if it is a very formal occasion. Indian or Western formal attire is appropriate for ladies.

5. **Grooming**: Has to be impeccable. Don't wear very strong cologne or perfume. Personal cleanliness and hygiene are essential in all respects.

Becoming a charismatic speaker

Q: What is Charisma?

A. Charisma leaves an impression on the audience, large or small, that makes them want to come back for more. A Charismatic Public Speaker is a Popular Public Speaker. People will want to hear what you speak, and you, in turn, get the chance to become their leader.

Politicians, film actors, and other celebrities have charisma. They may not have the best looks or wealth, but when they speak, people stop to listen. Steve Jobs and Satya Nadella are classic examples.

***Figure 8.8**: Make them feel something, and they'll follow your voice anywhere*

***Figure 8.9**: Like Satya Nadella said, If they love hearing you, they'll trust following you.*

A few simple steps to build charisma

1. Show enthusiasm: the audience's biggest excitement is your passion! Steve Jobs used to present Apple products with such immense pride and passion!
2. Avoid unnecessary criticism, condemnation, or complaining: Stop being a cribber!
3. Involve your audience. Ask questions, talk to them! Don't talk down to them.
4. Learn to love people. Be a people person. A good way to cultivate this is to join a meet-up or social networking group, develop some hobbies and interests outside of your area of work.
5. Give honest and sincere appreciation and praise.
6. Be a good listener.
7. Use your common sense.
8. Be prepared for Murphy's Law. Things will go wrong at the worst possible moment. Always have a Plan B ready.
9. Always give credit when quoting others or borrowing materials for making the presentation. Respect others' intellectual property. No one respects a cheater or an obvious cut-and-paste job.
10. Leave your personal problems at home when you are out `there' in the Real world.

8.7 Platform presence and personality: The physical aspect of delivering the presentation

Your body language and attitude play a big role in not only appearing confident but also putting the audience at ease. How you say it is as important as what you say.

How you carry yourself says a lot about you and your state of mind. Remember that self-confidence is contagious. If you appear confident, your audience will express confidence in you as well.

The following should be kept in mind while delivering the presentation:

1. **Hands and gestures**: Do your hands seem as if they weigh 5 kgs each while you are speaking? Often, we see speakers who don't know what to do with their hands while presenting. The best way is to keep one hand over the other and bring them to the front of your body. Let your hands rest lightly over your belly button, with your elbows resting lightly on your hips. If you need to make a gesture, bring your hands out and bring them back in. This way, your hands will have a `parking space,' and you won't be stressed about what to do with your hands.

Do use gestures while speaking. Your hands can sometimes complement your face and body to convey a deep emotion or idea.

***Figure 8.10**: Your posture speaks before you do*

2. **Legs:** Have you ever practiced judo or some other martial art? Seen the judoka stand with their legs slightly apart, with their feet pointing outward in a `V' Shape. The reason for this is that the fighter remains `grounded' and is not uprooted easily from their stance. It is the same with good speakers.

   If your feet are together and parallel to your chin, then your body will start swinging from side to side. This is called the `pendulum', where the weight of the body will shift from one leg to another. This is very distracting for the audience and should be avoided. Hence, the feet must be in a V shape, pointing outwards, legs slightly apart. Feel free to move around while presenting, but come back to this stance once you're still and stationary.

3. **Voice:** Speak loud enough so that the people at the back of the room can hear you. The microphone must be placed below the chin, pointing upwards. Try to bring a variation in your voice. No one wants to hear a boring monotone. Also, the rate of speaking must be such that people can keep up with you. Don't speak too fast or too slow. Practice pronouncing each word separately so that you don't `eat up' your words. A voice recorder is very helpful for this.

4. **Eye Contact**: Most speakers are guilty of not making eye contact with the audience. The tendency is to focus only on one or two people in the room, ignoring the rest. Good speakers move their faces and eyes to look at different parts of the room while speaking. This makes everyone feel included and thereby interested.

Tip: Mentally divide the room into three parts. Focus on 1-2 friendly faces in each part and look at them alternately throughout the presentation.

8.8 Summary

All of us have to do public speaking to succeed. So instead of shying away, we should try to acquire this important skill. The number one requirement to become a good public speaker is to practice constantly. Ensuring that the occasion, audience, and location are all under control. Define your aim and objectives; gather the required materials and visual aids.

Organize your speech according to the Talk Organization formula.

Speak loudly and clearly. Speak in terms of the other person's interest and speak from the heart. Observe great speakers like Obama and Amitabh Bachchan. Finally, don't be disheartened if you don't get success at first. Believe in yourself and look for opportunities to speak.

Knowledge Check:

1. Define Glossophobia. Explain the importance of public Speaking.
2. Explain five ways to overcome the fear of speaking.
3. What is COPTA? Explain each point in detail.
4. Explain the four parts of the TOF organization formula
5. Give examples of how the TOF can be used while introducing yourself to a recruiter
6. Name four ways of beginning a speech or presentation.
7. List out the things to be kept in mind while making a PowerPoint presentation.
8. What is Charisma? How can one develop Charisma as a speaker?
9. How does one develop a powerful platform personality?

Additional resources for self-development

- **https://www.youtube.com/@thecoachprashant**
- Steve Jobs: **https://www.youtube.com/watch?v=x7qPAY9JqE4**
- Roger Federer: **https://www.youtube.com/watch?v=pqWUuYTcG-o**
- Amy Cuddy: Fake it till you make it: **https://www.youtube.com/watch?v=Ks-_Mh1QhMc**

Get Ready for the Real World

Ramesh Yadav, a General Manager at a Multinational Bank, met his friend Rocky, a soft skills trainer, and shook his hand and said. "I have a problem I want to share with you: I am good at making prepared presentations and speeches. But in the office, when someone asks me to speak without any preparation, I get equally nervous and flustered. At social occasions, I

don't like to meet new people as I feel shy and I don't know how to start a conversation".

Rocky said, "That's perfectly normal. Don't worry; speaking without preparation or impromptu speaking, as it's called, is not easy. It comes with practice."

"So how do I practice? Can you tell me a trick to make impromptu speaking easier?"

"Yes," Rocky said, "POST IT!"

"Post it? What's that?" asked Ramesh.

Rocky said: **Connect with your audience through:**

1. **Preparation:** Always be alert in a new situation. Always be ready with some jokes or anecdotes. Have your visiting cards handy at all times.
2. **Organizing:** Organize your delivery and message properly. Speak logically. Always complete one sentence and then jump into the next. Use the Speech Organization Formula.
3. **Style:** Your voice & appearance have to match the audience you are speaking to.
4. **Tailoring:** Nervous energy into +'ve energy.

Speak with confidence anytime and anywhere by following the above principle. By the POST IT framework, you can talk to anyone, anywhere. No more anxiety of meeting or talking to strangers.

Applied knowledge

1. How can we overcome the fear of speaking without preparation?
2. Apply the POST IT framework to your daily lives by meeting at least one new person every week and striking up a conversation with them.

Build your vocabulary

Learn and use the Words and Business phrases used in this chapter to improve your Spoken English Skills:

1. **Let their guard down**
2. **Double-edged sword**
3. **Have something `handy':** Have it close by or nearby or even on oneself so that you don't have to search for it.
4. **Embrace the Opportunity:** Grab your chances, don't waste any opportunity to make yourself look good.
5. **Murphy's Law:** Prepare for the Worst and Hope for the Best. Always have a backup plan ready

Chapter 9

Non-Verbal Communication

Beyond words: Mastering Body Language, Listening and Non-verbal cues

LEARNING MILESTONES

This chapter will enable you to:

- Understand the distinction between verbal and non-verbal communication.
- Identify and appreciate the various types of non-verbal communication.
- Master the lesser known areas of non-verbal communication such as silence and touch.
- Enable you to develop powerful body language.
- Become an effective listener.
- Use non-verbal communication to develop conversational skills.

Expert Quotes

"You haven't got dressed till you wear your smile"

"Actions speak louder than words."

"He who does not understand a look will not understand a long explanation either.."

9.1 Essentials of non-verbal communication (NVC)

Non-verbal communication is the transfer of messages without using words. Body Language is the most commonly understood interpretation of NVC. The way we stand, look at others, our posture and walk, our smile, the clothes we wear, the vehicle we drive, or the office space we occupy, all communicate ideas to others. Telling others what we want or how we are feeling without speaking is the essence of non-verbal communication.

Your energy introduces you even before you speak.

Some examples of NVC from our day-to-day life: "The boss seems to be in a good mood today." "She is frowning...looks angry because we lost that contract." "See how her team is looking so worried and feeling scared." "How do you know that? How did you communicate that?"

People communicate many messages to others by their actions, facial expressions, gestures, body language, and other characteristics without speaking or writing.

Your non-verbal behavior should be in sync with what is verbally communicated to others. In other words, act in a way that shows that you are consistent with what you say. For example, in a job interview, if you wish to highlight some achievements proudly, your body and behavior should reflect this.

Case in Point

Aaron is appearing for an on-campus interview with his dream software company. During the interview, the interviewer casually asks him about his experience with organizing the Annual college fest. Aaron had spent almost 3 weeks hunting for sponsorships, chasing celebrities to perform. In fact, he was the Head organizer of the entire event. It was a huge feather in his cap when the chairman of the board of trustees took his name at the closing ceremony and congratulated him on stage for such a successful event. He mentioned this fact in his CV as well. However, during the interview, when the interviewer asks him about this experience, Aaron looks disinterested and bored. He does not appear to be smiling or excited while talking about it. His pride in his achievement does not seem to be in line with his facial and bodily expressions. The interviewer even tells him, "Aaron, you don't seem happy at having organized this event." The end result is that Aaron does not get an offer. He realizes later that he should have looked and sounded animated and excited as the interviewer was trying to evaluate his leadership skills. He understood that extra-curricular questions are as important as technical questions in job interviews.

The central idea is that what you communicate *non-verbally* to others can be as important as what you communicate verbally.

Positive and Negative Non-Verbal Communication

A positive example of non-verbal communication is illustrated by a manager greeting his team who have delivered an important project within budget and timeline with friendly eye contact, a smile, and a pat on the back for some of the team members.

A negative example may be illustrated by the same manager, body totally rigid and erect, lips closed, breathing fast, unsmiling, eyes narrowed, arms tightly folded, and head shaking from side to side. The team automatically comes to know that something is wrong today!

It is important to be aware of the messages you are sending to your team through your behavior. Make sure you communicate both verbally and non-verbally the messages you want your players to receive.

Can you guess what each of these people is trying to communicate?

***Figure 9.1**: Your body communicates constantly*

9.2 Importance of NVC

It is also important to understand the non-verbal communication of others, as it is easy to be misled or confused by their body signals. For example, a team member smiles during a team meeting: is the person laughing at the manager? Amused with the idea that the manager just gave? Or thinking of something funny that happened at home? The manner in which the manager interprets that person's actions will determine their reaction. And if this interpretation is wrong, then it can lead to misunderstanding and conflict.

Often, when verbal and non-verbal communication give out different messages, we tend to believe the non-verbal, mainly because we realize that most non-verbal behavior is involuntary and unconscious, difficult to control, and, therefore, displays what the person actually feels inside.

9.3 Types of Non-Verbal Communication

Non-verbal communication is not just about using the body to communicate. In fact, we can use our immediate environment for communicating non-verbally. Remember when we were in school, how we used to use objects to `reserve' our space or territory? For example, placing a handkerchief or water bottle on a seat to reserve that place for a friend on the bus going to the school picnic. That object was an unspoken communication that told the others not to sit on that seat. The various types of NVC that we normally exhibit are:

- Silence
- Touch
- Eye Contact
- Space & Territory
- Body Language
- Listening

9.3.1 Silence

You prepare for days for a presentation. You practice hard, and when D-Day comes, you think you have made a fabulous speech, and you ask your audience

to ask any questions – The response? Pin-drop silence! How would you feel as a speaker? What will go through your mind? All those fears and insecurities creep up into the mind and dent the self-confidence? That is the negative power of Silence!

***Figure 9.2**: Your silence can be the strongest message in the room*

The popular saying goes: "silence is golden". But in this case, you want anything but silence; you need some feedback, applause, questions, anything but the torturous silence!

We are social creatures, and we are constantly seeking approval and responses from others. When we don't receive this desired response, we become insecure and take action to get some response or some feedback from society. We treat that feedback as validation and approval for our actions.

Think about it: Solitary confinement is one of the worst punishments that can be inflicted upon another human.

Silence builds walls, and walls are barriers to communication.

A long period of silence may be ok for some people in certain circumstances, but at times it can be embarrassing, awkward, and even rude. It could suggest disinterest, boredom, rejection, disagreement, or agreement.

Business Communication demands that every message or communication needs to be responded to. If you cannot reply immediately, then provide some acknowledgement or acceptable responses like: "received", "noted" or "will come back to you shortly", and then followed by the action. Lack of response leads to miscommunication. Avoid silence in business communication. In the professional world, silence is not a response.

Case in Point

Whenever Shreya makes a mistake, her manager screams and shouts at her and the team. He is a very volatile person and makes his feelings known. Over a period of time, the entire team has come to expect this behavior and take it for granted. However, last week, there was an obvious error in her report, and she went to the office fearing the worst. She expected another shouting. Instead, her boss was quiet and maintained silence in the office. He

just didn't say anything. His silence bothered everyone, and they were very confused about how to react. No one knew what to say or do. The silence was a mystery to them!

9.3.2 Space & Territory

Before we try to understand the movements of the various parts of the body, we should first examine the space in which that movement takes place.

Space can be used in the same way as silence, and time can be used as a communication tool.

We have seen animals marking their territory by showing aggression or using their body movements. We humans are very similar.

Concept of Personal Space

Every one of us has their own concept of personal space. Physical space is the physical area surrounding our bodies that is also a part of our bodies. When another person comes into this space, our body responds with a stimulus. This could be in the form of acceptance, acknowledgment, repulsion, aggression, or any other emotion. The kind of emotion that our relationship with that person determines that our brain exhibits. We let some people get close to our bodies, while we hate it when others come that close.

This personal space also extends to objects that we call our own. If someone borrows something that belongs to us without asking, we feel a sense of irritation. This is called `invasion' of personal space.

Case in Point

How would you feel when someone invades your territory?

Example of an executive who is thinking: My chair in the office. It doesn't belong to me. I haven't bought it. It belongs to the office. It is their property. But it is mine. I have been assigned that chair. It is my personal space. My identity, my position in the hierarchy, and my seniority are tied to the chair. I feel violated if anyone uses my chair without my permission. I think they have used a personal item of mine! Why do I feel this way?

***Figure 9.3**: When your seatmate chooses you over the headrest*

Appropriate distance

So then, how do we determine what the appropriate distance that we should keep from other people is? The illustration below is helpful when interacting with another person, be it in a social, personal, or professional setting.

Proxemics - Distance	Distance from the other Person
Intimate distance (with lovers or people with whom we have personal or physical relations, very close friends)	0 -18 inches
Professional distance (with colleagues, professional contacts, and other business stakeholders)	18 inches to 3 feet
Social distance (with people whom we are not very familiar with, recent contacts, strangers)	3 to 8 feet
Public Distance (events, conferences, large gatherings)	8 feet to the limit of sight

9.3.3 Touch (Haptics)

Touch is probably the earliest form of communication. Before language was developed, humans used touch to communicate. People who are unable to speak use touch and sign language as a communication tool. Touch has the incredible power to reverse negative emotions.

The study of touch as nonverbal communication includes:

- Handshakes
- Holding hands
- Self-touch
- A pat on the shoulder
- Sign language

However, over a period of time, our society and culture have introduced inhibitions or rules related to touch. Some of these rules are necessary, and these are:

1. **Dealing with children**: We must be extremely careful when communicating with children, keeping in mind the concept of `good touch and bad touch.
2. **Dealing with the opposite sex**: Casual touch can be misunderstood to be meaningful or intimate touch if one is not careful. Hence, it is essential to be very careful how and where one approaches and touches another person. If you are unsure, just ask!
3. **At the workplace**: There are very strong laws against sexual harassment, which occurs when a person is victimized, touched, or exploited by another in the workplace for personal favors or gain. Again, it is essential to be familiar with POSH rules and be compliant with your organization's policy on touching and sexual harassment.

***Figure 9.4**: Respect boundaries or face repercussions*

4. **Inter-cultural situations:** Different countries and cultures have different standards of touch. Asians and Arabs generally are more `touchy-feely' than those in Western countries. It is very necessary to know the culture related to the country with which you are dealing.

Handshake

Handshake is an integral part of one's personality. A firm handshake accompanied by good eye contact and an occasional touch of the arm and smile can solve even the most complex misunderstandings. A good handshake can greatly improve first impressions.

***Figure 9.5**: A firm handshake gets instant respect*

1. Shake hands for 2-3 seconds at the maximum.
2. Practice a strong, firm, and well-gripped handshake. Shake hands in an up and down motion, never sideways.
3. Shake only with your hands, not your full arms.
4. Never ever offer a weak and limp handshake. There should be a slight pressure applied to the other person's hand when you shake hands.
5. Never shake hands when your hands are wet. Ensure that your hands are completely dry and then offer a handshake.
6. Shake hands with both men and women.

9.3.4 Body Language

NOT Body Language. Your Body as Language

Body language is the language communicated through posture, clothes, gestures, and facial expressions. It is the unspoken communication that goes on in every encounter with another human being. It tells you others' true feelings towards you and how well your words are being received. Body Language is the sum total of various parts of your body and etiquette that you use to communicate with others. A powerful or strong body language is interpreted as confidence, and weak body language is considered a sign of a weak personality!

Parts of Body Language

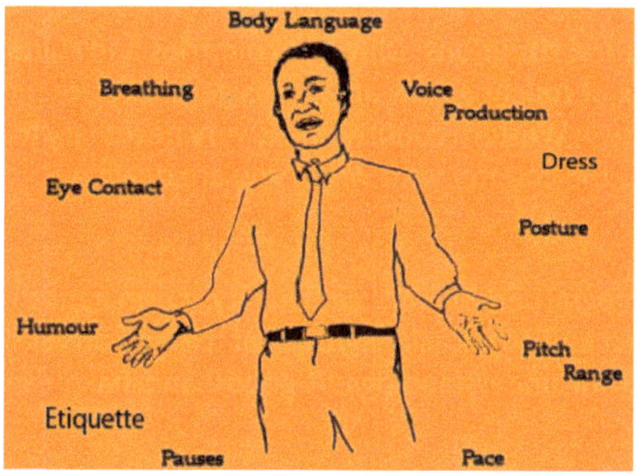

***Figure 9.6**: Understanding the different types of body language*

Features of Powerful Body Language

A survey conducted by the author and the resulting interviews with top leaders, managers, and coaches revealed a few common body language features that good professionals display:

1. **Being Involved**: Move among your colleagues or friends so that they feel you are spending some time with each of them. Vary the distance and position you maintain between yourself and others to communicate your intention. For example, standing very close and facing your team or another person rather than standing further away suggests a desire for more direct interaction.
2. **Make regular eye contact** with those you meet.

   "The eyes are the mirror to your soul."

   Essentials of eye contact

   a. Maintain eye contact long enough to see the color of the other person's eye. Looking at the other person for a duration longer than that makes them uncomfortable. When speaking to a group, ensure that you make eye contact with all members of the group at least once.

b. To avoid staring, when speaking with another person, make a mental triangle on their face consisting of 3 points: their eyebrows and the top of the nose. Look at the region of this triangle, as this gives the illusion of making eye contact without staring.

c. When your mind wanders, and you begin thinking of something or someone else, your eyes show your disinterest. And the person speaking to you is well aware that you are not paying attention.

d. Avoiding eye contact when asked a direct question shows a negative intention or a chance of telling lies.

3. **A pat on the back or shoulder,** a firm grip on the arms, or an arm around the shoulder are powerful ways of conveying appreciation, concern, and support.

Figure 9.7: *Not all care is spoken, some of it is shown by touch*

4. **Facing the person or group** that you are speaking with or listening to. Turning your back is a sign of boredom or disrespect.

Our Head and Body language

We shake our heads up and down or from one side to another. In some cases, it is done at different speeds. There are many reasons and implications. Could be a yes, no, go on, I want to intervene and speak, encouragement, disagreement, agreement, and so on.

Case in Point

Indian `wag' of the head

Generally, we humans move our head up and down to indicate agreement and from one side to the other side to indicate disagreement. But foreigners are often confused when interacting with Indians who move their head `sideways' with the ears almost touching each other alternately. This is a confusing gesture that can be a `yes' or a `no'. Here, the listener has to understand the communication not just by looking at the head but also by

facial expressions and other sounds. These are some cross-cultural situations that create confusion due to non-verbal communication.

Posture

People from the Defence forces can be spotted a mile away. Erect shoulders and a straight back, with a brisk walk and purposeful gestures, give an impression that they are confident and Self-assured persons. This discipline is ingrained in their rigorous training because stooped shoulders give an impression of an under-confident person. And under-confident people are soon defeated by their enemies!

It is the same with others as well. A confident, upright posture shows your state of mind and conveys to the other person that you are ready, able, and confident to do business with them.

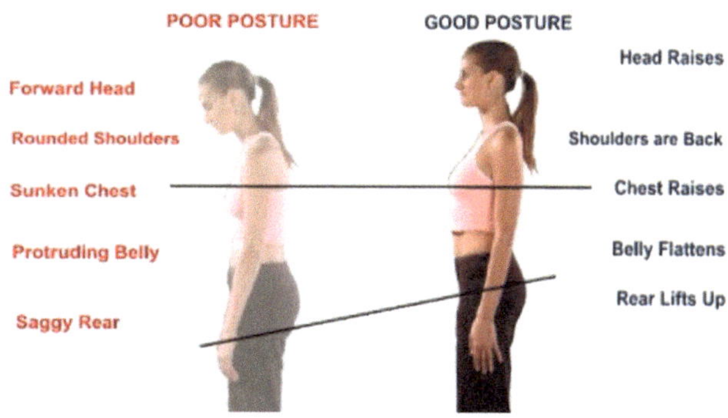

***Figure 9.8**: Poor posture undermines confidence*

Mirroring

Two people talking to one another, standing in the same pose, indicate that they are in agreement with each other, and they like each other. For example, if one person is speaking with their head slightly bowed and hands folded, this is the mirroring technique.

Tips to demonstrate powerful body language

- Be Energetic! Don't be lethargic or slow.
- Display variety in your gestures. Try to mix it up so that you don't come across as boring or monotonous
- Exercise and stay fit: A fit body shows a healthy mind. That's the impression that you give out by being physically fit
- Don't keep touching yourself.
- Maintain appropriate distance and eye contact.
- Pay attention to your posture and fitness
- Dress and Grooming should be modern and appropriate.

***Figure 9.9**: Fit body, sharp mind: people notice your presence*

9.3.5 Listening

> *"We were given two ears but only one mouth,*
> *because listening is twice as hard as talking."*

The True Meaning of Listening

***Figure 9.10**: Good listeners win trust without saying a word*

Listening is the most important and underrated communication skill. In fact, when the majority of people are asked about areas of improvement in their personal development, they rarely mention listening. In the author's experience with corporates, listening is a skill that can propel professionals to the top positions. In our quest to consume data and get connected digitally, we have stopped practicing the art of listening. But the fact is that whoever masters listening skills will succeed in the real world much faster than their competition.

Most people tend to be "hard of listening" rather than "hard of hearing."

What then is listening? Listening means not just hearing words using one's ears. It is a process involving the mind and body, which involves a more sophisticated mental process than hearing; It means acting upon the words being heard, giving feedback with due consideration, and showing empathy, respect, and courtesy to the speaker.

Ways to become an effective Listener

Good listening is a difficult communication skill to learn well. Like all skills, it takes practice to be a good listener. The following techniques can be used to improve your listening skills.

The difference between being a good listener and being a great listener is using your heart in addition to your eyes and mind while listening.

9.3.6 Hearing v/s Listening

Many times, we tell another person: Can you hear me? Other times, we demand: Are you listening to me?

Have you ever wondered why we use two different words for two different situations? In both cases, we want the other person to have absorbed our words. The difference is that by hearing us, the other person has only allowed our words to enter their mind. It is like sounds coming in. Hearing is just a small part of listening.

When this hearing gets converted to listening, the sounds take on the shape of a coherent message. We understand, give feedback, and act upon those sounds. That's the magic moment when hearing becomes listening

Case in Point

Avi is getting really agitated. Another team meeting has come and gone, and still the project is behind schedule. His reportee, Ronit, is in charge of circulating the minutes of the meeting. However, the minutes are often incomplete. Ronit seems to be taking lots of notes, but when the minutes are emailed to all, important bits of information are omitted. He always says sorry and resends, but it makes Avi look unprofessional with his leadership.

In the next team meeting, Avi observes Ronit. When someone is presenting, Ronit appears to be writing. But when Avi asks to see the notes. Ronit is reluctant. With great coaxing, he shows his notebook to Avi, who is shocked to see doodles and cartoons filling the pages instead of the team meeting notes. No wonder Ronit keeps making errors in his team notes! After the meeting, Avi speaks to Ronit and asks him for an explanation. Ronit says that he gets bored in meetings as no one asks him to contribute. He is made to sit at the end of the table, far away from the presenter. This makes him sleepy. Avi hears him out.

In the next meeting, Avi makes it compulsory for all those who are present, including Ronit, to say something, give feedback, or make a presentation. No one is allowed to stay silent. Ronit is placed close to the speaker and given the additional charge of assigning the order of speakers. This time, Ronit takes brilliant notes. He tells Avi later that because he was giving feedback, speaking, and placed closer to the speaker, he was more attentive and hence was less distracted. Previously, he would hear the words and drift off into a daydream. Now, each speaker seems different, and this makes their message more interesting. He has actually started listening!

- Hearing is like breathing; it is an automatic process. It is physical in nature.
- Effective Listening is a skill that can be achieved only through Practice. It is intellectual in nature.

How to Improve Your Listening Skills

Have you ever found yourself finishing someone's sentences for them? If a friend or a colleague tells you about something wonderful that has happened to them, you usually interrupt with something similar that you have experienced. Another person comes to you complaining of a headache, and you tell them about your relative who is experiencing similar pains. Rarely do we share joy or happiness or sympathize with others' pain. Rarely do we just let others speak.

The result is that people think that you are a selfish and boring person who is absolutely uninterested in their lives. No one wants to associate with such selfish people.

People with Emotional Intelligence have great empathy skills. These people have exceptional listening skills.

Tip

To improve your listening skills, practice with those who are closest to you. Be conscious of the urge to interrupt another person while they are speaking. When family members or friends share their thoughts and feelings, resist the urge to relate what you hear to one of your own experiences. Literally bite your own tongue just as you are about to interrupt. Let them finish their sentence and then speak.

1. **Maintain eye contact** with the Speaker. Eye contact maintains self-discipline. It keeps you focused on the job at hand and keeps you involved with the speakers' words. It is a visual lock that doesn't allow your mind to wander. Sit up straight or lean forward slightly to show your attentiveness through body language.

***Figure 9.11**: Eye contact is the cheat code for staying attentive*

2. **Focus on the content**, not just on the delivery. Have you ever counted the number of times a speaker clears his/her throat in a twenty-minute period? If so, you weren't focusing on content. You were instead distracted by the speaker's mannerisms, which took your mind away from the words.

3. **Be conscious of your bias**: Have you ever been frustrated by another person who is `selective listening'? In other words, they hear only what they want to hear. When you approach a conversation with an emotional lens or bias. Or are you too emotional or have already passed judgment on the speaker, you tend to hear what you want to hear--not what is actually being said. Try to remain objective and open-minded. Wait until the speaker is finished before deciding that you disagree. Try not to make assumptions about what the speaker is thinking.

4. **Avoid distractions:** Don't let your mind wander or be distracted by your environment near you. If the room is too hot or too cold or if there is too much external noise, try to find a solution to that situation if you can. It could be a common-sense solution like looking away or even maybe changing the room. Itself.

Figure 9.12: *Control the room or change the room*

5. **Stay active** by asking mental questions. If the speaker has made a point, ask yourself How does this affect my team or me? How can I use this to my advantage? What can I pick up from the presenter that I can use later? Active listening keeps you on your toes. Use the gap between the rate of speech and your rate of thought. You can think faster than the speaker can talk. That's one reason your mind may tend to wander.

6. **Give Verbal Cues**: Respond verbally appropriately to show that you understand. Murmur ("Ok", "uh-huh", and "um-hmm") and nod. Raise your eyebrows or nod your head. Say words such as "Really," "Interesting," as well as other such phrases.

The Golden Rule: To know how to listen to someone else, think about how you would want to be listened to.

Case in Point

Ria, wife of a celebrity, is very popular in her own social circle as well as in her husband's business network. She and her husband get invited to many parties and events where she is a much sought-after guest. Her popularity has created many lucrative business opportunities for her husband.

One day, Saina, a friend, asked her: "Ria, how is it that you are so popular? Everyone wants to talk to you." Ria smiled and replied, Saina, you won't believe this, but my conversational skills are directly related to my listening skills. As my listening skills have improved, so has my aptitude for conversation. The other day, Mr. Bezos once complimented me by commenting that I had such great speaking and conversation skills, and I was so easy to talk to. When in fact, I had not said more than five words, but I had listened to him for more than 25 minutes!

9.4 Summary

Non-Verbal Communication is the sum total of the various parts of the body speaking to another person, without the use of words! It is an unspoken language that conveys complex thoughts. Body Language can be as effective as verbal communication in conveying our innermost thoughts, feelings, and emotions. Silence and touch are extremely useful tools, especially as negative reinforcement. We need to listen with all our being, so as to become the popular and gifted communicators that we aspire to be. Correct Body Language helps to build relationships, solve problems, ensure understanding, and resolve conflicts. At work, effective listening means fewer mistakes and more productivity. At home, it helps to build bridges, reduce the generation gap, and helps members solve their own problems. In this age of social media, listening builds lasting friendships and careers.

Knowledge Check:

1. What is non-verbal communication? Give two situations where you have encountered non-verbal communication today.
2. What are the different types of Non-Verbal communication?
3. Give 1 example of each type of Non-verbal communication from your own life.
4. What are the ways to develop a powerful body language?
5. Give the difference between Hearing & Listening.
6. What are the ways in which you can practice effective listening?

Additional resources for self-development

1. Amy Cuddy: Body Language: **https://www.youtube.com/watch?v=Ks-_Mh1QhMc**
2. Characteristics of Great listeners: **https://hbr.org/2016/07/what-great-listeners-actually-do**

3. Emotional Intelligence and Listening: **https://www.huffingtonpost.com/anne-loehr/four-ways-to-amp-up-your-_b_7513982.html**
4. Understanding the psychology of Body Language: **https://www.psychologytoday.com/basics/body-language**
5. Essentials of Successful Communication: **https://youtu.be/VJ3uLTFdkW8?si=kiGD8q7X8lhaKgsO**

Get ready for the real world!

"Are you listening to me, young man?" Professor Siva shouted!

Dev sat up with a jerk. "¡Y.y.y.es, sir!" He shouted back.

The entire class laughed. Once again, Dev had been caught daydreaming in his MBA class.

"Can you repeat what I just said? Why are you staring at me like that for 15 minutes? Get out of class if you don't want to pay attention."

That evening, feeling low and dejected, he met his friends Tina and Akash, who had just started as interns in a multinational food chain.

They exchanged their stories of the day! "What? You too, cried Tina? Can you imagine yesterday, Akash got an earful from our supervisor, and today I was reprimanded for the same thing. He said we don't listen! What does that mean? I don't know, she cried! We hear whatever he is saying, but he speaks so fast and gives so many instructions to us that sometimes the customers' orders get messed up."

Akash, who was in the HR department, said, "My boss told me to file the salary slips for the month, but I heard that he wanted me to scan the salary slips. I spent one full day doing that, and he shouted at me for wasting time in the office!"

Ahmed, their common friend, was listening to this talk. He said, "It's strange that my uncle Anoop, who is a communications teacher at First Personality, was telling me that effective listening is such an important communication skill, but it's a skill that almost none of the people he meets possess. Let me call him now!"

Anoop agreed to meet them at the market. They sat at a coffee shop, and once he had heard their complaints, he said. "You know you all are making the classic mistake that almost everyone makes: You are confusing hearing with listening."

"But they are the same thing," Ahmed cried!

"No, they are not," said Anoop. "Hearing is totally different from speaking."

"Hearing is simply the act of perceiving sound by the ear. Listening, however, is something you consciously choose to do. Listening requires concentration so that your brain processes meaning from words and sentences. Listening leads to learning.

Many times, too, as soon as the other person starts speaking, we're busy preparing our answer before they even have ten words out of their mouth.

Anoop said: "Dev: Do you know that by Effective listening, you can attain academic success? You can improve your marks by 25%! Your professors will take you more seriously. If you have any queries, they will go out of their way to accommodate you. You won't need to keep running here and there to have your queries answered."

He continued: "Tina and Ahmed! You can have a better relationship with your boss by listening effectively. He will be more receptive to your request for leave and extra facilities. He will go out of his way to give you a good appraisal.

'That's true,' said all three glumly! 'But why does it happen to us only?' asked Ahmed. 'Why do others seem to get ahead, while we are constantly told that we don't listen properly?'

'You will be surprised said Anoop. Lack of listening skills is one of the most common issues that people have in their soft skills. Most employers who are quizzed will lack soft skills as a primary problem in the employability of the potential candidates.'

"There is no other way! If you don't start to practice effective listening, you will forever find yourself receiving from your superiors. Do you want to spend the rest of your life getting shouted at and eventually be left behind in the race of life?"

"No!" they all cried in unison.

"Then learn to listen", Anoop said.

Applied knowledge

1. Why were Akash, Tina, and Dev dejected and sad?
2. According to Anoop, what were the reasons for their low morale?
3. What, according to him, was the one main communication that could help them?
4. How will you practice Anoop's suggestions in your real life?

Build your vocabulary

Learn and use the Words and Business phrases used in this chapter to improve your Spoken English Skills:

1. **In sync:** In agreement with.
2. **Feather in the cap:** A great achievement.
3. **D-Day:** The day on which the event that you have prepared for will happen.
4. **Decorum:** The way of behaving in a particular situation.
5. **In Unison:** All together.

Join our Discord space

Join our Discord workspace for latest updates, offers, tech happenings around the world, new releases, and sessions with the authors:

https://discord.bpbonline.com

Chapter 10 Building Online Presence

Creating impact and Visibility in Virtual Meetings, Interviews and Calls

LEARNING MILESTONES

This chapter will enable you to:

- Make yourself more visible and showcase your efforts working from home
- Make the best impression in online Interviews, meetings and sales pitches.
- Master your online executive presence and personal brand
- Develop a striking and unique camera presence and personality
- Make high-impact online presentations and product pitches

Expert Quotes

" Your Online Presence needs to work in unison with your offline ambitions."

10.1 Importance of building your Online Presence

Online work has always been an option for both students and professionals. Whenever there were constraints on budget or travel, physical limitations, or after-hours work, online meetings and work-from-home have been used ever since online meeting tools were developed. However, these were usually an option, not the norm.

COVID has disrupted the learning and meeting space forever. In this online work era, developing a virtual presence has become a foundation for building one's personal brand. Changed work and learning habits post-COVID have forced organizations to offer a hybrid option to their employees or students.

While online meetings, webinars, e-learning, and video-based instruction have been around for several years, it is only now that these mediums have become the standard. Zoom, MS Teams, Google Meet, WhatsApp, FaceTime, etc., are the default new meeting places. Not just mere options.

With corporations under economic stress, budget cuts have impacted business travel. Routine meetings are being held online, with professionals now being told to make complex decisions without their physical presence. Truly, the world

has shrunk into our computer screens and mobiles. From functioning human beings of different races and cultures, we have now become a 2 x 2 square on someone's screen!

***Figure 10.1**: Let your energy travel through the screen*

In such a scenario, people from all walks of life, whether they are students, consultants, corporates, trainers, or entrepreneurs, all have to learn to project themselves online in the best possible manner.

10.2 Offline v/s Online Presence

So what's the big deal about meeting online?

The reality is that while there is a difference between meeting face to face and meeting online, the same rules of physically creating the best first impression, verbal and non-verbal communication rules apply online as well.

The main difference between the two media is the absence of physical cues in online media. When we meet someone face to face, we have the benefit of observing their body language, micro-expressions, and we can feel the energy of the room once discussions take place. However, in online communication, one has to be extremely observant and conscious of vocal cues, eye contact, and others' participation to actually gauge whether your message has gone across in the most optimal way.

In Virtual, the communicator is almost alone, operating in isolation, looking at the camera and trying to express thoughts and words into a screen or microphone. How well they are able to adapt to online can make the difference between success and failure.

While communicating virtually, there are two modes of communication that need special attention:

1. Virtual Verbal Communication
2. Virtual Non-Verbal Communication

10.3 Virtual Verbal Communication

In Online Verbal Communication, there are three main components that play a very important part:

1. Voice
2. Presentation
3. Packaging

These are the three components that determine whether one has been able to make the best first impression across the screen.

As we have seen in the previous chapters, first impressions can make or break the meeting. The stakeholders are impressed with your ability to communicate your message in the most appropriate way.

10.3.1 Voice

Voice is one of the most important components of good communication. A good, strong voice with proper modulation makes the communication interesting. The chances of convincing and influencing others increase by using one's voice properly.

There is no better example of this than actors who have to communicate with their audiences via camera. Small nuances, the proper context, depth of feelings, and mood, and a wide range of emotions can be expressed by using one's voice in the proper manner.

Case in Point

Aniket has a very important video call coming up with his skip-level manager, who has just joined remotely. Aniket is desperate to make the best first impression. He does virtual calls with his team regularly, and 1 minute before the meeting time, he logs on.

Two minutes into the meeting, his manager tells him, "Aniket, I cannot understand you....slow down a bit. And I can barely hear you, your voice is very faint."

Aniket increases the volume to max, but the same issue. He requests that he log out and log in again. But the same problem.

He starts panicking when he sees his boss getting restless and irritated. He knows he has not been able to make a good impression.

Later, he discusses with his colleague Ita about his bad first meeting. To his surprise, Ita says: 'Yes, that happens often in your calls."

"But why didn't you ever tell me? No one has ever told me of this problem."

Ita replies: 'You never asked anyone."

Ways to ensure proper voice and sound during online communication

- One must pay attention to the 4Ps of Voice:

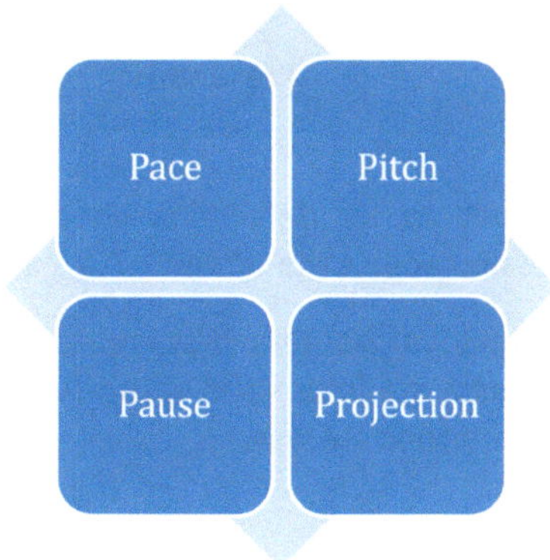

***Figure 10.2**: It's not just what you say — it's how you say it*

- Invest in a good microphone (mic) if your system does not have a good internal mic. A hands-free headset with a mic works best. Check online for the best deals.
- Test the mic before important meetings. Check for volume and whether it is compatible with the meeting platform that you are using.
- Ensure that your mic is in mute mode when not speaking. This is true especially if you are not able to conduct the online meeting in a noise-free environment.
- Your mic must always be on while speaking. Before speaking, it is a good idea to ask: "Am I audible?" If possible, ask for feedback on whether your voice level is OK.
- Do voice intonation and modulation exercises. This will ensure that there is variation in your voice and you get clarity. You can refer to the author's YouTube channel for more information on the same.

  Exercise:

  Mouth Yoga: Stretch your mouth and jaw to the maximum 6 times every morning and night before sleeping. You should feel relief in your jaws. Discontinue if you feel pain. Loosening your jaw results in better voice clarity

10.3.2 Presentation

Whether you are giving a status update, having a department meeting, making a pitch, or showcasing work, presentations are an integral part of professional work. While PowerPoint and other presentation software have made it easier to present, online presentations need far more planning and detailing than face-to-face.

Here are some things to keep in mind while planning online presentations:

a. **Rehearse:** There is absolutely no substitute for rehearsals and practice before any public speaking event. Online Presentations are no exception. The speaker needs to rehearse all the parts of the presentation offline and then come online to present. Ensure that you know the platform limitations and capabilities beforehand. AI tools built into presentation softwares can provide you with real-time feedback on your presentation delivery, the same way as an offline coach does.

b. **Presenting as a group**: If you are presenting with others or if you have co-presenters, ensure that you have rehearsed as a group beforehand. The audience gets restless and disoriented if there is no unity and cohesion between a group of presenters. It also shows an embarrassing lack of preparation. Preparing as a group before the online meeting shows extreme professionalism.

Case in Point

Rani, Sabrina, and Yang-Chin are startup entrepreneurs. The three women got together as college friends, and now they have a food delivery startup. They have an important online pitch coming up with an investor who has given them only 20 minutes to make their presentation. They are in the process of preparing the pitch deck. They have decided to divide their work so that each presenter knows their role beforehand. So Rani, who is good at designing, is in charge of preparing the actual presentation and the pitch. Sabrina is a good speaker and has the best camera and microphone setup, so she will be the primary speaker. Yang-Chin will be the producer- i.e., the one who will handle the technical details of the platform, coordinate the Q&A session, and ensure that there are no technical glitches in the presentation.

The presentation is conducted very smoothly. The investor compliments the trio on their pitch and says he is very impressed, especially when they inform him of the kind of preparation they did. He makes the decision to invest in their company.

c. **Don't just read out from notes**. It is always good to have a conversational style where you look at the camera for the majority of the time. It is boring for the audience to see you read out from notes, and it also shows a certain lack of confidence if the speaker cannot present without reading.

***Figure 10.3**: Stop reading. start presenting. big difference*

d. **Set your presentation rules in advance.** Inform the audience beforehand when you will take questions, what the format will be, and whether they can communicate on mute or chat, etc. Otherwise, it remains a guessing game. If you want the cameras to be on or off, this will need to be informed prior to the presentation as well.

e. **Use the chat:** The chat is a valuable feature in all platforms for audience interaction and should be used extensively as much as possible. It also keeps the audience involved without interfering with your speaking flow. Acknowledge chats as they come in, else the others feel you are not listening to them. Gen Z participants mostly prefer chat to verbal communication. Hence, use the chat to communicate better with this age demographic.

f. **Call people by their name.** The participants become alert the moment they hear their name. It also gives everyone the feeling of being accountable and being part of the presentation. In case of complicated names, maintain a small diary and write the pronunciation down. As far as possible, call the participants by their names at least once in every meeting.

10.3.3 Packaging

Whether it is food or a product, the seller or creator makes all efforts to package it before selling. The reason is that, however good the product might be, if the first impression and look & feel are not good, there will be no takers for it.

It's not just what you say, but how you say it that also matters in online communication.

As with anything else in life, packaging plays a very important part in online communication as well. Good virtual presenters know that the physical aspects of their presentation are determined within the first 10 seconds, whether the audience will remain interested or not.

Aspects of packaging to be kept in mind:

a. **Design:** Don't have too much text on the screen. Remember that Less is more. A cluttered screen puts people off, and you don't want them to feel that they will be subjected to a verbal overload. While designing the slides, ensure that there are not more than 20 words on the slide. For example, Steve Jobs, who is supposed to be one of the best presenters, used nineteen words in the first 3 minutes of his iconic iPhone introduction speech.

b. **Infographics and images:** these help to convey complex emotions that words sometimes cannot. A picture is worth a thousand words, and your slide should have keywords displayed as bold headlines. The audience will remember the headline words far more than a bunch of text. Infographics can be easily created using free software.

c. **Customize look and feel of the slides**: Customize this to the culture and image of the audience. So if the corporate colours of a company are orange, grey, and black, then the slides can be designed to maintain that look. This gives the audience the feeling that you have taken the time and effort to understand their look and feel and culture, and this shows respect. They will reciprocate that respect by listening to you.

d. **Pay attention to your Executive Presence**: Your Personal Brand is the sum total of your executive Presence and how others experience you. In online meetings, ensure that whatever you say or present is consistent with your brand. Just because the other person is not present face-to-face with you, it does not mean permission to lower your guard and say things one would normally not have said in a face-to-face meeting.

***Figure 10.4**: Your executive presence doesn't log off just because you're online*

10.4 Virtual Non-Verbal Communication

Most audiences will notice your non-verbal cues, much before you start speaking into the camera. Your comfort level, your ability to engage with the participants, your eye contact, dress, and body language are all under scrutiny. In fact, online,

the non-verbal communication, often 55% of the effectiveness of the message, gets magnified even more than face to face.

The following are certain aspects of non-verbal communication that require special attention in an online scenario:

a. **Camera**: It is essential to have a good-quality camera. If your system camera does not capture your image correctly, please make a small investment in a good-quality external webcam. This is extremely crucial to how you appear to others in an online meeting.

   Imagine a face-to-face meeting or interview, where you show up without dressing properly, or no grooming, or makeup. What sort of impression would that give? A pretty poor one, right?

   Your camera is the eyes of the viewer.

   What your audience sees is dependent upon what your camera captures. So please do not underestimate the power of your system camera. Make sure that you have a good one.

   The camera needs to be placed at eye level.

b. **Lighting**: Once your camera is sorted, it becomes necessary to get the right lighting. Ensure that the light falls directly on your face. However, the lighting should not be very harsh or bright. Proper lighting ensures that the audience is able to see your complete self, similar to the experience they would have if you met them face-to-face.

   1. Test your camera with proper lighting beforehand so that the proper silhouette of your face and upper body is highlighted.
   2. If the light is too weak, add more or use a more powerful light source. If it's not possible to add more light, then try to get closer to a natural light source like a window. However, do not have the window exposed behind you, as the light will be behind you. Remember to have blinds or curtains drawn on the window.
   3. If it's too bright, diffuse the light by going for indirect light or putting tissue paper on the light source to reduce brightness.
   4. Avoid lighting placement, which is directly over the head, as it creates dark shadows on the face and under the eyes.

c. **Background**: Having a good background or backdrop for the online session ensures that the viewer is not distracted by the physical environment behind the speaker. Ample thought needs to be given to having a good background.

   1. **Remove the clutter:** Ensure that the background is free from clutter or misaligned objects that appear out of place. The more plain the background, the better. If possible, some green plants or flowers serve as a fresh and natural backdrop.

a. **Virtual background:** Many platforms provide the option of having a Virtual background. If you cannot have a natural background that is suitable, then go for the Virtual option. Please choose a backdrop that is professional and not very loud. If in doubt about what backdrop to use, you can choose the `Blur background' option.

b. Keep in mind that some virtual backgrounds can distort the overall figure of the speaker. So please test the virtual background beforehand.

c. Virtual backgrounds can be used to display your brands, logos, or any other statement that you would like to make. Showing off your brand constantly as a background reinforces that image in the viewer's mind.

2. **Frame yourself:** For the viewer, often the speaker is a small window on the screen. In that case, it becomes important to be visible. The speaker should be placed in the center of the camera frame. Depending upon the type of presentation, the upper body, up to the chest or stomach, should be visible.

***Figure 10.5**: Visibility online builds opportunity offline*

3. **Body language:** Use gestures in the same way that you would have used in face-to-face meetings.

   - Let your hands show. Smile and do not move your head too much unless necessary.
   - Dress the same way you would dress in a face-to-face. Dressing well for the meeting shows respect for the viewer. The audience takes you and your message more seriously.
   - Do not sit on the bed and conduct meetings. If there is no provision for an office set up, sit on the dining table or on a chair that has a firm back.

4. **Smile:** Your enthusiastic smile shows that you are happy to be there. Smiling is contagious, and the viewers also get relaxed. Once the environment is friendly, rapport building becomes easier. So don't forget to smile. Prior rehearsal can make you look relaxed and get that smile going on your face.

5. **Look enthusiastic:** using words and positive body language shows your eagerness to be there in the meeting. This enthusiasm is very infectious in online meetings, and the viewers really appreciate enthusiastic, energetic presenters. Enthusiasm in body language must also be supplemented with using happy, powerful, image-evoking words. Your audience is expecting you to show enthusiasm. If you're not excited about your idea, they certainly will not be.

Case in Point

Steve Jobs is considered one of the best presenters of all time. His presentations, especially his annual introductions of new Apple products, were like a pilgrimage for tech lovers across the world. What made Jobs such a compelling speaker and ambassador for his company? It was the language that he used.

Jobs would use words such as "cool," "amazing," or "gorgeous" because he believed it. While introducing the iCloud, he used three simple words to describe the simplicity and ease of the service: "It Just Works". He genuinely was proud of his message, and it showed on stage. Not only speaking the words, but Jobs would also display these words on the giant screens behind him. The viewers would read those words and get mesmerized by the imagery of words with awe. The reader would do well to view Steve Jobs' best videos on YouTube and be inspired.

***Figure 10.6**: Steve Jobs unveiling the iPhone with 3 iconic words*

6. **Eye contact:** Ensuring good eye contact with the participants in online meetings sustains interest. The participants feel that you are speaking to them directly and trying to make a personal connection. This helps in getting a better response for your presentation.

Pro tip: Looking at the camera rather than the screen makes the audience feel that you are making eye contact with them

7. **Listening:** Active Listening is as important in online communication as it is offline. Listening involves giving the participants time and opportunity to speak, ask queries, give feedback, and interact with you. No one appreciates a speaker who hogs the limelight. Listening is a key skill, and the speaker would be well aware of using their minds and bodies to eliminate distractions and give the viewers their undivided attention when they are speaking. Asking questions, giving verbal feedback, and paraphrasing are effective listening techniques used in online communication. Taking notes also helps in retaining and recalling information.

***Figure 10.7**: Write it down or watch it disappear from your brain*

10.5 Best Practices for Effective interviews, sales calls, and meetings

Online meetings are of different types. Different people use online as a medium to conduct different types of meetings: Ranging from personal 1-1 Coaching and Training, to large webinar formats. Job interviews, new joinee onboarding, daily scrums, stand-up meetings, status updates, and promotion boards are now being conducted online.

10.5.1 Easy ways to crack online Job Interviews

1. **Be professional:** The same level of professionalism that one would show in face-to-face must be maintained online. Log in 2-3 minutes prior to the interview time. That's like your waiting room. Cool down, compose yourself. Practice positive self-talk during this period.

2. **Display Positive Body Language:**

   2.1 **Dress**: Wear a formal top even if you're taking an official call from your home or in transit. Remember, online requires the same level

of effort and professionalism as offline. Good professionals are ready for any situation. What if the power goes off, or if you need to change your location, or you need to stand up? And your informal lower becomes visible, even if briefly? Would you show up for an interview in pyjamas or shorts? No? In that case, make the effort to wear appropriate attire for job interviews. Top to bottom.

2.2 **Eye contact**: make eye contact with the participants on the other side of the screen, the same way you would in face-to-face. Do not look away from the screen often, as that can make you appear distracted.

3. **Manage the environment:** Reduce external noise or disturbance to a minimum. Try to schedule interviews at a time when there is minimal noise around you. Request the organizers for the same by explaining to them your limitations. Most people will understand and accommodate you. Remember, you don't get unless you ask.

4. **Prepare-Practice-Rehearse:** There is no substitute for the same. Testing all the hardware and doing a rehearsal with someone prior to the interview can help you deal with any unforeseen situations. Having a power and Internet backup is a must. If your Internet connection is not strong enough, test your phone's wifi data as a Wi-Fi hotspot. This prep can help you appear calm, cool, and composed, all qualities that potential employers really admire.

10.5.2 Conducting effective online Presentations and Meetings

1. **Prepare for the eye more than the ear:** Online communication needs to be more visual than any other medium. What appeals to the eye, on the screen, will get more attention from the participants. The slides, the presentation, and the content need to be designed in a way that makes it easy to read and absorb.

2. **Involve everyone:** Audience participation is essential for the successful outcome of a virtual meeting. Ensure that you call people by their name, give others a chance to speak, and ask questions. Encourage Introverts or camera-shy people to use the chat if they are not comfortable switching on their cameras.

***Figure 10.8**: Collaboration turns potential into performance*

3. **Call to action**: Ask for the outcome you want. State it out explicitly, by speaking it out. In online communication, there are no assumptions. You need to be clear on what the result is that you want from your online communication. And this focus on the end result needs to guide whatever virtual planning you do.

4. **Look for blended models:** Many times, having a stand-alone online model might not be the most optimal. In this case, people wishing to conduct online communication can opt for a suitable online + offline blended model, where some of the communication is online, and the rest is face-to-face. This is especially beneficial for learning & development and critical meetings that require a personal contact.

10.6 Summary

Online Communication is not a fad. It is here to stay and has become the primary means of consuming and sharing information. From school children to corporate executives and entrepreneurs, from NGOs to religious organizations, online communication is being used to reach out to a mass audience. In such a scenario, it becomes important for all professionals and students to adopt the best practices of online communication. Get familiar with communicating with your screen. It requires a paradigm shift in the way we have been communicating so far.

Online Communication is a very powerful opportunity and an accessible medium to build your Personal Brand.

The future belongs to those who invest in their Online Presence and can balance their skills between online and offline communication effectively.

Knowledge Check:

1. What is the basic difference between Online and Offline Communication?
2. What are the three components of Visual Verbal Communication?

3. What is the Importance of Packaging in the online communication context?
4. Outline any three components of Virtual Non-Verbal Communication along with the importance of the same.
5. What are the things to keep in mind while planning for online interviews?

Additional resources for self-development

1. Free Slides template download

https://www.slidescarnival.com

2. Speaking up in meetings

https://youtu.be/F8F6yqlFN-o?si=kVsURBVT9E7D8SZu

3. Voice Development: **https://www.gcu.edu/blog/performing-arts-digital-arts/how-improve-singing-voice**

Get ready for the real world

Paul received a meeting invite from a potential client. At last, he thought! He had been waiting for months for this call. The changing AI landscape has been very tough on his new Digital marketing business, and he wanted to leave no stone unturned to impress this potential client.

He preferred Teams or Meet for conducting his online meetings. Most of his clients, friends, relatives, and other contacts were comfortable with Teams as well, so it worked well for him.

He was also familiar with Zoom and Webex. However, in these platforms, he had attended a few meetings as an attendee, but not as a presenter.

When the client's calendar invite came, it was for a meeting on Zoom. No worries, all good, he thought.

The meeting began, and the client had a different agenda in mind. They had invited three other vendors and immediately announced that each vendor would be placed in a separate Breakout room. One by one, they will be called from their Breakout rooms into the main room and make their pitch to the client's global board. This was to ensure that the other vendors could not get access to, hear, or see their competitor's pitches.

Paul had never used the Breakout room, so when the screen prompted him to join the Breakout room, he was confused. He kept asking the host how to do it. 3-4 people from the client's side kept trying to prompt him till finally someone called him and showed him through screen-share. He had already delayed the meeting by 8 minutes.

Then, when he was in the waiting room, he wanted some info, and instead of using the 'Ask for help' feature, which pings the host privately, he started

typing his queries on the chat window. He did not realize that everyone in the meeting, including his competitors, could see his chats and queries!

Finally, when it was his turn to speak, he started to share his presentation. But instead of clicking on the 'Share Window' option that would have opened only his deck, he clicked on the 'Share Entire Screen' option. His entire computer screen opened with the different windows that were open on his desktop. His competitors' websites, his Excel sheet with costings, and an adult website. All was displayed to everyone in the meeting room.

He realized his faux pas, but it was already too late. His impression of the clients had been spoiled. They didn't ask him any questions. The meeting ended soon.

He has not heard back from the clients since the meeting.

Applied knowledge

1. Why was Paul not able to operate basic Zoom tools, despite being a seasoned techie?
2. What is the biggest lesson or takeaway from Paul's experience?
3. If you were in Paul's place, would you have prepared differently for the meeting? If yes, how?

Build your vocabulary

Learn and use the Words and Business phrases mentioned in this chapter to improve your Spoken English Skills:

1. **Micro expressions:** small facial expressions or visual cues that are caused by an emotion that is not yet expressed.
2. **Faux pas:** A mistake or error, generally that causes a breakdown in plans.
3. **Blended:** generally used to imply a mix of something. So online + offline training is a blended model.
4. **Pitch deck:** A Presentation that start-ups make to send to potential investors. Also simply called a deck.
5. **Disrupt:** Generally used in corporate to describe some event, person, or product that causes a major change in the industry. For example, AI, Apple, or Nvidia are disruptors in their respective industries.

Chapter 11 High Performance Leadership

Leading with purpose: Professionalism, Inspiration and Innovation

LEARNING MILESTONES

This chapter will enable you to:

- Understand the true meaning of Leadership.
- Discover everyday leaders in your life and be inspired by them.
- Adopt the ways in which leaders inspire others.
- Practice the best qualities of inspiring Leaders.
- Master the true meaning of professionalism.
- Know how to become a high-performing professional.
- Learn the importance of creative thinking as a means of getting ahead.
- Familiarize with techniques to develop creative thinking.

Expert Quotes

A leader is one who sees more than others see, who sees farther than others see, and who sees before others see."

"Kites rise highest against the winds...so do leaders."

One of the tests of leadership is the ability to recognize a problem before it becomes an emergency.

Leadership is probably the Number 1 quality that most people aspire to possess in their lives. Whether it is in college, at work, in business, or in one's family, leaders are respected and revered. We look at Leaders in our lives and get inspired by them. And wish that we too developed their characteristics. Millions of Books have been written on the subject of Leadership. Books, blogs, podcasts, Reels and Tik-Toks, and YouTube videos provide vast information on how to become leaders.

We want to be Leaders. In fact, more than desire, it is the realization that it is indeed leadership that will help us beat our competition. How do we stay ahead of the pack? How do we ensure visibility for our efforts? The answer is simple: By becoming Leaders.

11.1 What is Leadership?

- Leadership is the process of inspiring others to give their best to achieve a desired result.
- It is about getting people to move in the direction that they want, gaining their commitment, applauding their achievements, and motivating them to realize their goals.

***Figure 11.1**: Kings don't push pieces rather they inspire movement*

11.2 Everyday Leadership

One question that most people want to know is: Are leaders made or born? The answer is that Leadership can be acquired through observation and practice. This is possible by understanding the concept of Everyday Leadership. Often, we are given examples of famous people, living or dead, who have led an inspiring life. Their deeds and actions are quoted to motivate and energize us. However, we find that we fail to make a connection with them. People whom we haven't met or will never meet are like characters in a movie. We see them but can't get to know them. We cannot know what made them do the things that they did. Biographies and books written on these celebrities and historical figures don't allow us to go into their minds. Simply put, there just isn't any connection. Then how can we be inspired by them?

On the other hand, there are people in our lives with whom we live. Work with, play with. Parents, relatives, family friends, social contacts, professional colleagues, or people within the organization. They may belong to different strata of society. Someone may be a manager; the other may be a cleaner. But they sometimes perform a task or do something that makes you go Wow! A task that no one else wanted to do, they do! Against all odds, they succeed in the same environment and variables that you operate in. You wonder how they do it! And they are around to tell you. Show you. Demonstrate to you. They are everyday leaders! And they demonstrate the power of everyday leadership.

From the Chairman to the Doorman, everyone can be an inspiring leader.

We don't have to go far to see everyday leaders. They are all around us. A parent who defies all odds to educate their child. A girl from a small town who rebels against societal norms and prejudice to appear for her Engineering exam and clears it with flying colors. Everyday leadership is all around us. It is a constant presence in our lives. We need to be aware of such leaders and pick up the best qualities from them. In this way, leadership becomes accessible and practical to learn.

Case in Point

Sudhakar is a peon in a small company consisting of the owner, his son, and about 20 employees. It is a very profitable trading company. The owner, Mr. Gupta, is uneducated but a self-made millionaire with a sense of fair justice towards his employees. Over a period of time, Mr. Gupta appears dissatisfied with his employees. He feels they have started taking their jobs for granted. And they are not giving their best. These same employees who used to work day and night in the field are now becoming complacent.

One Monday, the employees come to the office and see a chair placed in the middle of the entry to the office. They are puzzled, but one by one they punch in and enter the office by squeezing past the chair. The chair is clearly blocking the entry, but no one bothers to find out why it's there. Mr. Gupta is watching from his office. Sudhakar comes a little late on Monday, and he too squeezes past the chair.

The next day, the chair is still there, and one by one, everyone goes through the same routine of going around the chair. Sudhakar comes in, and this time, he does something about it. He actually lifts the chair to remove it from the entry to keep it in its place. Just as he lifts the chair, he sees an INR 500 note under the chair. He keeps the chair near a table, and the entrance is now free from any obstacle. He takes the INR 500 note to Mr. Gupta and tells him he found it under the chair. To his surprise, Mr. Gupta takes him out to the main office area and announces, "Sudhakar has just received an INR 500 bonus from me." Everyone is surprised, why? Mr. Gupta continues: "Since yesterday, there has been an obstacle to coming to the office. Everyone avoided the obstacle, but no one removed it. Sudhakar is the only person who removed the obstacle for everyone else to walk unaided, without being told. He is a true leader." The others were a little ashamed, but the message that Mr. Gupta conveyed was driven home so effectively.

Sudhakar proved to be an everyday leader for them.

11.3 How do Everyday Leaders Motivate Others?

1. **Inspire:**

Every day, leaders show that it is possible to do something if one applies their mind to it. They motivate by their vision and make sure that this vision is achievable.

Case in Point

Dhanush's father works as a tailor in a small factory. Dhanush did menial jobs to support his family and got a job in a computer hardware shop as a cleaning assistant. Often, when the electricity would fail at night, he would go under a street lamp and study. He completed his education from an open school and enrolled in a distance learning college, and due to his high grades, received a scholarship to do his Master's. Despite his poor English skills, Dhanush was selected for a multinational due to his technical skills. He is a star employee today and does not hesitate to share his story with others. He tells others from vernacular backgrounds: "If I can do it, you can also do it!" His colleagues are inspired by his grit and cheerful disposition despite having led a hard life.

***Figure 11.2**: Where there is will, even a streetlight becomes a classroom*

2. **Influence:**

Leaders have the knack to get people to do what they don't want to do. They set boundaries and timelines that are achievable, and once these are achieved, they develop a reputation that influences others. Their reputation precedes them.

Case in Point

Sejal is a homemaker in a small town in Gujarat. She studied in a local school and married at an early age into a traditional and conservative family. Sejal is meticulous and disciplined. She has a sharp memory and doesn't forget names and dates easily. She realized this early on and reads books and hears podcasts to develop her memory. She is an expert in mental maths. Once she completes all her household activities, however tired she is, Sejal does the kitchen accounts and reconciles the finances. So, over a period of time,

her very rich father-in-law, who never lets even his sons touch his finances and does not believe in risky investments, begins relying on her sense of numbers. He gets Sejal to make some investments in crypto and stocks. Sejal, with her shrewd mathematical ability, has made several investments for him, which are paying rich dividends. Now, not only her father-in-law but also their neighbors ask her for investment advice. The common refrain in the area is: if Sejal has recommended it, then it must be good. Such is her reputation! A true self-made leader.

3. **Empathy:**

Leaders have an in-built radar that senses when something is not right in their immediate circle. They are sensitive to changes in their immediate environment and immediately pick up when something has changed or when something is not right. They don't ignore it or sweep it under the carpet. Instead, they get to the root of the problem and don't rest till the issue has been resolved. Not only that, every day Leaders stimulate, urge, provoke, and energize everybody around them. They push people to perform much beyond their capabilities. They continue to perform and raise the bar for themselves and for all those around them.

Case in Point

Vikrant is a sales professional on the fast track in his organization. He is rising fast in the company and is tipped to be the future CEO. He is usually in the field, meeting clients and making big-ticket sales. He visits the head office once a month to give a presentation to the MD and the Board. Every month, he enters the building, and the guard greets him with a cheerful 'Good Morning, Sir!" Vikrant nods back and usually moves on without exchanging a word.

The next month, Vikrant comes into the Head Office lobby as usual, and there is a guard. Vikrant passes him and enters the elevator. However, at the last moment, he changes his mind. He steps out. His colleague calls after him, but Vikrant moves on. He goes back to the guard, who looks up. Vikrant asks in Hindi: "Balraj, today you didn't wish me." Balraj, the guard, looks up, surprised, with a sad face, and replies: "My son has been in the hospital for the past week. The doctors don't know what is wrong with him." Vikrant asks him for the medical report, which Balraj is carrying with him. He takes an image of the report and sends it via WhatsApp to his close friend, a Doctor, who tells Balraj there is nothing to worry about and suggests some basic medication. Balraj is happy and thanks Vikrant profusely.

Back in the office, his colleagues admire Vikrant for his empathy and people skills. They ask him how he knew about Balraj's problem. Vikrant replied: "I didn't know about his problem. But what I did know is that a person who wishes me without fail every time he sees me didn't do so today. So, I knew something had changed, and therefore something was wrong."

No wonder Vikrant is adored by all and tipped to be the leader!

4. **Create possibilities:**

Every day, leaders innovate. They think out of the box. They always look out for ways to do the same thing faster, cheaper, and better. Quality is an obsession with good leaders. They don't hesitate to get their hands dirty. They look for different ways to succeed at the same thing. Leaders innovate and force others to think differently. To quote Shiv Khera: "Leaders don't do different things. They do things differently."

Case in Point

Prasad is a septuagenarian, the president of the local senior citizens club. He enjoys the company of his grandchildren and has various hobbies and interests that keep him busy. Recently, the digitization wave that has spread across India has also touched him. Going to the bank to withdraw his pension was not always convenient, as the bank was situated far away from his house, and he had to be dependent upon his family members to take him. One day, the bank manager met him at the bank and asked him why he didn't get a debit card or open an online banking account. Prasad was hesitant at first, as he thought ATMs were unsafe. But gradually he started using his debit card at the ATM. He then asked his grandchild to teach him how to access his bank account online! What a thrill it was to see his account details whenever he wanted without going to the bank. He started shopping online for himself and his family by using his debit card. He also updates himself on cyber-frauds and changes his passwords frequently.

At the senior citizens club, his friends were amazed at how quickly he had learnt these things. He was glad to share his knowledge with them, and it has made such a positive difference to their lives! They are forever thankful to Prasad for freeing them from the dependency they had on others. And yes, he is a true leader!

11.4 Qualities of a good leader

Leaders come in all shapes and sizes, and while it is difficult to compile an exhaustive list of qualities of a good leader, at the same time, it is important to recognize that inspiring leaders have certain similar qualities. The first step to improvement is awareness. Once we are aware of the leadership qualities, we can motivate and inspire others, and it becomes simple for us to practice the same.

Some qualities of a good leader are:

1. **Leaders are role models:** When children are asked what they want to become when they are older, they usually respond by mentioning someone close to them. Or someone who has a strong influence on them, like their parents, a sportsperson, or an actor who is very popular. These people are role models for the children. In the same way, our role models are leaders who influence and motivate us so deeply that we want to become like those leaders. We want to emulate them. This is the impact that leaders have on their teams.

2. **Professionalism:** Leaders are proactive. They just don't wait for things to happen. They make things happen. They exhibit a very high level of professionalism. Due to their attention to detail, they anticipate events, issues, and problems before they occur. They take corrective steps to ensure that mistakes don't happen and, more importantly, are not repeated. This ensures stakeholder satisfaction and builds bridges of cooperation.

A good leader has the ability to be at the right place at the right time

3. **Ownership & Accountability:** Leaders recognize the concept of Risk & reward. At the same time, they recognize that decision-making gives great rewards, bonuses, and success. At the same time, decisions that backfire can have grave consequences on their team as well as their own careers. While others shy away from taking tough decisions, Leaders take full responsibility for their actions and accept the results with equanimity. The buck stops with the leader.

Case in Point

Saurabh J. is the MD of a Shreeraj Group, a large cement-to-computer conglomerate. In his cement division, a competitor has been constantly poaching people from his team. Saurabh has tried everything to motivate his team members, who are unable to resist the temptation of a salary hike in the competitor company, twice as much as that being offered by Shreeraj. Saurabh hears the news that his senior-most salesperson is planning to put in his papers. He panics on hearing the news and calls the President to inform him of the same. The President orders Saurabh to match the competitor's salary. Saurabh is resistant to this strategy as he feels this will create a bad precedent, and he will have to do this for anyone who resigns, which the budget cannot allow. The President is adamant, but Saurabh holds his ground. The President even threatens to dismiss Saurabh if he continues to defy him. But Saurabh is convinced that letting him go is the best option. Soon enough, the Sales Head leaves and joins the competitor company. Two months later, Saurabh gets the news that the sales head has been accused of stealing company secrets and has been terminated by the competitor. It is now revealed that he had a drug habit that he had not revealed to anyone, and was stealing due to that. Saurabh stands vindicated, and his decision to let that employee go proved to be correct despite the short-term conflict and inconvenience.

Leaders have conviction. They believe in themselves.

4. **Communication skills:** Good Leaders are masters at communication. And communication, as we have seen in the previous chapters, is not just speaking. In fact, Leaders use Listening and silence at the right time to convey different emotions. Leaders know how much to push and when to hold back. Leaders can read the non-verbal signals of their teams and act accordingly.

5. **Empathy:** Leaders love people and empathize with them. They are sounding boards and agony aunts when the need arises. The true test of leadership is when a team member has the rapport with them to share problems and ask for help, when no one else bothers to listen or help.
6. **Physical Fitness:** Leaders realize that a fit body leads to a fit mind. And fit minds can work wonders. Since Leaders are role models, their overall physical health is also a reflection of their respect for their bodies. This attitude rubs off on the teams, who also get inspired to take up physical activity.
7. **Storytelling skills:** Leaders are great storytellers who like to think in narratives. They like to tell stories from their own experiences that inspire others. Through these stories, they are able to relate their vision and align it with that of their teams. Transporting their audience into an ideal world through their stories, leaders are able to ensure that even the most complex tasks get done without resistance.

11.5 Professionalism

What is Professionalism?

Professionalism is one of the key traits of a good leader. Professionalism should not be confused with the word Professional.

While a Professional is a person who gets paid to do a particular job, professionalism is the technical expertise that person exhibits, combined with the demonstration of the intent to do a 100% great job!

Professionalism is the skill, good judgment, and courteous behavior that are expected from a person who is trained to do a job well. It is not just knowing how to do your job, but also demonstrating a willingness to learn, cooperating, and ensuring the satisfaction of others.

***Figure 11.3**: How you behave at work defines your brand*

Professionalism is a trait that separates high performers from average performers. Excellent professionals believe that they are not just doing a job. Rather, their focus is on doing things right every time. Every task is given the same level of attention and detail orientation. In fact, every true professional gives their 100% by showing commitment through their work and positive attitude.

Case in Point

Shalini is a high-end garments retailer with her own store. She has a saleswoman called Priya who is much liked and very good at her job. Shalini is the last to leave every day and locks the store herself by locking the shutters. One evening, she shut the store but forgot to switch off the lights and fans. There has been a previous incident of a short circuit fire in her store, and normally, she is very careful. But on that day, she forgot to switch off the electricity mains. Priya had gone out for a late-night movie with her friends, and on her return, she passed the store. She saw the light coming out from under the shutter. She noticed the lock on the shutter, so she realized that her boss had forgotten to turn off the main switch. She hesitated calling, as it was very late in the night. Her friends kept telling her to forget it and go home. But Priyanka thought about the store and the short circuit danger. She went home, got her spare key, went back to the store, switched off the mains, and then went home.

In the meantime, Shalini too realized her error and took a cab to the store with the intention of switching off the mains. When she reached there, she saw the lights were off. Amazed, she called Priya, who told her she had already done it a short while ago and sent Shalini a text regarding the same.

Shalini was very thankful for having such a professional employee and soon gave Priya a big salary raise and bonus for her extreme professionalism.

11.5.1 Qualities that display excellent professionalism

1. **Do the right thing and do them right:** Professionalism is the means by which the task is done correctly and at the right time. True professionals don't waste time on non-essential tasks. Rather, they pick and choose their battles, and whatever they do, they do it right. And ensure that they don't repeat a mistake.

The Mantra of Professionalism

Under Promise & Over-deliver

Don't Over-Promise & Under-Deliver

2. **Follow up:** The job and the subsequent payment are not the end of the transaction. Professionalism is exhibited by following up on the job, whether the task has been done correctly, and there are no subsequent problems, and the client is satisfied. This part is very important, as most people simply provide the service and move on to the next job.

Case in Point

Prabhat is a delivery manager at an IT company. Once the software is delivered and installed, the team moves on to the next project and client. However, Prabhat makes a point to call the client at least once every 2 months after delivery and ask if everything is going OK. Or is there any issue that he can help with? This is not required as per the SOP, but Prabhat still does it out of sheer professionalism. A simple call from him results in a lifetime relationship with the happy client who feels that Prabhat is always there to support them, whether they need that support or not. Now the client insists that Prabhat should be heading every project of theirs.

3. **Ask for feedback:** Good Professionals always ask for feedback. They want to know how they're doing. And if there is room for improvement in their performance or service. They use this feedback as a means for continuous improvement. They recognize that improvement is the only way to progress and success.

4. **Deep sense of integrity** and adherence to values and ethics. Professionalism entails adherence to:

   a. Organization rules and regulations

   b. Personal values and beliefs

While it is essential to be aware of rule changes and follow the laws, rules, and regulations, good professionals naturally demonstrate such behavior through their actions. They don't wait to be told to comply with the correct behavior. It comes naturally to them. They don't make a distinction between what is illegal or unlawful. In their life, everything has to comply with their sense of integrity and justice. They not only comply but also inspire others to do so as well.

Integrity is doing the right thing...when no one is looking.

Case in Point

Atif, a Medical doctor with a successful practice, is going for a movie with his wife and two children, 10-year-old twin boys. He sees the light turning red and speeds up. He passes it when it has turned red and is promptly caught by the traffic police on the other side of the intersection. There is another car ahead of him. Both cars park on the side. Atif can see the policeman arguing with the car driver ahead of him. Taking advantage of this, he slowly starts reversing his car, and all of a sudden accelerates and drives away. It is a dangerous maneuver and also absolutely illegal to run away from the law. He tries to joke with his family, who remain serious. He realizes that his family is upset over his behavior and tries to justify it by saying they were getting late. His sons tell him that what he did was not right. His wife also looks at him with a disappointed look. She asks him: Atif, what if tomorrow a patient runs away from your clinic without paying? How will you feel?" Atif realizes

that he has set a very bad example for his children. He reverses and goes back to the intersection. He meets the cop, who is really surprised to see him. He pays the fine. He comes back to the car where his family is smiling proudly!

11.6 Creativity: How great ideas are born

What is Creativity?

Creativity is an inborn trait combined with a set of skills that can be learned, developed, and utilized in daily problem-solving.

Creative Thinking is another characteristic of High-Performance leaders.

In this dynamic and ever-changing world, only those with the ability to innovate and think differently get ahead. Status Quo is no longer accepted. The only constant is change. Professionals are hired for a technical job, but are often called upon to do multiple tasks due to pressures on the bottom line. In such an environment, only a professional who is able to think differently can survive and hope to get promoted.

Creativity is always in the top #5 lists of things that managers want from their teams. It is a key soft skill.

Creativity means thinking of new, innovative ways to do the same task. Right from the history of humans, there has been evolution in the processes. But the digital age has made it mandatory to be creative, think creatively, be different, and act innovatively.

Practical application

Creativity for its own sake has no meaning. Only when creative ideas can be applied to the real world and used for financial and other benefits, do these ideas have any value. Hence, it is important to think of creativity and innovation as means to save the organization: time, money, and effort.

Case in Point

Aliya, a call center executive, is unhappy with her boring, monotonous job. She always complains that she is always getting shouted at by her clients and bosses. She just can't understand why it is important to read from the prepared script when the clients are so impatient and angry that they don't want to hear a word of her sales pitch. But the management insists that this is what their competition is doing; hence, it needs to be done that way only.

Arunima, her manager, is an amateur theater artist and acting enthusiast who realizes that her team of callers is struggling. She comes up with a series of role-plays that involve a client with a problem and a call center executive who solves the problem. However, there is no script. The call center executive has to use speech & drama techniques taught by an expert trainer to improvise.

The result is that all center executives are energized. They no longer have to read from a script. Instead, they can change and customize the sales pitch depending on the reaction of the client. The results are amazing! Clients are now more receptive. the callers sound more empathetic and human. Profitability increases.

The entire organization now adopts speech & drama techniques in client interaction. Extensive role-plays and simulations help in anticipating objections and increasing sales.

Arunima is promoted and made innovation lead for her project.

Ways to become more creative

While many creative people seem to have been born with this trait, creativity can be acquired and perfected through practice. Some easy and practical ways that can be applied to solve almost any problem are:

1. **5W+1H method**: also known as `Five Wives & 1 Husband.'

   Each time that you are confused about making a particular decision or having to solve a problem, ask yourself the following questions:

   a. **Who?** (Actor or Agent) Who are the people involved in the problem? Who did it or who will have to do it? Who uses it, wants it? Who will benefit, be affected, included, or excluded?

   b. **What?** (The actual Act) What should happen? What is happening? What was done, should have been done, or simply not done? What will be done if it happens? Or vice-versa? What were the factors that resulted in success in similar situations in the past or experienced by others? What are the motivations of the stakeholders?

   c. **When?** (Timing) What are the time frames for completion? Is it flexible? What are the tolerances accepted for delays? What is a realistic time frame with buffers? Can it be hurried or delayed?

   d. **Where?** (Location) Where, will, or should this occur or be performed? Where else can this be done?? Where else did the same thing happen In the past? What is the effect of this location on the stakeholders?

   e. **Why?** (Purpose) Why was or is this done, not done, or even permitted? Why should it be done? Why should anyone do it? Why that particular action, rule, idea, solution, problem, and not anything else?

   f. **How?** (Method) How can it be done, or avoided? How can it be started, finished, prevented, destroyed, made, improved, or altered? How did the start lead to the end?

2. **Brainstorming:** Brainstorming is a technique for generating new ideas. It involves pooling of ideas as a group. It is a free-flowing and random process where nothing is held back. A group of people gets together and is encouraged to come up with whatever idea comes to their mind. No idea is considered too silly or important. All ideas are put into a central pool and then fine-tuned to arrive at a final solution. Its main goals are:

    1. To move away from the conventional, linear thinking process.
    2. To produce a larger set of ideas from which we can choose.

Brainstorming is useful for attacking specific, rather than general issues. It is ideal where a collection of innovative, fresh, new ideas (rather than cold judgment or complex decisions) is needed. Alex Osborn, the inventor of the brainstorming technique, recommends an ideal group size of twelve for brainstorming.

Case in Point

A specific problem, like how to come up with a more cost-effective package of a mobile phone so that it does not get damaged in transit, would lend itself to brainstorming. However, a general problem like getting approvals for setting up a new manufacturing plant for the mobile phone will not be very productive using brainstorming. Here, the 5W + 1 H technique will be very useful.

3. **Mind mapping:** Tony Buzan is the inventor of mind mapping. A **mind map** is a diagram used to visually organize vital information. It is created around a single idea, drawn as an image in the center of a blank page, to which associated ideas, such as images, words, and parts of words, are added. Imagine a tree with roots going in all directions and sub-roots joining those roots. All connected to a single idea. Like the nervous system of our body. Major ideas are connected directly to the central idea, and other ideas branch out from sub-ideas.

    According to Tony Buzan:

    1. Start in the CENTRE of a blank page turned sideways. Why? Because starting in the Centre gives your Brain freedom to spread out in all directions and to express itself more freely and naturally.
    2. Use an IMAGE or PICTURE for your central idea. Why? Because an image *is* worth a thousand words and helps you to use your Imagination. A central image is more interesting, keeps you focused, helps you to concentrate, and gives your Brain more of a buzz!
    3. Use COLOURS throughout. Why? Because colors are as exciting to your Brain as are images. Color adds extra vibrancy and life to your Mind Map, adds tremendous energy to your Creative Thinking, and is fun!
    4. CONNECT your MAIN BRANCHES to the central image and connect your second and third-level branches to the first and second levels, etc. Why? Because your Brain works by *association.* It likes to link

two (or three, or four) things together. If you connect the branches, you will understand and remember a lot more easily.

5. Make your branches CURVED rather than straight-lined. Why? Because having nothing but straight lines is *boring* to your Brain.

6. Use ONE KEY WORD PER LINE. Why? Because single keywords give your Mind Map more power and flexibility.

7. Use IMAGES throughout. Why? Because each image, like the central image, is also worth a thousand words. So, if you have only 10 images in your Mind Map, it's already the equivalent of 10,000 words of notes!

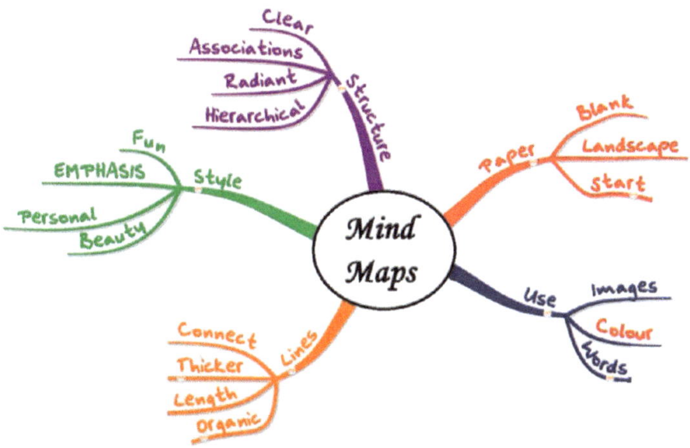

Figure 11.4*: Mind maps turn thoughts into clarity*

4. **The Six Thinking Hats Method:** Edward De Bono is a world-renowned expert in creative thinking. His 6 Thinking Hats is a world-famous and very effective technique that has been applied and adopted to creatively solve problems in all kinds of organizations: from Fortune 500 companies to SMEs.

How does the 6 Thinking Hats technique work?

There are six imaginary hats. The main idea is to have the group only "wear one hat at a time" when considering a problem. The wearing of the hat is imaginative. At any one time, everyone will wear the same colour. What this means is that everyone together will look at the problem at hand from only one common perspective, the perspective indicated by the hat colour.

Each hat enables the problem solver to separate their thinking into six clear functions and roles. By mentally wearing and switching "hats," you can easily focus or redirect thoughts, conflict, problem, or issue.

The six thinking hats are:

1. **White hat:** recognizes that information is power. It is gathering information and focusing on facts.
2. **Blue hat:** manages the process. It involves listing the rules of engagement and how the problem will be solved in steps.
3. **Green hat:** focuses on new ideas, creative concepts, and alternatives.
4. **Yellow hat:** helps explore the feasibility and identify value and benefit.
5. **Red hat:** signifies feelings and emotions. It could be the use of intuition and gut feeling.
6. **Black hat:** is the use of judgment or playing the "devil's advocate." Identifying what can go wrong and assessing potential problems.

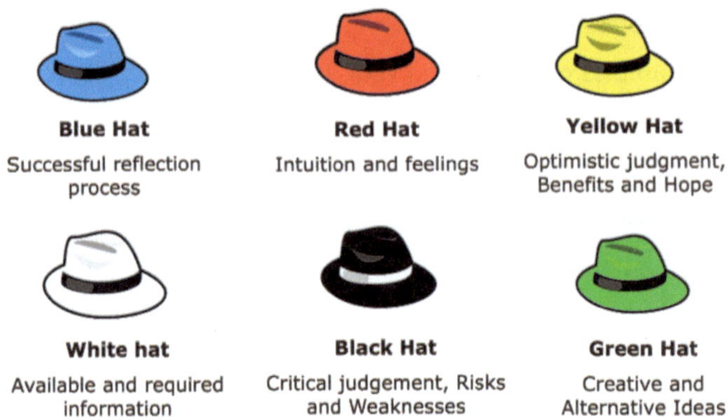

***Figure 11.5**: The Six Thinking Hats by Edward De Bono*

The Six Thinking Hats require some training and application. But once understood and adopted, it is a very powerful tool for fostering creative thinking in all spheres of life.

11.7 Summary

Leadership is a skill that can be acquired with organized training coupled with awareness of basic concepts. Leaders are made, not born. A combination of human relations, technical knowledge, initiative, humor, common sense, and ambition is required to build successful leadership qualities. It should be kept in mind that leadership is a constant `work in progress and not a one-time effort.

Leaders exhibit extreme professionalism. However, remember that you don't just "become" a professional overnight. It takes dedication and awareness of other professionals from whom you can emulate their best behaviors. Pay attention to your own behavior at work, as well as the way others behave. Take notice of your colleagues who are most respected and whose work or opinions are most valued by others.

Creativity involves coming up with new solutions to problems. This involves using questioning and experience analysis to ask specific questions to get a wide body of answers. 5W + 1H, particularly, is a very easy and practical approach to creative problem solving, especially for students and young professionals. It involves asking: What is the problem? Where is it happening? When is it happening? Why is it happening? How can you overcome this problem? Who do you need to get involved? When will you know you have solved the problem?

Knowledge Check:

1. Are leaders made or born? Comment in 50 words.
2. What is Everyday Leadership? Why is it important?
3. How can we learn motivation from everyday leaders?
4. What are the qualities of a good Leader?
5. Define professionalism.
6. Give examples of 5 people in your life who are very professional with two qualities that they exhibit.
7. What are the ways in which a person can become more creative?

Get ready for the real world!

"And the winner of the residents' welfare elections is: Mr. Monish Thapar!"

"What? I lost the election? How is that possible? It can't be! I was the sure-shot winner. Everyone told me so!" Vivek cried!

His friend Asit asked him: "What's the matter, my friend? Why so dejected?"

Vivek said, "What should I tell you! I really tried hard to get the maximum votes. I canvassed, I thought I was so popular...then why did I lose?"

Asit smiled....and said: "Vivek, the residents of our colony don't want just a president...they want a leader! So even though you may be popular, you didn't exhibit the leadership qualities that your team was looking for."

"Leadership? What is leadership?" Vivek asked?

Asit replied: "At its essence, leading is all about relationships— developing the connections among individuals that foster co-operation, collaboration, and creative thinking - all leading to success! Leadership is the sum of many traits-a combination of emotional, spiritual, physical, and mental abilities that influence others to take action. So, my friend, whilst you were busy campaigning, your competitors were busy engaging with the residents, meeting them, motivating them, listening to their problems, working with them to solve their colony's problems. That's what leaders do. And that's what leadership is. Showing initiative, going first, and boldly going where no man has ever gone before!

While you showed interest in winning, your competitor was interested in Leading."

Asit asked: "Vivek, you are only interested in giving orders. Telling people to vote for you is not the right way to lead. You have to think differently, cooperate with people, and control them when things go out of hand. Did you do that?"

"No", replied Vivek

"Were you there when the residents required someone to represent them at the annual meeting with the municipal council?"

"No"

"That's why the colony did not get funding this year. See, those are the times when you have to stop being part of the crowd. And instead lead from the front."

"What else could I have done as a leader?" Vivek asked?

"Well, leaders perform many tasks and functions simultaneously. Leaders have the habit of juggling between various responsibilities at the same time, making sure that no issue remains unresolved and a win-win is attained in all spheres.

"Is it too late for me to develop leadership qualities? Am I too old to learn now?"

Asit said: "No, it is not true that leaders are born, not made. Leadership is a skill that can be acquired."

Vivek asked: "But how am I supposed to develop these leadership qualities?"

Asit said, there are many ways. Lead by Example: delegate but don't hesitate to get your hands dirty. Show Commitment: Your words and actions should be in harmony. Work smart and hard. Don't shy away from taking ownership of your problems.

In the next year, stand again for elections and success will definitely be yours."

Applied knowledge

1. Name three reasons why Vivek did not win the elections.
2. What are three things that Vivek can do to win the next elections?
3. What are three ways in which Asit thinks Vivek could become a leader?

Build your vocabulary

Learn and use the Words and Business phrases used in this chapter to improve your Spoken English Skills:

1. **Ahead of the pack:** To be ahead of the competition. To beat the others, to come out first.
2. **Complacent:** taking something for granted.
3. **Have the knack:** the ability to do something.
4. **Sweep under the carpet:** To ignore something, to hide it.
5. **Big ticket:** Something of a high value.
6. **Backfire:** A decision that goes wrong.
7. **To hold your ground:** to be firm in your decision. To not waver.
8. **Stakeholder:** Every person involved in any way in a job or transaction.

Chapter 12 Meetings and Business Writing

Running effective meetings , impactful emails and business writing

LEARNING MILESTONES

This chapter will enable you to:

- Understand the essentials of Verbal Communication.
- Develop high impact business writing skills.
- Master business english fundamentals.
- Learn to write effective emails.
- Know frequently committed errors in emails.
- Avoid mistakes in verbal communication

Expert Quotes

"Your words make your listeners feel your attitude"

12.1 Essentials of Verbal Communication

How many times have you met a person who dressed well, looked fresh and well-groomed, had excellent manners, and great technical skills? But when they spoke, they just couldn't make the right impression! Their manner of speaking was boring, and you just couldn't wait to move on to the next person. Or when they sent you an email, it was full of mistakes, and the language was very annoying and inappropriate?

Poor verbal skills can kill a great First impression. However, it is not just enough to be able to talk. One needs to be able to speak at the right time, at the right place, and to the right person. This is the essence of verbal communication.

From speaking to family &friends on phone or chat to business presentations by using various media, verbal communication is everywhere.

Verbal communication is often confused with speaking. But verbal communication consists of:

1. Written Communication
2. Spoken Communication

Good verbal communication can help us to differentiate sounds from speech, news from noise.

For a student, good verbal skills are tested right from their performance in interviews and Group Discussions. Soon, they are thrust into the professional world where business presentations are a part of work life. From presenting to internal and external customers, day after day, people are required to speak or send emails. Gone are the days when you could just put together a quarterly report in PowerPoint and hope to hide behind the slide projector. With AI, however, it is the quality of verbal presentations that is the differentiator. Emails have come of age in this era of AI, and people view the quality of your verbal skills as a reflection of your personality.

Often, you are given one chance to perform. Now you have to ensure that your message actually relates to your audience and gets the desired response on the first attempt. Good verbal skills can perform this task for you.

Whether it is information, feelings, desires, thoughts, or memories, you can share them by using verbal communication skills!

12.2 Writing and verbal communication

Yes, writing skills are also a part of verbal communication. This is because verbal communication means communication with words, whether spoken or written. Words have been used for centuries as carriers of meaning. Though we may communicate in many different languages, if we use words, we can define our communication as verbal communication. verbal communication means sharing things by means of words.

Words consist of both spoken and written. Not just spoken. Hence, written communication like emails and instant messaging like WhatsApp are also categorized under verbal communication.

Examples of verbal communication

Verbal Communication can be in the form of a monologue where one person speaks or presents, and the others listen. Or it could be a dialogue where there is an exchange of words. Group discussions, debates, arguments, interviews, and romantic conversations are all examples of verbal communication.

12.2.1 Various media of verbal communication

1. Face-to-face:

This is our daily interaction with others. Words have the power to heal and the power to hurt. Whatever the intention, words are like arrows. Once the arrow leaves the bow, it cannot be retracted. Words once spoken can never be taken back. Hence, it becomes even more important to use our words carefully. Words said in extreme emotion are usually regretted later. Hence, choose your words as carefully as you can. However, use the opportunity to speak and strike up conversations, for these may have hidden opportunities.

Case in Point

Ajit is travelling to Hyderabad from Pune by train. He is a 22-year-old Assistant sales manager in a small pharmaceutical company, unhappy in his current profile and looking for a job change. He is a voracious reader and tries to read at least one new book every 3-4 months. The middle-aged man sitting next to him looks upset and keeps shaking his head. Ajit decided to ignore him. Halfway through the journey, Ajit finishes his book, a new novel by a famous Indian author. He keeps his book on his lap and looks around. His neighbor is looking at his book! Ajit smiles and says, "Nice book. I just finished it." His neighbor says: I had packed this same book for this journey, but I left it in the cab while coming to the station." Ajit is quiet. After a while, he turns to his neighbor and says: Why don't you take my book. I've finished reading it. His neighbor is delighted and offers Ajit his gratitude and his business card, "CEO of one of the biggest medical supplies companies," it says. He asks Ajit what he does, and upon hearing that Ajit is looking for a new job, asks him to come and meet him for a new position once he is back from his trip.

Ajit realizes that his conversation with his neighbor resulted in a huge promotion in life for him. He decides that he will carry his business card on all trips and on all journeys, and he will try to strike up a conversation with his co-passengers. You never know what good luck face-to-face conversations can lead to!

2. Meetings:

A meeting happens when people come together and communicate with each other. Most corporations complain that they spend too much time in meetings and too little on work. While this may be partially true, the fact remains that meetings tend to take up more time than scheduled if not planned properly.

Meetings have evolved over the years. From formal meetings in conference rooms to Virtual meetings, people meet everywhere: in coffee shops, near water coolers, at the gym, while commuting, just about anywhere where they can have a dialogue.

Meetings, whether these are personal meetings or business meetings, are most fruitful only when:

1. The participants come prepared or have the necessary information to make a decision at the meeting.
2. The meeting starts and ends on time.
3. Participants listen and speak as agreed and respect others' views.
4. The meeting is to the point, adhering to the agenda.
5. The participants learn something or gain something that they did not have prior to the meeting.
6. The meeting concludes with a plan of action, and minutes are kept and circulated.

Case in Point

THE 2-PIZZA RULE

Jeff Bezos, the Founder and CEO of e-commerce Giant Amazon, realized that meetings are very necessary considering the huge Amazon operation. Decisions had to be made and communicated across the world by his team members. However, given the diversity of the teams and the worldwide operations, the meetings would go out of control and often be unproductive. He decided to make a 2-Pizza rule for meetings at Amazon. The rule is that all meetings will have only the number of people who can be fed on 2 pizzas. This ensures that there is a limited number of people in each team and in each meeting, thereby reducing the discussion and decision-making time. The 2-pizza rule ensures that the meetings are short, to the point, and decision-making is faster.

Meetings Etiquette

Figure 12.1*: Plot twist: no one knows why this meeting exists*

1. **Formal Meetings**: These are held in a professional setting and have a predetermined agenda and defined outcomes. meetings can have varied venues: From conference rooms to places of leisure. For example, a meeting while eating. Sometimes meetings are held in vehicles, for example, a CEO and his team having a meeting in the car on the way to the airport. Participants should ensure their participation and visibility in the meeting for optimal results.

2. **Breakfast meeting**: Often, executives or prospective job candidates are invited by a senior person for a meal, typically breakfast. The invitee should arrive a little early and can observe what kind of meal setting it is. Whether à la carte or buffet. Be familiar with the correct table manners and etiquette. Do not overeat. In fact, stick to non-messy foods like fruits and other foods that can be eaten with a fork and juice or tea/coffee. Remember that at such meetings, you are being observed, and how you deal with support staff, your mannerisms, and decisions about you are being made accordingly.

3. **Standing meetings**: Quick meetings between a few people where fast decisions need to be made and communicated. These have no chairs, no formalities, and are often more effective than long sit-down meetings. Ensure that you adhere to the spirit of the meeting and do not allow it to extend beyond its stated purpose.

4. **Offsites and company events**: These are unstructured encounters in a social or informal setting. Office off-sites and after-office parties can become surprising venues for meetings. Sometimes decisions can be made at such meetings faster than formal meetings because people are free to speak their mind and hence more forthcoming with their views. Such meetings should also be taken seriously, and you are advised to maintain proper decorum and professional etiquette at all times.

12.3 Online Calls

Web calling has become an integral part of our lives. Most apps from Zoom, Teams, and Google Meet have become default modes of video communication.

This enables organizations to save valuable time and the expenses of their executives in making expensive business trips. It enables people to reach out to a global audience.

***Figure 12.2**: Communication fails when clarity fails.*

12.4 Social media communication

With so many options in social media for people to air their views, it is no wonder that the average person is overloaded with information. On social media, celebrities and common people have a level playing field as far as the opportunity to speak is concerned. Verbal communication has become extremely easy and one-sided in this era of social media. Remember that social media is not private. Irrespective of privacy settings, assume that your message will be read by someone other than the intended receiver. Hence, it is prudent to be careful while disclosing information or sharing views on social media.

Figure 12.3: *Stay connected online. Stay human offline*

12.4.1 A Clean Digital Footprint

Your Digital Footprint is the messages that you leave on social media. This has proved to be the downfall of many leaders and prominent people. Seemingly stable and intelligent people have let their guard down and regretted it. In this era of trolling, people get abused and criticized on social media, sometimes for unintentional errors. Countries like the USA are now vetting social media messages before granting visas. Hence, it is very important to use words on social media with care, as these are a permanent record. When your words are viewed out of context later, they can do real damage.

12.5 High Impact Business Writing

Basics of Writing

The need to write clearly and carefully arises in virtually every situation, especially as you enter into the professional world. From CVs to emails, business-writing skills are used as a benchmark to gauge the candidate's communication skills. Good writing is one of the most highly prized competencies of an employee or potential hire. Emails, status updates, letters, or formal reports each have their own special requirements, but these fundamental principles apply to all business writing:

- **S.T.O.P**: Stop-Think-Organize-Proceed. Just as a student is taught to cross the road without getting hurt, the STOP principle is extremely important in ensuring that poor writing is not sent out. STOP enables the writer to compose their thoughts, write correct communication, and send it out at the right time.

Flaming: It happens when your mind is filled with negative emotion. Situations or other emails that make you angry, stressed, irritated, etc. These are flaming situations where the mind's natural reaction is to retaliate. In this state of anger, written communication is very toxic in nature and can seriously damage one's career and relationships. STOP prevents you from

doing such communication and instead helps your mind to cool down. In a more cooled-off state, your mind is able to make more rational decisions, and most times you end up changing your own text, thereby preventing mishaps.

- **Planning & Purpose**: What outcome or result do you want out of that writing? The 7Cs are a good way of planning your writing. Good written communication has to be result-oriented communication. Words just can't be thrown together and sent out by text or email at random. It is absolutely necessary to keep the expected result in mind while framing the words. In fact, if you already know what is on your mind and what you want out of the reader, the words will come to your mind much more easily, and you won't have to struggle to find the right words.

"If you don't know where you are going.... any place will take you there." This old saying is very true for business writing.

- **Knowing your Audience**: Knowing who you are writing to, their culture, status, and motives, is a good way to say the right thing to the right person. This also reduces culturally related miscommunication.
- **Tone & Packaging**: Striking the right tone, matching the most appropriate words to be used to the right person. The tone is body language in words. The right tone can ensure the right connection.
- **Revising and proofing**: Spellcheck and proofreading your message to ensure that no wrong or inappropriate words are used.
- **Correct Business English**: While it is important to know and use good, correct, and appropriate grammar and rules of English, the same is not always possible. Good English comes with practice and training. It is not something that can be learnt overnight. The author strongly advises you not to fall into the trap of Spoken English institutes that claim to work miracles and turn you into English experts in 30-60-90 days! These are false claims. AI-based Speech-to-text and Translate-to-English tools are getting more sophisticated, so please explore these for better English writing.

Good English can be mastered by following these basic fundamentals:

1. **Don't get obsessed with Grammar**: This rule is contrarian and might sound strange to many readers who are not native-English speakers, but it is one of the most important rules. If you want to pass exams or IELTS, then study grammar. However, if you want to master Business English, then you should try not to get too deep into English grammar rules, as this will generally slow you down and confuse you. You will think about the rules when creating sentences instead of naturally saying a sentence like a pro. Instead, learn idioms and phrases instead of getting fixated on vocabulary and word meanings.
2. **Learn and study phrases**: Mugging up a dictionary may be difficult, but not impossible. But is it of any use if you can't recall those words

in the correct situation? Instead, one should study Business phrases, idiomatic phrases, phrasal verbs, and idioms. When children begin to learn a language, they learn both words and phrases together. Likewise, you need to study and learn phrases.

If you have a vocabulary of 1000 words, you might not be able to say one correct sentence; But if you know one phrase, you can make hundreds of correct sentences.

3. **Don't translate**: When you want to create a sentence in English, do not translate the words directly from your mother tongue. The order of words, context, and grammar is probably different, and you will be both slow and incorrect by doing this. Instead, learn phrases and sentences so you don't have to think about the words you are trying to put together.

   There are both free and paid apps that can help you practice using the right words in different situations. The more you practice, the better you get. The best way to master English is to actually start speaking it. Choose an app, an AI, or a friend who wants to learn as well and start reading the newspaper out to each other. Hearing each other speak. Go on YouTube and see videos and clips of English movies. Try to understand what they are saying in the video and mimic their accent and speech. You will start becoming more confident and hence more eager to speak. Surround yourself in English.

12.6 Email writing workshop

Email is a preferred method of communication in most situations, and despite AI tools, it's one that many people still struggle with.

Email writing skills are very important because they are instant, fast, and convenient. Words used in the email have the power to convey one's state of mind and body language. If that is the case, then the writer must ensure that the correct rules of grammar, protocol, Internet syntax, and other rules are followed. The 7Cs of communication framework is very much applicable to emails.

***Figure 12.4**: Some conversations deserve a voice, not a subject line*

Correct email etiquette rules have to be followed by keeping in mind:

Professionalism: By using proper email language, you convey a professional image.

Efficiency: emails are instant and get to the point, and thus are much more effective than poorly worded messages.

Protection from liability: By committing yourself to writing, you can save yourself from potential liability. Verbal communication can be without witness or proof, but emails are a written record.

Emails have the power to make or break careers.

Email writing is a very popular corporate training workshop for the author, and below are the important points covered in these trainings.

Given below is an illustration that has been used to highlight the most common errors committed in email writing.

Under each wrong point, the correct alternative has been given. The reader is well advised to keep these points in mind while framing emails and use the correct alternatives given below to write powerful emails.

A detailed analysis of these errors and ways in which we can remove them from emails can convert average writing into high-impact email writing.

Frequently Committed Errors in Email Writing

Sample E-Mail with correct alternatives

(email from client to supplier)

From: RAHUL KUMAR (rahulxyz1234567890@gmal.com)

To: Sudhir420@niceeteamz.com

Cc: team@teamz.com

Subject: Systems (1)

Date & Time: Friday, April 1, 2017, 4.30 pm

Dear Sudhir,

The computers that you installed recently are not working properly. Send your technician immediately (2)

Rgds (3)

Rahul

(reply from supplier to client)

From: *SUDHIR S. (sudhir420@niceteamz.com)*

To: rahulxyz@gmail.com

Cc: team@teamz.com

Bcc: legal@teamz.com *(4)*

Subject: *problem (5)*

Date & Time: Monday, April 25, 2017, 1.20 pm (6)

Hi (7) Rahull (8)

BEEN BUSY MAN! (9). GUD 2 HERE FRM U! U HAVE NOT CHKD IF THE CABLES R PLUGGED INTO UR SOCKET ; (10) ?!!!!!!!????!!!! ROTFL! (11)

I WILL CALL U LTR. C YA

SUD

1 & 5 Subject line

In this case, the subject line is a single word and incomplete, and can cause confusion in the reader's mind.

The subject line is a very important part of your email. It is necessary, like a headline in the newspaper, to tell the reader what the email contains. It can fetch a faster reply or desired result if framed correctly. The subject line must be 3-6 words and should inform the reader what the desired action is.

Alternate Subject: Need urgent repair of systems installed by you

Similarly, in pt. (5) Sudhir, in his reply, has changed the subject without Rahul's permission. This can create further confusion. Maintaining the same subject enables all parties to follow the same chain of correspondence, as everyone knows what they are referring to.

2. **Wrong Tone**

The tone of this statement is curt and too harsh. It sounds like an order. Even if one is speaking to someone lower in the hierarchy, such as a subordinate or team member, vendor, or support staff, basic courtesy demands that the request must be made politely. The `Courtesy' of the 7Cs must apply here as well. People respond more positively to requests rather than orders. With clients or superiors, an extra effort must be made to sound polite. For e.g., A simple "Please send this..." can be substituted by "Can you please send this...?"

Alternate: Can you send your technician immediately?

Note how the statement has been converted into a question to improve the tone

3. **Wrong use of short forms**

Avoid cutting words short: like `Tks' for Thanks, `Rgds' for Regards, `K' for OK, `U' for You, `Gr8' for Great, `2' for Two, etc.

Clipping of words shows that the writer is in a hurry, or just lacks respect, or has a careless attitude. And we all know that work done in a hurry is often not 100% successful. All these convey a negative impression on the receiver. Hence, it is advisable to use and write the complete word even if it takes a little more time.

4. **Misuse of CC and BCC**

CC should be used only to keep people informed about an ongoing communication. People in CC are not expected to take any action, but are put in cc to be `kept in the loop'.

BCC: In this case, Sudhir has included someone on BCC and made them part of the email, without letting Rahul know. BCC should be used only for general announcements that concern everyone in the organization. For example, a policy, a timing change, or a new initiative for all. In all other cases, BCC must be avoided. It should not be used as a means to keep the receiver in the dark, and can create all kinds of problems for the sender if the person in BCC uses the `reply all' option. That's when the original receiver realizes that someone else was also part of the email without their knowledge! This can cause great miscommunication.

5. **Change in subject** already discussed with pt. 1 as above

6. **Acknowledgement & speed of reply**

In this case, the reply has been sent after almost 25 days, which is very unprofessional! Typically, emails should be replied to in the same time frame as one would reply to a missed phone call. While organizations have their own standards as part of their systems or culture, the time frame for the reply must be reasonable. A reply within 24 hours is reasonable. If the receiver cannot reply immediately or does not have the necessary information asked for, then at least an acknowledgment must be sent.

Silence is not a response. Every email must be acknowledged.

Correct usage: Noted, I will come back to you by (date)

7. **Wrong salutation**

Sudhir has used the salutation: Hi. In this case, it is wrong. The correct method is to use the `mirror' technique. i.e., if the sender uses the salutation `Dear...', then it must be replied with 'Dear...'. When the sender uses Hi... you can switch to Hi.

All emails must have a salutation, unless it is a chain email between two people that has an ongoing thread over a long period of time.

Correct: In this case, Sudhir should have replied: "Dear Rahul..."

8. **Wrong spellings**

Here, the receiver, who is also a client, has had his name misspelt. This is unacceptable. Manual Proofreading and spell check are a must before sending the mail. An effort must be made to spell all names properly.

9. **Use of full caps**

Full capital letters are equivalent to shouting or screaming. Full caps should never be used in professional communication.

10. **Use of bad humor**

Humor is a double-edged sword. It can work in some situations and cause bad problems in others. Unless the sender is sure of the appropriateness of the joke, humor should be avoided. People can take offense, and it can cause miscommunication.

11. **Use of Emoticons and Excessive Punctuation**

While correct punctuation is essential, use of emoticons and excessive punctuation should be avoided. It makes the text appear juvenile, and the writer appears immature. Similarly, terms like LOL and ROTFL, etc., have no place in business communication. A clear distinction must be made between social media conversations with friends and professional communication.

12.7 Topics to Avoid

a. **Avoid controversial topics**: these include conversations of a personal nature. Some topics of a personal nature that should be avoided in most communication are:

1. Race, caste, creed, and religion
2. Politics
3. Personal salary details
4. Choice of occupation or activity
5. Sexual preference
6. Marital status and choice of having children

b. **Self-praise** or constantly highlighting self-achievements repels others.

c. **Use of negative language**: Write in the positive, using passive voice, which is more courteous and non-confrontational. For e.g., instead of writing:

"Applications will not be accepted after 5 pm today."

Instead, you could write:

"Kindly ensure that all applications must be submitted by 5 pm today."

12.8 Summary

Good Verbal skills are constantly tested in this competitive world. Whether it is a job interview or business meeting, CV or email, good writing skills enable an aspiring candidate or business professional to communicate their true potential. Meetings and social media are various forums for communicating verbally, and these should be used professionally and to one's advantage. Good Business English further enhances business writing and phrases, and idioms are a very

good way of acquiring spoken English skills. Emails need to be framed keeping the 7Cs of communication in mind, and the writer is advised to refrain from composing emails in flaming situations.

Knowledge Check:

1. List 3 advantages of Good Business Writing
2. What are some kinds of meetings? Which do you think are the most effective and why?
3. How can one acquire good spoken English skills?
4. List out the frequently committed errors in email writing.
5. What are the topics that should be avoided in professional verbal communication

Get ready for the real world!

Hi Mike (*senior in hierarchy*)

Hows you? How's the weather? It's hot this side

OK, anyway, I want you to understand my tech problem. For this, you blame my team!!

The software keeps rebooting on its own, and I don't know what's got into it.

CAN'T U DO ANYTHING FAST? ▯ ;)

I want to call you, so carry your mobile with you everywhere.

Tks

Arvind

Applied knowledge

1. What are the different errors that you can spot in the above email
2. Please rewrite this email to use the correct language, grammar, and etiquette rules.

Build your vocabulary

Learn and use the Words and Business phrases used in this chapter to improve your Spoken English Skills:

1. **Come of age**: To become ready for something.
2. **To adhere to**: To follow, to comply with.
3. **Bombarded with information**: Have too much information coming in from all channels
4. **Decorum**: The way of behaving in a particular situation.

Join our Discord space

Join our Discord workspace for latest updates, offers, tech happenings around the world, new releases, and sessions with the authors:

https://discord.bpbonline.com

Chapter 13 Etiquette and Grooming Habits

Presenting yourself professionally through dressing, hygiene, and good manners

LEARNING MILESTONES

This chapter will enable you to:

- Understand what etiquette and good manners are?
- Appreciate the importance of etiquette.
- Realize the benefits of good manners and etiquette.
- Explore ways to develop good etiquette and manners.
- Find practical ways of personal hygiene and grooming.
- Adopt the benefits of good grooming.
- Master the tips for maintaining good hygiene and grooming.

Expert Quotes

Etiquette is the fine-tuning of education."

— Nadine Daher

"Manners are the ability to put someone else at their ease."

You are your greatest asset....Put your time, effort, and money into training, grooming, and encouraging your greatest asset.......

Dress for the job you want....not the job you have!

13.1 Importance of etiquette & good manners

It is common knowledge that proper etiquette, grooming, and hygiene are major factors in setting the best First Impression. So much has already been written and discussed on this subject. This highlights the need to grasp and adopt correct grooming and etiquette to make an accelerated impact on others.

Etiquette refers to guidelines that influence the way a responsible individual should behave in society. Good manners refer to polite, humble, courteous, respectful, and well-thought-of social behavior. A person is known and talked about positively on account of his or her good manners.

Manners and grooming are important in the overall professional image you project.

As a professional, you must adopt a code of personal behavior that demonstrates respect for your organization and the people who work with you. This creates a good reputation early in your career. You should give careful attention to personal behavior. Many people have been high achievers who projected an appropriate image in their appearance, and yet failed in their careers because they did not take responsibility for their personal behavior.

13.2 Importance of professional appearance, grooming, and good hygiene

Professional appearance is a combination of your professional dress and attire and your grooming. The message communicated by these results is in the powerful non-verbal communication, which either attracts or repels others. **Professional** dressing can be defined as dressing in such a manner as to enhance your authority, command respect, and promote your advancement in the workplace. Personal grooming habits are also very important for developing a powerful professional image.

The maximum impact that good etiquette and professional appearance can have on one's personality can be highlighted by the following case studies. These have been adapted from real-life cases as encountered by the author in the course of soft skill training. Each case in point is complete in its takeaways and learnings:

Case in Point 1

Etiquette & good manners

"Get out of here! You have no manners thundered the Principal!"

Aniket and Dosco ran out of the room, sweating, and almost crashed into Jimmy Sir, their soft skills teacher.

"What happened?" asked Jimmy.

"Principal sir is getting angry. He asked us to meet him for a meeting on the student council, but I kept getting WhatsApp messages and missed calls from my friends who wanted me to go with them to a movie. When I put the phone on silent, Dosco got an itch in his nose and put his finger in his nose. He wanted Sir to hear his point of view, so he kept interrupting him."

***Figure 13.1**: Professional grooming builds credibility*

Jimmy said, "Look at how you are dressed. You knew there was a meeting today. Yet you went in wearing slippers, and your t-shirt is so loose! Frayed, low-waist jeans and unshaven, dirty-looking guys, both of you. No wonder he was angry about your lack of etiquette and manners."

Aniket said, "By mistake, when the tea came, I grabbed the first cup on the tray. That was his sugarless tea, which I drank by mistake and then wasted. Dosco grabbed the biscuits and ate all of them. Finally, when another professor from a visiting college came in, we forgot to stand or wish her. She remained standing as there was no other chair in the office. After she left, the principal really shouted at us, and when I said something in a loud voice, he told us to get out!"

Dosco kept on giggling, hearing this.

Jimmy said, "You both think this is funny! Let me tell you it's not. In fact, this lack of manners and etiquette is the reason why you may not be able to get a good job, and even if you do, you will not be successful at it."

Aniket said! Really, sir, why is that? We are only having fun!"

Jimmy said: "What seems like harmless, frivolous fun to you appears to be immature and downright lack of manners to another person. And let me tell you. Good manners and etiquette are one of the most important soft skills. 85% of your success will depend upon your soft skills. So even though you are studying in the best engineering college, your chances of professional success are only 15% if you rely only on your technical knowledge. My advice is to improve your manners and etiquette immediately.

Let me tell you something about this subject:

Manners and etiquette are not quite the same thing. Etiquette means "the rules of behavior" and will change from culture to culture, depending on the local customs, and is also different within cultures. For example, there are different etiquette rules for cricket as opposed to ballroom dancing.

Manners are all in how the individual treats people, whether according to etiquette or not. It's simply a matter of behaving in a way that's thoughtful to others. Good manners across cultures or countries would be different, but definitely expected to be as defined in the etiquette of those countries. Bad manners are when the person fails to behave according to the etiquette of the culture where they are currently living or operating.

Why are etiquette and good manners important?

Jimmy continued: "You all are about to graduate soon and enter the real world. Do you think your future employers will want to hire people like you who have no manners, who can't get along with others? Because of your lack of good manners and etiquette, it appears that you have no respect for the institution that you belong to, for your colleagues. Believe me, no one wants such people to work in their organization.

No employer wants to have to train people on the things that they should have learned in their childhood years. So, they get rejection letters and are never given another shot at working for that company. And for a moment, let's forget your employers: You tell me, would you like to work with such people? Would you like to have a person in your team who doesn't listen, dress, and speak in a manner that disturbs others?"

Both Aniket and Dosco were quiet.

"No? Correct?" asked Jimmy. "That's why I am telling you, good manners and etiquette are very important because they result in:

- Increased Self-Confidence
- Positive Attitude
- A spirit of Collaboration
- Improved Professional Image
- Enhanced Career Opportunities
- Leadership Skills
- Deep Respect for Self & Others

Benefits of Etiquette and Good Manners

Jimmy said, "You know, there are so many actual and perceived benefits of good manners and etiquette. Irrespective of the fact that you are just students, this is a soft skill that benefits everyone, whether you are working or not, young or old. I will tell you some benefits across situations of good manners and etiquette:

1. **First impression:** Good etiquette allows you to make the best first impression on recruiters, colleagues, and people that you encounter. This impression goes a long way in getting you positive results for your actions.
2. **Conflict management:** Fights, escalations, and disagreements can be resolved by good manners. It can protect everyone from internal and external conflicts by setting a high standard of behavior for all.
3. **Happy customers:** Proper etiquette sets a tone for clients and customers that the business has a productive and cheerful environment. Everyone loves to deal with such positivity, resulting in higher sales. The impression created when everyone displays professional manners helps the company's profitability.
4. **Social life:** Good manners help you to make friends and influence others. New relationships are formed and bridges built. Difficult people can be won over by good etiquette. Leadership has its foundation in good people skills and good etiquette, helping you make and keep friends. Good online and email etiquette helps you become more popular on social networks.

Tip: **Inside an elevator, avoid making eye contact and keep your bag on your shoulder. This is to avoid bumping into others. Please allow others to exit first.**

Ways to develop etiquette and good manners

Dosco said, "Jimmy, sir, all this is ok. But we are only students. Young people who don't have much guidance. We are lucky that you are giving us all this information. We are about to graduate soon. Can you give us tips and tell us ways on how to develop good manners and what we should do to observe good etiquette when we enter the professional field?"

Jimmy said: "Very good question, Dosco! Rules of etiquette, whether for everyday life or for the office, or for children or students, are very similar. You must show the same standard of behaviour at all points in your life. The focus should be on caring for others' needs, respecting your environment, and listening to others.

Jimmy said, "I will give you the Ten Commandments of Business Etiquette for improving your manners in the professional field:

1. **Keep Decorum:** It must be clearly understood that the office is not your home, where you can do whatever you wish. Keep professional decorum during office hours. The office must be treated with respect. Coming to the office must be given the same respect as doing any other private activity. Avoid family or personal talks during office hours

2. **Calm & Professional behavior:** No one in the office is your enemy. However, they are not your best friends either. They are colleagues with whom you must maintain an appropriate distance. This means that one must be as formal as possible in the office. Informal behavior can distance you from your co-workers, and they will not give you the respect you deserve. Address your seniors politely according to the culture of the organization. Encourage others to observe good manners. Do not tolerate bad manners and try to correct others discreetly when they display bad manners.

3. **Teamwork:** Work like a team in the office, and help others whenever required. The ability to form and work in teams is perhaps one of the main requirements of a successful manager. No one can succeed alone in this world. We are all connected and hence interdependent. That's the power of teams, and working according to the team norms is a key soft skill.

4. **Avoid Gossip:** The Grapevine is an informal means of communication in any organization, which is used by people telling each other bits of information that they heard from someone else. Sometimes this information is correct, other times it's not. The grapevine is used deliberately by others who have a hidden agenda to spread misinformation or gossip. If someone is spreading a rumour about you, it is best to ask them the reason directly, in front of others. Avoid gossip or long cigarette or tea breaks for complaining about the organization or others, as this usually will come back to affect you only badly.

5. **Meeting etiquette:** Be on time. Every time! There can be no excuses in the professional world. Stick to the agenda. If the meeting is going off course, try to make it come back. People will respect you for it. Remember the names of people by addressing them directly. Put your phone on silent and give everyone a chance to talk and contribute. Lastly, offer to make **minutes of the meeting (MOM)**, which recaps the next steps for everyone.

6. **Dining etiquette:** It is important to understand the culture of the place where you are dining. Familiarize yourself with basic rules for using cutlery. Avoid food that has a strong odour. Do not make `slurp' noises while having soup or sipping tea. Do not overeat. Wait for everyone to order before placing yours. Do not be rude to the serving staff, even if they make a mistake. Thank the host for inviting you before and after the meal. Do not talk loudly on your cellphone if you have to take a call in an emergency. Place the napkin on your lap and wipe your mouth after every bite.

7. **Telephone etiquette:** Do not take calls in public transport, movie theaters, or meetings. This has to be strictly followed. Place your phone on silent mode so that you can go outside and take calls without disturbing anyone. Whenever calling anyone, start the conversation by following these three steps: (a.) greeting them by name, (b.) introducing yourself, and (c.) asking them if they are free to talk. If the other person doesn't answer the phone in 4 rings, cut the call. They may be busy. If they don't call back within a reasonable timeframe, call them back. Use the hands-free option if speaking while driving. Reply to phone calls within a reasonable time frame, preferably within 4-6 hours.

8. **Video calls Etiquette:** Ensure a quiet location with a neutral background. Place the camera with your back against a plain curtain or wall. Check the sound and video before the call. Download the software being used by the other participants and familiarize yourself with it before the call. If invited for a call, ensure that you are on time. Have a power backup handy. Look at the camera while speaking, not at the other participants. Dress should be appropriate, even if speaking from home. Speak slowly and clearly.

9. **Use the Golden Words:** Make 'Please', `Thank you', and `Sorry' part of your daily vocabulary. Use extreme courtesy when speaking with superiors and clients. Even otherwise, practice using words and refined language, which is appealing to others. Avoid slang and abusive language even with friends.

10. **Appreciation:** Appreciate and applaud others and give praise and feedback. Tell people how pleased you are with their performance. Call others and tell them how much they mean to you. Be genuine in your praise and likewise accept compliments graciously. An attitude of gratitude goes a long way.

"And finally, in case you forget all this, just remember to *soften yourself,*" said Jimmy with a smile.

"Soften! What's that?" They both asked.

Jimmy said: SOFTEN is the quickest and easiest way to remember the etiquette rules:

- **Smile:** Show friendliness towards others.
- **Open posture:** Be attentive to others.
- **Forward Lean:** Look alert while talking or listening.
- **Tone:** Show courtesy and interest through your voice or written tone.
- **Eye Contact:** Make direct eye contact for 2-3 seconds, without staring.
- **Nod:** Show your understanding by giving feedback by nodding.

Case in Point 2

Power Dressing, Grooming & Hygiene

"What is that smell?" said Shruti. Sitting in her cabin, she could detect a bad, stale smell coming from a nearby cubicle. She went to investigate and found Daljeet sitting there. "Hey! Why have you taken off your shoes? Are your feet giving out such a foul smell? Don't you realize it is causing all of us so much discomfort?"

Daljeet laughed and didn't pay any attention.

Figure 13.2*: Professional success begins with personal care*

A few days later, he walked into the office and was promptly called in for a project meeting. During the meeting, he started talking, but he found no one was paying attention to him. People were looking at him and laughing and joking. He realized that something was wrong, but continued.

These sorts of incidents became quite common with him. End of the year, during appraisal time, he realized that neither was he promoted nor did he receive an increment.

Dejected, he sat and skipped office for 3 days. On the fourth day, his friend Clayton from another company, who had recently been promoted and was soon leaving for the UK on an onsite project, came home. He asked: "What's wrong?"

Daljeet told him that he felt very lonely and depressed. He didn't have any friends, and people always seemed to talk behind his back. His reportees poked fun at him and had seniors treat him badly. In his personal life as well, he didn't seem to connect with anyone.

Clayton said, "Just look at you! Filthy! You have not had a bath for days, it seems. Your mouth is smelling, this room is stinking. Look at your clothes, they're dirty! Unwashed utensils in the sink, no ventilation in the room. How do you expect to get ahead in life when you have no sense of personal hygiene and grooming?" he asked.

Daljeet said, "What grooming? Where is the time? I do wash my face daily, but I am too lazy to wake up early when the water supply comes on. Many times, I miss the water supply and go without taking a bath. But what has that got to do with my work? I have the most technical knowledge out of all my colleagues!"

Clayton said, "Personal grooming, also referred to as personal hygiene, is the act of taking care of your body through proper cleanliness and self-care. The way that you look and the way that you act determine what people think about you. If you smile, people think that you are pleasant; If you wear wrinkled or badly maintained clothing, people think that's how you perform your professional work as well.

How you feel about yourself from the inside has to show on the outside. Some of us know this; some of us do not. If we want the outside world to respond to us in a positive way, we must look and act positively."

Benefits of personal hygiene and grooming

Clayton said: "There are certain skills and actions that you can use to be successful in getting what you want – especially in getting a job. You must keep in touch with the latest grooming trends and have detailed information on how to look and act your best. The objective is to increase your confidence and to help you present yourself. Looking at other good dressers and lookers provides detailed guidelines on appropriate attire, grooming, and presentation for individuals seeking employment.

Remember that it is very important to look your best because of:

1. **Respect:** Your physical appearance is the first impression that people have of who you are. Bad Grooming or poor hygiene shows a lack of respect for your own body. And if you can't respect yourself, how will you respect others?
2. **Self-Confidence:** Good grooming helps to increase your self-esteem and confidence as you present yourself to potential employers. You feel more in tune with the latest trends are able to `fit in'. Personal grooming

not only affects the way others see you, but also has an impact on how you feel about yourself. When you look and feel your best, you are able to present yourself confidently to others.

3. **Pride:** Bad grooming or hygiene tells others that you do not take pride in your work because you don't take pride in your appearance, or that you are someone who cannot be taken seriously. Demonstrating that you care about your personal appearance communicates to the person you are meeting with that they are important to you.

4. **Disease:** Not showering or brushing your teeth immediately after exercise increases your risk of MRSA disease, which can lead to potentially life-threatening infections.

5. **Details:** Paying attention to the details of your appearance sends a message to others that you are a detail-oriented person and will take care of the needs of your customers and clients.

Tips for maintaining personal hygiene and grooming

Daljeet said, "But how can I suddenly start looking good?"

"It won't happen overnight, but you have to make a start somewhere. Remember: If you take care of your personal grooming, your boss will take care of grooming you for the promotion! Isn't that enough incentive to start immediately?" asked Clayton.

Daljeet said: "Yes! Can you give me tips for good grooming? How do you always look so clean and fresh? Do you keep looking at yourself in the mirror all the time?"

Clayton smiled." No, it's not necessary to do that. Just some basic common-sense techniques and things can make you look and feel good and clean.

These practical tips are very important for good grooming and dressing:

1. You need not have the looks of a supermodel, but should always try to look neat and tidy.

2. Your hair should not cover up your face, but be held back. No excessively oily or smelling hair.

3. For Ladies, the makeup should be natural and light, not bold and bright.

4. One may not wear very expensive clothes, but just make sure that the clothes are well-ironed and crisp, and not wrinkled. During an interview or a job, one should dress formally. The rule to be followed is to dress one level above what is normally the culture of the place. For e.g., if the culture of the company is jeans or casual clothes, go for the interview wearing formal clothes, e.g., a formal shirt and trousers.

5. The shoes make a huge statement, too, so wear the appropriate ones for the right occasion. Many people can gauge your personality just

by looking at the state of your shoes or feet. So, wear polished, clean footwear at all times.

6. No fiddling with hair, crotch, nails, feet, etc. in public.
7. Pay attention to your diet and eating habits. Excessive garlic and other foods that result in a loud mouth and other odours can be offensive to other people. At work, especially, carry food that is non-smelly and easy to eat without making a mess.
8. You should always dress to impress clients, investors, and customers, because a winning sales pitch is not enough to seal the deal.
9. Dirty nails of the hands and feet, Nail art, and nail jewels are not acceptable for business meetings.
10. Bath daily. Shave your underarms and keep your private parts and feet free of smell. Take care of bad breath, underarm sweating, or other body odour. Ask your friends and family for feedback.
11. Make a checklist of your grooming schedule and stick to it to ensure nothing gets left out.
12. Do not leave a messy desk or bed at home, as it reflects on your poor attitude towards life or work.
13. Make your own style; follow popular trends, but remember: We are not all the same: an outfit you see on the young man next to you may or may not work for you.

    (illustration 58a)

The right clothing combinations

" But how do I know what clothes to wear. What clothes to match with what, asked Daljeet."

Clayton said: "Let me tell you:

1. For Men, the belt, socks, and shoes must match in colour.
2. If wearing blue, grey, or black trousers, wear a light coloured shirt with a black belt, dark coloured socks, and black shoes.
3. Brown shoes must never be worn with blue or black trousers. Brown shoes must be worn only with olive, green, brown, and beige colour combinations.
4. White socks must be worn only with sportswear. Never wear white socks for office or formal occasions.
5. For women: Indian or Western formal is ideal.
6. Use minimum Accessories like jewelry, bags, and shoes, which must be in light, subtle shades, so as not to attract undue attention.

" Wow! Thanks, buddy," said Daljeet. "You have opened my eyes regarding staying clean and healthy, and I will ensure to look presentable and well-groomed at all times."

Clayton said, "No problem, take care of your personal appearance and watch the world appear so joyful and full of opportunities."

13.3 Summary

Good Manners, appropriate grooming, and dressing are the start of a Best First Impression. The correct Etiquette and Dress mean acting appropriately in a way that is socially acceptable and respectful, and to display respect, care, and consideration for others. Excellent manners can help you to have better relationships with people you know and those you will meet. Looks have always played a very important role in everything a person does. However, no matter how talented a person may be or possess sound technical skills, speech, etc., if a person looks untidy and acts uncivilized, that person creates a bad impression immediately. You should always dress to impress your boss, clients, investors, and customers, because a winning sales pitch is simply not enough to steal the deal. A person's professional appearance needs to support their professional accomplishments.

Knowledge Check:

1. Why is it important to practice proper etiquette rules and have good manners?
2. Name the ten commandments of correct etiquette.
3. Give one example from your own life of each of the Ten Commandments.
4. How will you practice to SOFTEN in your own life?
5. What are the ways in which you can improve your dress and grooming?
6. Discuss the importance of wearing the right clothes for a certain job. (dress codes, neat dress, uniforms, safety equipment)
7. Write down your dream job; Write a description of the appropriate dress for the job. Give reasons for the type of clothing choices.

Build your vocabulary

Learn and use the Words and Business phrases used in this chapter to improve your Spoken English Skills:

1. **Internalize:** Something that becomes a part of your basic nature. Not artificial or put on.
2. **Give it a shot:** Give it a try, attempt something for the first time.

3. **To win over:** To influence someone positively. To get an agreement from someone.
4. **Grooming:** A combination of correct dress and good personal hygiene.
5. **Next steps:** The next course of action to be taken. What everyone has to do from this point onwards.
6. **Amiss:** Something that is not right, or something that is out of place.

Chapter 14 Resume Writing and Job Applications

Showcasing your best-self in applications and CVs

LEARNING MILESTONES

This chapter will enable you to:

- Understand the need for a high-impact resume.
- Differentiate between Bio Data, CV and resume.
- Apply practical resume writing tips.
- Master the Dos and Don'ts of Resumes.
- Write impressive covering letters and job applications using AI tools.
- Showcase inspiring resumes and covering letters.

Expert Quotes

A Good Resume is A Simple Marketing Brochure for YOU !!!

The interview gets you the job, the resume gets you the interview!

The Resume is a self-introduction by the candidate to the prospective institution or company. Much before the company actually selects you, they come to know you through your Resume. In fact, if we can visualize it, the Resume is actually you. Would you go out in public intentionally wearing the wrong clothes and displaying bad manners? The answer is an obvious No! So if you take care of your grooming, appearance, and personality, then the same care must be shown while preparing the Resume. Now with **Applicant Tracking Systems (ATS)**, digital portfolios, and so many GenAI tools, crafting a good resume is no longer optional. It is essential.

14.1 Why invest in a high-impact resume?

In this age of digital media, there is a lot of virtual noise. Attention spans are very limited, and recruiters now have to deal with thousands of profiles just for one single opening. Not many people have the time or patience to read beyond a few lines. The Resume has to appeal both to the human reader (Recruiter) and the machine reader (AI tools).

Resumes are also evolving. Whereas in the past, Educational background and Work Experience were the key highlights.

Now, in this Intelligence Age, Adaptability, Emotional Intelligence, AI fluency, Remote-collaboration ability, and a Learning mindset are the key requirements.

Resumes present a snapshot and highlights of your life and allow the prospective recruiter to scan through the document visually or electronically, to see if your skills match their available positions.

The bottom line: Use a well-crafted Resume to increase your chances of getting a job. And a CV for all purposes other than professional.

Advantages of a good resume

- **Filtering and shortlisting:** The sole purpose of a resume is to get you a job interview and to pass the employer's screening and shortlisting process. If the Resume does not pass the ATS or has been poorly formatted, it might never make it to the shortlist for human readers.
- **Advertisement:** You are the product, and your resume is an advertisement for yourself. Like any other product, you need a medium to tell others about your benefits and the value you can add to their lives. A good resume does exactly that. It positions you in the mind of your employer recruiter, thus differentiating you from the others.
- **How can I help you?:** Your resume is the answer to the unspoken question every recruiter asks: *"What can you do for me?"* It helps to make the first impression about you, thus making the recruiter more in sync with your capabilities and their own requirements.
- **Self-Assessment:** Enable you to assess your strengths, skills, abilities, and experience - thereby preparing you for the interview process. It also gives an insight into the recruiter's personality, without even meeting you!
- **Top of the mind recall**: Your resume helps the recruiter recall you as soon as an opening comes up, sometimes long after the interview has been conducted. Many times, recruiters need to justify to their clients why they have shortlisted or hired you, and your resume is a basis for this.

Think of your Resume as your Launch Pad

14.2 Difference among CV, Resume & Bio-Data

Gone are the times when one had to send 6-7 page novels of self-praise to companies to land a job. These were the days of bio-data when every possible information on oneself had to be put down on paper and sent to the employer. However, this is the age of instant gratification and brevity. This makes it important to understand the various formats of a resume and when these should be used.

People use the words **RESUME**, **C.V.**, and **BIO-DATA** interchangeably for the document highlighting skills, education, and experience that a candidate submits

when applying for a job. However, there are fundamental differences between the three:

1. **RESUME:**

   - Resume is a French word meaning "summary", and is actually a basic summary of one's employment, education, and other skills. Personal information such as age, sex, religion, and marital status is never mentioned in a resume. Many people include such particulars in their CVs. However, this is neither required nor considered appropriate and sometimes even unlawful in many countries.
   - A resume ideally should be one side of an A4 sheet or sometimes more (depends upon your experience) or a complete infographic.
   - A resume is not a comprehensive list of accomplishments. Rather, it only highlights specific skills customized to target the required job.
   - A resume is usually broken into bullets and written to appear objective and formal to the third person. For example, the Personal Statement in a resume will start with a Professional summary: "Prashant is a seasoned professional with deep experience in sales and marketing. He thrives in a high-energy environment……"
   - A good resume starts with a brief Personal Objective Statement, Key Result Areas, Summary of Qualifications, followed by Industry Expertise in keywords, followed by Professional Experience in reverse chronological order.

2. **CV - CURRICULUM VITAE**

   - CV is a Latin word meaning "course of life". Curriculum Vitae (CV) is much more detailed than a resume, usually 2 to 3 pages, but can run even longer depending upon the requirement.
   - CV generally lists out every educational or vocational qualification, such as skills, jobs, degrees, and professional affiliations, which have been acquired by the applicant, usually in chronological order.
   - A CV is a document of general talent rather than an attempt to match specific skills against any specific positions.

3. **BIO-DATA**

   A Bio Data, the short form for Biographical Data, is the ancestor of the CV and Resume. It is traditionally personal in nature. The emphasis in a bio data is on personal details like education, experience, date of birth, religion, sex, race, nationality, residence, marital status, etc.

14.2.1 Practical resume writing tips

Your resume is representative of not only your KRAs, skills, and accomplishments; it is also a reflection of your personality, your attention to detail, and your ability to be short, sweet, and effective.

Here are some practical tips to keep in mind when you set out to write a high-impact resume that impresses, highlights your strengths, and ultimately lands you an interview:

1. **ATS Friendly:** The focus should be on `keywords' related to the job description that are in demand with recruiters, and the formatting should be simple to make it machine-readable and human-friendly. AI tools can be used to validate whether the resume is ATS-friendly and if there are any areas of improvement.

2. **Format** your resume properly. Remember that you are competing with thousands of others. The recruiter is spoilt for choice. You must therefore format your resume in such a way that it grabs attention at a 10-second glance. A neat, nicely structured resume is the way to do it. A great way to do this is to present your resume clearly and crisply with headings. Use the same font across the entire resume. Maintain consistency in language, fonts, and tenses. Maintain a `master version of your resume that can be used as a template when you send it to different recruiters or organizations.

Case in Point

Tip: Use action verbs rather than passive voice to demonstrate that you are a person who is action-oriented and proactive.

Action verbs for Resumes

Organized	Communicated	Directed
Planned	Created	Assisted
Supported	Initiated	Solved
Reported	Edited	Analyzed
Described	Developed	Managed
Led	Sold	Designed

3. **Focus:** Keep relevance in mind. Ask yourself, does this bullet point help me in selling myself for this job? If not, be ruthless with your editing. Target the job advertised, the needs of the recruiter, and the keywords used in the **JD (job description)**. Then set out to customize your resume according to the needs of the recruiter. A one-size-fits-all approach does not work in a resume application. Instead, the resume must be focused on the job, not just on the applicant.

   Don't make the reader go through the entire resume to understand what your profession is or what you can do. There should be a balance between hard and soft skills.

Customization is the key to telling the recruiter that you are trying to have a direct dialogue with them. One size does NOT fit all.

4. **Proofread:** The following three steps have to be followed before sending out a resume:

   Step 1: Compose and format the resume. Then use the spell check function in your software to check for spelling and grammar.

   Step 2: Take a physical printout and manually read each and every word yourself. Go line by line, word by word, using a pencil to mark the changes. Revise the resume based on these corrections.

   Step 3: Ask a professional or use AI tools to read your resume and suggest changes.

5. **Step by Step**: Build your resume in a sequence:

   1. Statement of Interest and personal Summary, personal statement, your key objectives, e.g, "I am a Digital marketing enthusiast who is always looking for the next big thing......"
   2. Accomplishments and strengths, work experience.
   3. Culture Fit or what you can do for the organization.
   4. Moving on to your academic experience (College onwards) and finally your interests. Imagine that you are telling someone about your strengths and suitability, in written words, without the benefit of body language.

14.2.2 Checklist for making resumes

Below are the key points that must be included in your resume. These will ensure that your Resume is complete in all respects. The amount of detail will vary depending on the position applied for. However, a good Resume includes the following:

- What are the key qualifications that the employer is looking for?
- What are your qualifications that will be most important to them?
- What are your Key Result Areas? Facts, Figures, and Numbers to back up these KRAs have been included?
- Which of these are your greatest strengths?
- What are the highlights of your career that need to be highlighted?
- What weaknesses or gaps should be de-emphasized?
- What is your USP? What are the things about you that set you apart?
- What are some other skills you possess?
- What keywords describe you best in your personal statement? (Like "innovative, game-changer, rainmaker, strong interpersonal skills, high energy")

- What were the two or three accomplishments of a past job?
- What were the key skills you used in that job?
- What did you do in each of those skill areas?
- Research what sort of results are particularly impressive to recruiters in your industry?
- Latest and current jargon or buzzwords, unique to your industry or vertical, that recruiters would expect you to use.

14.2.3 Things to avoid while writing a resume

These are the things to avoid while writing your resume:

1. Don't use too many graphics, photos, or non-text elements, as it might confuse the ATS.
2. Do not indicate what you expect out of a job. Instead, focus on how you can contribute to that profile.
3. Do not go back further than college in your academic experience.
4. Do not list names or give unnecessary references unless specifically asked for.
5. Do not be wordy or use paragraphs. Instead, use bullets when listing job duties, use bullets like small dots or squares in a consistent style.
6. Do not omit a previous position because it does not relate to your desired job. Gaps in employment should be avoided as these raise unnecessary questions and doubt.
7. Do not indicate expected salary unless specified.
8. Do not mention hobbies, marital status, etc., unless specified.
9. Do not forget to put your name on the second page, in case it is separated from the first page.
10. Don't use generic words, especially if you don't know their meaning. Rather, demonstrate what you have achieved.

14.2.4 Write your own resume

There are many professional websites, apps, and AI tools that claim to write professional, job-oriented resumes. These services are often costly and clubbed as part of job portal services. Ensure that you do your due diligence and complete research on whether these resumes actually work. Use these services only if you feel that you are unable to write your resume yourself. Otherwise, take help or advice from friends and family and craft it yourself.

Writing your own resume will give you a sense of control over yourself, and you will be able to expand on it better in interviews. LinkedIn is a great hiring platform now, and a good LinkedIn profile provides the same opportunity and benefits as any other portal. And the best part is: it is free!

The samples given below are pretty representative of modern resume trends, which can be used and downloaded online as well.

14.2.5 Using AI tools

AI tools like Chat GPT, Claude, and Copilot can generate a great first draft. These tools can help you save time and energy by getting an overview going. But one must personalize and customize! AI tools are accelerators. Not crutches. Blindly copying AI prompts can result in your resume matching many others who have done exactly the same thing. If you want to stand out, you have to add your own personal touch. Your Resume must look and sound authentic, as opposed to having been written by a machine.

14.2.6 Sample resumes

1. **Fresher -5 years experience:** The following is a resume for someone straight out of college or having limited work experience:

Neeraj Bajaj
Sales & Marketing

Male | 25 years | English, Hindi, Marathi
Email id | phone

Academic Qualifications

Degree	Stream	University / Board	Institute	Year	(% / GPA)
B.E.	Mechanical	Subharti University	A1 College of Engineering, Meerut	2012	74.7
12th	Science	C.B.S.E.	DAV Higher Secondary School, Kollam	2008	75.4
10th		C.B.S.E.	St. Xavier's High School, Mumbai	2006	86.8

Summer Internship – Amrapali Ltd. - Pune — 2 months

- **Analysis of Channel Partners to amplify Company reach and Market share** (May'16-Jun'16)
  - **Sales Profile**
    - **Market activation** for the New product launch –instrumental in getting business revenue worth **INR 1 crores** through channel partners
    - Conducted **pre-launch and post-launch surveys** of **100 channel partners** to evaluate the impact of marketing activities during the launch window
    - Performed **competitor analysis** for similar inventory in the luxurious & high end customer segment
  - **Marketing Profile**
    - Conceptualized & recommended a **Digital Marketing framework** for enhanced Customer Engagement

Professional Certification

- **Google Adwords Fundamentals Certification** for online advertising

Work Experience — 24 months

- **Engineer,** Production Line at **BMR India Pvt. Ltd,** Chennai (Mar'14-Aug'14)
  - Responsible for **Supervising** the production line and **Designing** a 'New Process Layout' for production line
- **CAE Engineer,** Mercedes drive train at **Infotraining Ltd.,** Pune (Aug'12-Mar'14)
  - Involved in **Leading and Supervising** the team of 4 Engineers for Mercedes drive train projects
  - Was awarded the **'Employee Spot Award'** during 3rd quarter of 2013

Key Projects

- **Everest – Virtual Marketing Intern** (Sep'16)
  - Developed a database of relevant Q & A on Marketing & Advertising trends
- **B.E Final year Project** on **'Designing and Manufacturing of a Hybrid Vehicle'**, (Sep'11-May'12)
  - Alterations in Rear wheel differential and including two way drives on it. Awarded **'Best Project'** in college

Achievements

- **National Winner's** at **Markopolis, 3M & Christ College-Bangalore, Pre-Placement Interview** with **Apple** (2016)
- **National Runners up** at **L'oreal Brandstorm, Pre-Placement Interview** with **L'oreal** (2016)
- **National Winner's** at **EXCELSIOR**, Live case study challenge, **Great Lakes-Chennai** (2015)

Positions of Responsibility

- **Member, Guest Lectures Team,** Subharti, Meerut (Jul'15-Present)
  - Organize guest lectures on contemporary business issues by eminent personalities, from the corporate sector
  - Enhance student learning experience through exposure to best corporate practices in various business functions

Extra-Curricular

- **Volunteer** at **Learn India** : a CSR initiative, Shapath: CSR cell at Subharti (2015)
- Member **(Team Myrmidons)**, SAE- BAJA, SAE India, Indore (Jan'11)
- **Other interests** – Yoga and Meditation, Travelling, Writing

***Figure 14.1**: Sample CV1*

2. **5-15+ years' experience:** The following is a sample resume for those with more work experience.

Mahesh Lala

SYNOPSIS

Recognized for outstanding product deliverables and quality assurance as evidenced by long-term client relationship (17+years). Strong ability to deliver results in dynamic and unstructured environments. Creative problem solver used to working in high energy and deadline driven situations. A curious mind for solutions and a thorough understanding of multi-cultural issues. An impressive communicator with a proven ability to lead teams across diverse and multi-disciplinary skills.

EXPERTISE

- Strategic Planning and Execution
- Penetrating New Markets
- Key Account Identification and Planning
- Customer Relationship Management
- Vendor Development
- Growing Revenue
- Project Management and Process Implementation
- A 360-degree perspective on all aspects of running a business

KEY RESULT AREAS

- Significantly contributed to changing product focus and introducing innovation, resulting in CAGR of sales of 40% from 2007-2010.
- Changed the product mix from a majority high volume/low margin model to an 80% high-end, design driven / 20% volume-low margin driven business. This resulted in an incremental revenue growth and increased bottom line.
- Framed and executed a business process redesign for a faster turnaround of inventory levels, resulting in a decrease in cycle times by 30 days (33%).
- Planned supply and logistics system and delivered US $800,000 of orders within a very compressed time-frame, boosting the top line by 70% in 2010.
- Introduced employee development programs aimed at increasing throughput resulting in an increase in operational performance by more than 15%.

PROFESSIONAL EXPERIENCE

General Manager, Business Development and Strategic Planning

TARANG LIFESTYLE EXPORTS ™ (1997- Present)

Home Textiles Industry

Co-founded the company, dedicated to sourcing, designing and exporting of the highest quality home textiles and accessories for clients in the UK, Australia and New Zealand.

Responsible for:

Business Development and Market Penetration

- Led prospect meetings and managed the follow up.
- Managed the end-to-end sales cycle: Right from cold calling to negotiations.
- Ensured that all terms and conditions of sale were accurately incorporated into binding contracts.
- Established points of contact with domestic retailers for increasing focus on the growing Indian market.
- Provided creative direction for the company website, promotion events, photo shoots and trade events.
- *Vendor Management*:
  - Developed expertise in sourcing raw materials both from India and overseas.
  - Ensured quality and timely supplies and handled the contract renewals and management.

Select Achievements

- Secured orders from two customers with annual revenues in excess of US $40 Million, despite a very tough economic climate.
- Identified and developed a diverse range of international customers from mid-size retailers to large importer corporations.

Client Management

- Extensive experience working with demanding buyers, owners and senior managements of several British and Australian-NZ companies.
- Worked closely with the team designing the sales proposals and the service level agreements.

***Figure 14.2**: Sample CV 2*

3. **Infographic resumes**

Resumes are undergoing a gradual change. Increasingly, the use of infographics and images in resumes is becoming popular. An illustration

of one's experience and qualifications rather than simple text gives relief to the reader's eyes.

However, recruiters advise that the candidate must be familiar with the company's culture and the nature of the job before using graphics. Jobs in the creative, performing arts, Design, and Digital media fields ideally lend themselves to such resumes.

The Reader is advised to be aware of the changing trends and ensure that the resume is modern and fresh.

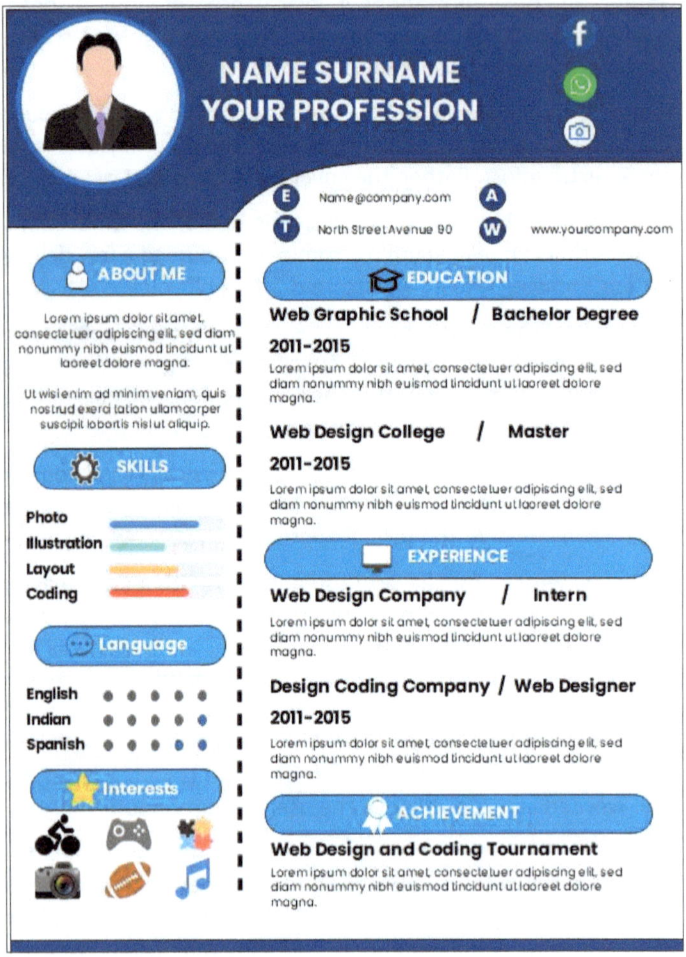

***Figure 14.3**: InfoGrapic CV Sample*

14.2.7 Cover Letters or Job Applications

When applying for a job, a cover letter should be sent or mailed with your resume. A cover letter is a job application, typically a short, one-page message that

explains to the recruiter why you are an ideal candidate for the job. It acts as a perfect introduction to yourself in the eyes of a stranger. It helps the recruiter to go beyond your resume and to explain in detail how you could add value to the company.

The receiver may get surprised or confused, receiving just your resume without any context, background, or supporting information. The cover letter provides the necessary introduction to your Resume.

Tips for creating an effective cover letter

1. **Gather all the information:** A logical presentation of ideas always creates a good first impression on the reader. No one wants to hire people who appear disorganized or confused.
2. **Spend** as much time on the covering letter as you would on your resume. The same attention to detail must go into the covering letter as well. It is not an extra effort. Rather, the covering letter is part of your resume.
3. **Write & Re-write:** A covering letter is not a one-time effort. It is a process that can take anything from a few hours to a few days. Keep on writing, showing it to an expert, re-drafting till you are satisfied.
4. **Personalize:** The chances of a best result usually come from personalizing each covering letter to fit the specific job, organization, position, or organization. If you are unsure, ask for opinions, advice, and feedback from someone in a similar profession.
5. **Proofread:** Read, check, spell check, and physically read your message, especially to check for correct formatting, spellings, and grammar. Go for the conservative and formal approach in your covering letter.
6. **Show excitement for the position and end with a Call to action:** e.g., Start with: "I am excited to come across the position of ...." Avoid weak endings such as "I hope to receive your reply" or "Please call me at your earliest convenience." This shows a lack of confidence. Instead, appear positive and confident and use words that convey that you are the right person for this job. An appropriate ending would be: "I look forward to meeting or connecting with you soon." The covering letter should be well-worded and controlled in the use of the pronoun "I".
7. **Follow-up** is as important as the act of sending or mailing the letter. Design your own follow-up steps and reminder system. Follow up with the recipient, but do not harass them with messages or calls. Remember, you are dealing with busy people, and they will respond whenever they have a requirement.

Remember the KISS approach: Keep It Short & Simple

1. It is important to mention in your letter how you found out about the position, what you are looking for, and how you can add value to that company.

2. You might also mention a few keywords that the ATS might pick up.
3. Most importantly, be brief and concise.
4. Make sure that you compose your cover letter offline first before uploading it and sending it.
5. Check the email ID of the recipient before sending.
6. Follow up after a reasonable period of time, keeping your earlier mail in the same message.

14.2.8 Sample Covering Letter

Subject: First Name, LastName – Digital Marketing Manager Position

Dear Contact Person:

I am excited to express my interest in the Digital Marketing Manager position listed on your online job portal. I have extensive experience with AI and digital tools, building large, consumer-focused IT/ITES-specific content sites. While much of my experience has been with SMEs, I understand the impact of a large multinational corporation since I have dealt with large company clients during the course of my career. SMEs have taught me the importance of working in high-energy, deadline-driven environments. My business and corporate experience will be an asset to your organization as I can deliver cost-effective solutions in the assigned timeframes.

My responsibilities in my current profile include UI/UX prototyping, Creative Ideation and storyboarding, the development and management of the website's SEO, web design, and content, as well as the daily maintenance of the programming and production of the website.

I bring to the table a 360-degree exposure to all aspects of running a successful online digital marketing campaign.

Experience has taught me how to build strong networks and relationships with all departments at an organization. I have the ability to work within remote teams. I can work with web architects to resolve technical issues and implement technical upgrades, work with the development teams to implement design and functional enhancements, and monitor site statistics and conduct search engine optimization. This has resulted in savings of valuable time and money for my clients.

Please find attached my Resume for your perusal. Do let me know if you require more information.

I look forward to hearing from you.

Best Regards,
First Name LastName

14.3 Summary

A resume is not just another document about one's life history. Rather, it is a showcase of knowledge, skills, and experience. A well-crafted resume is the key differentiator between an interview call and a rejection message. Before making your resume, it is important that your resume answers these questions:

- Does it clearly and quickly communicate to the recruiter that you can do the job?
- Do your actual strengths come across?
- Does the information mentioned support the job you are targeting?
- Should anything be removed? Is anything extra?
- Does it really sell your skills?
- Is the formatting, spelling, grammar, quality of print, and fonts correct?
- Can it convince the recruiter that you are the right person for the job?

Knowledge Check:

1. Why is it important to build a well-crafted resume?
2. What are the topics that you must include in your resume?
3. What are the topics to be avoided in resumes?
4. Do you think it is important to include illustrations and graphics in resumes? Why?
5. Give one example of a good resume and one that you feel will have no impact. Compare your resume to the resume that you feel is an impactful one.

Chapter 15 Personal Interviews and Group Discussions

From preparation to performance: succeeding in the interview process

LEARNING MILESTONES

This chapter will enable you to:

- Practice what interviewers look for.
- Use the checklist for preparing for the interview.
- Understand what interviewers look for in an ideal candidate.
- Explore the different types of interview questions.
- Develop the Perfect Interview Etiquette.
- Practice Interview FAQ and role play -1.
- Excel at Group Discussions

15.1 The importance of Interviews

Interviews now are not just about assessing skills. Interviewers use interviews to assess potential and cultural fit. With AI and automation dominating routine tasks, Interviewers are now looking for soft skills and communication skills.

A question asked in a recent survey to recruiters: Would you select a candidate who does not have communication skills? A shocking majority of employers and recruiters said No! They have answered that they would not hire someone who does not perform well in the interview.

The reality is that recruitment or selection methods are still heavily focused on communication skills, particularly the job interview. Interviews favor those who can communicate their ideas fluently and come across as likable and able to convince the panel that they are the right candidate.

The personal interview is widely regarded as the ultimate test of selection. Irrespective of the industry or institution, the interview is a subjective methodology adopted by recruiters, often relying on common sense and first impressions to check the suitability of the candidate. The interview is assumed to reveal what the Resume and the technical qualifications of the candidate cannot.

The selection body or the recruiter wants to see and meet the person they intend to hire. Whether it is face-to-face or via mobile or video call, the interview reveals

personality traits that come forth based on sustained questioning. Training times and budgets have shrunk, and organizations require professionals who are capable of handling responsibility, showing teamwork, and exhibiting emotional intelligence from Day 1. Your ability to carry yourself with dignity and poise and answer questions with confidence and ease can hide deficiencies or gaps in your Resume. It gives the recruiter the confidence that Yes! You are the right person for this position! Hence, it is necessary to prepare well for your interview. The following chapter focuses on the essentials of interview success and FAQs for intensive interview preparation.

15.2 What do interviewers look for?

Success in the interview is a combination of many factors. While the interview itself is an event that takes place on the pointed date and time, the preparation for the interview is a process. A slow and steady process that needs to begin today! While technical and functional mastery are the foundation that must be exhibited, through an experience with interacting with and training thousands of candidates, the author has narrowed down the following behavioral qualities that interviewers look for in successful candidates:

1. **Technical competence:** As the popular saying goes, `you are hired for your technical skills, but can be fired for lack of communication skills. This means that technical knowledge and domain expertise are the necessary first steps towards getting selected. Interviews are generally competency-based, and thus a command over your subject or expertise is a must, and one must be able to answer all job-related questions to the recruiter's satisfaction. Recruiters look for people who require very little training and can start performing from day 1.

2. **Poise & confidence:** This shows itself in the first 30 seconds or so. The candidate's ability to answer unexpected questions confidently, deal with unfamiliar situations, and conflict scenarios via case studies or role-plays is tested by the panel. If the candidate performs well in these situations, the panel is impressed, as this simulates the conditions that the candidate will encounter in the real world.

3. **First impression:** In the first few seconds of the interview, the interviewer is evaluating your mannerisms, your dress, accessories, your handshake, grooming, and smile. This bunch of physical traits should result in the display of positive body language. It is this positive body language that helps the recruiter to make up their mind about you. What they are looking for is a person who fits into their organization's culture and value system. This `fit' is determined by the first impression that you make.

   Remember: Form does not always win over function. i.e., looks cannot substitute domain expertise.

4. **Preparation and fit:** Interviewers appreciate the fact that the candidate has done research on the company prior to the interview. Knowledge of basic information about the organization, their website, their financial performance of the previous year, their areas of operation, and recent news about them are some ways in which the candidate can display their research. Remember that research shows interest in becoming a part of the organization, and it is this interest that impresses recruiters. However, maintain a conversational flow. Don't appear over-rehearsed or answer questions verbatim as you have memorized them.

Case in Point

Diya received an interview call. She was not familiar with the area where the organization was located. So, the previous day, she asked her network, found the location on Google maps, and actually took a cab and went to the location. She found that the cabs were not allowed inside the main gate, and the walk from the main gate after completing all security formalities took almost an additional 20 minutes. On the day of the interview, she left on time, and since she was familiar with the procedures, she reached the interview waiting room 20 minutes before the allotted time. The room was empty! Just when it was time for her call, she saw another candidate rush inside the room, all hot and sweaty! Later, she found out that the other candidate was actually scheduled before her but had missed his appointment because he was delayed at the main gate.

During her interview, she was asked whether she had any trouble finding the location. She replied, telling them that she had come the previous day to see the location. Her phone was on silent, and she asked the interviewer for clarification on one question. This gave the impression that she listened actively to the questions. The panel was impressed, and she got the offer! When she went out smiling, she saw that other candidates were still coming in, well after their appointed time!

15.3 Checklist for the interview -preparation

Before you appear for the interview, please go through this checklist and answer each question. Be honest with yourself, as that may influence the manner in which you answer questions in the actual interview. It will also help in being prepared and do wonders for your self-confidence.

1. Have you done research on the organization?
2. Have you determined why you want to apply for that post?
3. What do you know about the post for which you are being interviewed?
4. Can you convince someone that you are the best candidate for that post?

5. What do other people say about that organization?
6. What are your short-term and long-term goals?
7. What are your salary and CTC expectations?
8. Are you willing to relocate, travel on the job, work in other profiles, etc.?
9. If changing jobs, what information is important to you in making a decision about this job change?
10. What questions do you plan to ask the interviewer, either about the job, financials, or any other issue?

15.4 Type of Interviews

Interviewers use five different types of techniques - Screening, Open-Ended, Case Study, Behavior-based, and Stress. Being aware of the different types can help you in the preparation and be ready for anyone, anytime, anywhere.

1. **Screening Interviews:**

This is used to shortlist candidates from a vast pool. For example, a recruiter who goes onto a job site and selects candidates. This is followed up with a phone or video call where the interviewer quickly determines the focus of your answers. Through this focus, they eliminate candidates who they think are unsuitable. This is a very important opportunity to create the best first impression, and the key trait to be displayed here is self-confidence. The information that the interviewer wants is very clear, and your answer should be very clear as well.

Case in Point

Question: *"Why do you think that you are good for this position?"*

Answer: Use the **STAR** method:

- **S**ituation – Set context
- **T**ask – What was expected of you
- **A**ction – What you did
- **R**esult – The measurable outcome

"I have done an internship where my primary focus and responsibility were aligned exactly with the requirements of your position. I used my excellent communication skills to make a lot of presentations to my superiors and potential clients. One of my presentations resulted in a big project for my company. I am confident that my background and your requirements are in sync, and I will be a good fit for this position."

2. **Open-ended interviews**

The questions that the interviewer asks in these types of interviews do not require a simple yes or no. Rather, you determine the focus of your answer. The interviewer asks a general question and does not ask for specific information. Instead, the interviewee answers based on experience and understanding of the

question. There is no right or wrong answer here. Just simple, the best answer that gets the best result.

Case in Point

Question: *"Tell me about yourself."*

Answer: "I have done B. Tech in Automobile Engineering and an MBA from the Northmain University, and have recently completed the course. I have 2 years of work experience with Toyota, where I had both production floor and administrative exposure. I was involved with the production of the XYZ model, where we introduced Branch Robotics to the plant. Robotics, as I can gauge from my research on your company, is also a focus area of your organization. I was given a 2-month training by Fokomura corporation, Japan, and during the course of this training, I also practiced my presentation skills as we had to make a lot of presentations about the plant. I am a volunteer with TeachBharat, where we educate slum children in Maths and Sciences.

Tip: Do not give any personal information about your family background or childhood experiences unless specifically asked.

3. **Case Study Interview**

Here, the interviewer tries to put the candidate in a real-world scenario and observes their response and reaction if faced with a similar situation. This simulates the challenges that the candidate faces in the real world. This is a good way to test creative thinking and problem-solving abilities. When answering this type of question, try to apply a simple problem-solving model – obtain the background information, evaluate the information, establish priorities, evaluate the alternatives, make a decision, communicate, and monitor the results.

Case in Point

Question: *"Suppose you are working on your first day on the production floor, and a key component catches fire in your machine. What will you do?*

Answer: "Before I start working on the production shop floor, I always locate the emergency equipment and speak with the Emergency Response Team in charge. This way, if any emergency strikes, I am prepared and also able to guide others. My training with the NCC has helped me develop a sense of danger. As soon as I notice the fire, I will shut down my machine and raise the alarm. I would ensure that the surrounding areas are kept clear of any obstacles, and evacuation and assembly of all personnel away from the fire are done in an organized manner.

4. **Behavior Descriptive or Behavioral Interviews**

Here, the interviewer wants to see how you reacted or behaved in a particular situation in the past. The assumption here is that the past performance is an indicator of future performance. What you did is more important here than what you will do.

Case in Point

Example: "Tell me one thing in your old job or in your past that you are proud of?"

Answer: I am very proud of doing an internship along with my studies. I utilized my vacations in 2 semesters to work for an Engineering casting company. Even though it was a small SME, it gave me exposure to aspects of running a business. I was able to relate and apply many theoretical concepts in the real-world environment during my internship.

5. **Stress Interviews**

Some interviews will turn out to be totally different from what you imagined! The interviewers or panel will create situations or ask you questions that will make you feel very uncomfortable. You will wonder why these are being asked or what the relevance is, but you must not ask so. Instead, take it in your stride and answer with creativity, maturity, and occasional use of humour. Life is full of stress, and the panel wants to know if you are mentally capable of handling stressful situations. How you react under pressure or in anger is the test of your leadership ability.

Case in Point

Question: *"If you were an animal, what type of animal would you be?"*

Answer: I would love to be a Lion. The king of the jungle and the master of all they survey! Lions are so majestic and calm, yet command so much respect. The Lion is at the top of the food chain, yet it is so important in the food cycle. To be honest, my impression of Lions was reinforced after I saw their lovely portrayal in the movie The Lion King."

15.5 Power tips for success in the interview

1. **KISS:** Keep it Short & Simple. Remember, be short, be brief, and be interesting. No long lectures on your past or strengths. No one likes a bore! It should not take more than 90-120 seconds to answer a question.

2. **Match your strengths** with those of the organization's requirements. Find the fit between yourself and the position, and tell the interviewer the same. Don't assume that they will know this. Tell them!

3. **Teamwork:** Speak like you are part of their team. Talk about the organization, what you know about them, and how excited you are at the prospect of being part of their winning teams. Show enthusiasm.

4. **Look, feel, and behave confidently:** Your dress and voice should match the organization's culture. An image is often as important as content. Don't wear a heavy deodorant or cologne. Dress as per the company's

culture, but one level higher than required. For example, if the company employee wears jeans and a t-shirt to work, they should dress in formal pants and a shirt for the interview. Here, a tie or jacket is not required.

5. **Ask questions:** This tells the interviewer that you are confident and curious. The types of questions you ask and the way you ask them can make a huge impression on the recruiter. Remember that Good questions require advanced preparation.

6. **Thank you note:** Keep an interview journal. As soon as possible, after the interview, send a thank-you message to the recruiter or the company for giving you the opportunity. Then write a brief summary of what happened. Note any follow-up action you should take and put it in your calendar.

7. **Sell yourself:** As if you are the product and the company is the buyer. Just like any other sale, the product has to be packaged and sold in the most pleasing and efficient manner. It is the same with job interviews.

8. **Know your resume:** You have to be the master of your own resume. Role-play each and every point in your resume with your friends and family and ask them to grill you on any gaps, terminations, short periods of employment, etc. You have to memorize the dates mentioned in your resume by heart.

15.6 Frequently Asked Questions

Presented below are some FAQs and their suggested answers. Once again, remember there is no right answer or wrong answer. The winner only gives the best answer out of all the other candidates. Below are some of the commonly asked questions and their answers as per a wide survey of successful candidates. The reader can use these as a template and build upon each answer based on the position and their own personal experience.

1. **Tell me about yourself. OR Tell me something not mentioned in your resume.**

My background to date has been focused on preparing myself to become the very best at this job. I have done this by studying (mention latest academic qualifications) and working (mention any internship or work experience). This has helped me match myself ideally to the position that you have open, and I am confident I am a good fit. My skills will help you save training time and result in quick efficiency.

2. **Why should we hire you? OR Why did you apply for this job**?

Because I sincerely believe that I'm the best person for the job. Compared to others with similar academic qualifications, I have an additional quality that makes me the very best person for the job--my attitude toward excellence. I can add tremendous value to a project as I have already experienced the potential problems and can help avoid time and resource wastage. I am not just saying

this, but have also demonstrated it by doing (mention any commendation, recommendation from an important person, or award that you have received)

3. **What is your long-range objective? Where do you want to be 10 or 15 years from now?**

I have given this much thought and feel that, ideally, I would like to break up my career into 5-year spans. Within the next five years, I want to develop an operational expertise in my profile by gaining valuable field experience. Based on this, in the next ten years, I would like to move into a managerial role leading teams and then build on my leadership skills. I would like to be a part of winning teams throughout my career and would focus on learning and training as a necessary supplement to my job.

4. **How has your education prepared you for your career?**

As Mark Twain said: I have not let my studies interfere with my education (say this with a smile). I have taken courses and electives in my academic career, keeping my desired profile and interests in mind. I also volunteered to be part of the fete organizing committee and was in the students' council. I have been a part of the NGO for teaching children. I was fortunate to study under some of the best academic teachers and professors, and through them I have learn the value of applied knowledge. I am eager to test out this knowledge now at your organization.

5. **Are you a team player? Do you like working in a team or solo?**

I feel no single person alone can succeed in life. Behind the success of every person lies the contribution of their team, network, and family. I believe in teamwork. All through my academic and professional career, I have volunteered to organize events. This has been possible only through working in teams. I also enjoy training people and creating teams. Teamwork and team integration are essential skills for a leader, and I displayed the same recently (give a good example of how you completed a project within budget and before the deadline through teamwork)

6. **Have you ever had a conflict or problems with your boss or teachers? How was it resolved?**

Yes, I have been in conflict situations in the past. In fact, I feel that not all conflict is bad. For example, in my previous organization, my boss and I had a disagreement on a particular team member's role. But we eventually sat and discussed the problem without getting personal. Both of us displayed the maturity and found a win-win solution. That's the benefit of conflict. It also enables us to see another's point of view and find multiple solutions to a problem together.

7. **What is your biggest strength?**

I feel my ability to understand people and technology is my biggest strength. I feel the future lies in a blend of the two, and one is incomplete without the other.

It's not just B to B or B to C. It's all about P to P, i.e., People to People. This is my strength, and it enables me to get along and work with people from different verticals and skill sets. I also like to read and, in fact, read the newspaper and the latest blogs related to my field. My favorite blogger, writer, newspaper, or book is (mention a specific name that you are totally familiar with)

8. **What is your greatest weakness?**

I would say my greatest weakness has been my tendency to overcommit to others in terms of time. I have in the past put my entire energy and time into doing a task at hand, with the result that other projects were delayed. However, after receiving the necessary feedback, I have invested in a time management tool (give the example of an app, productivity method, or technology that you use).

9. **How do others describe you? Or what did your colleagues say about in your previous job?**

Dependable and professional is how most people describe me, whether it is my superiors or colleagues. I believe in technology as a huge enabler, and others can reach out to me for the latest in tech and current affairs. I am a high-energy person, and others, too, have commented on my ability to keep going even in deadline-oriented environments. My recommendations on LinkedIn and other media show these traits. Could I show you? (If asked, show them this information)

10. **What is the worst feedback you have ever received?**

I was told that I need to brush up on my presentation skills. I took immediate action and enrolled in a good Public Speaking training program. This enabled me to overcome my weakness in a short time.

11. **What are the qualities of a good Leader or Manager?**

A Good leader is a perfect mix of IQ and EQ, i.e, Emotional Intelligence. Proactiveness and Empathy are the two must-have qualities of a good leader. By being proactive, the leader can anticipate potential problems and conflicts and take action. Empathy is displayed by good communication skills, whereby the leader is approachable and surrounded by good professionals and teams. The manager thus becomes a good role model. One such leader is (give an example of a leader that you admire).

12. **What are the biggest accomplishments of your life? Or accomplishments of the past job?**

"Although I feel my biggest accomplishments are still ahead of me, I am proud of (mention a project, paper, or task that you did successfully in the past for which you have received a recommendation. Ensure that this project or task relates directly to the position that you are currently applying for).

13. **How do you explain changing so many jobs? Or a big gap in your employment history? Or being terminated from your last position, particularly when that position gave you the skills that you'll need to succeed in your career field?**

I agree, I have changed several organizations in the past. Or changed my vertical or job profile in the past. It was a learning phase for me, and the Key thing is I have learned a lot from this experience. I was searching for a profile or organization that utilized my skills to the fullest, and I finally feel that your organization will give me this opportunity. I have made mistakes in the past, but I can assure you that I have learnt from these mistakes and have no intention of repeating them. In fact, I would be glad to share my experiences with others so that they can avoid costly mistakes.

14. **Why did you leave your last job?**

At the time of joining there, I was put in a team of my interest. The work and profile were interesting, and I was learning a lot. But over a period of time, I was shifted to another team where I continued to work and perform. However, that was not related to my chosen field, and I felt my skills were going unused. A sense of stagnation was building up, and I had several interactions with the management, who were unable to help me. In this scenario, we agreed that it was best that I look at opportunities outside the company

15. **Does that mean you don't like change? OR Are you willing to change your project/profile when required?**

I absolutely like change and, in fact, welcome it. I am open to working in other locations or profiles if the situation demands it. As a team player, I would give my best to whichever team I am assigned. If my manager is communicating with me and I am likewise communicating with them, then it's a perfect situation, as I know that my knowledge and skills will be utilized to the fullest.

16. **What is the Salary that you expect? Or do you have any other offer at hand?**

I am very confident that the salary offered is as per my experience and qualifications. Your organization has a reputation for salaries, which are as per industry standard and beyond. I have no doubt it will be a win-win for both of us. I do have some other offers and have had preliminary interactions with them, but I am very keen on the position offered by you.

***Figure 15.1**: When your preparation pays off in a handshake*

15.7 Group discussions

While many educational institutions are doing away with Group Discussions and instead opting for **WATs (Written Ability tests)**, GDs still have some relevance.

These have been taken from observation with numerous GDs. The most common questions that candidates have regarding GDs and their answers are enumerated below:

1. **How many panel members are there who evaluate?**

   There are usually 3-4 panel members who do the evaluation.

2. **Should I address the panel of judges or the other group members?**

   Never directly address the panel members. During the GD, don't make eye contact with the panel members. Ignore them completely. The GD is between you and the other candidates, not with the panel members.

3. **How should I address the other candidates?**

   If the GD starts with self-introduction, make a rough sketch of the seating arrangement and write down the name of each candidate in your notebook. Addressing them by name is a great way to impress the panel judges. If you can't remember their names, then just refer to the others as "Friends".

4. **Suppose I have a lot to say on the topic, should I say all of it?**

   The GD is not a talking contest. It is a myth that the more you speak, the more you impress. If you keep speaking, without listening, you will lose points.

   Remember the golden rule of a GD: Quality over quantity

5. **Should I encourage others to speak up?**

   While it is good to display empathy for others, avoid speaking to specific people in the group if they are silent. Your job is to put your point across and not put others in the limelight, positively or negatively. However, if someone is trying to speak but constantly getting interrupted, tell the others, "Can we let (name) complete their point?" and immediately after they have made their point, you should take the stage again.

***Figure 15.2**: Speak to contribute, not just to compete*

6. **Are we allowed to carry a pad or notebook during the GD for noting down important points?**

   Normally, yes, but the rules and regulations may vary. Carry a pen and pad to the GD, but check with the panel first to avoid embarrassment.

7. **Is there any particular seating position in a GD that is favourable to the participants?**

   If the candidates are asked to sit in a circle or a semicircle, then it really does not matter where you sit. But if you are asked to sit on either side of a rectangular table, then choose a position as close to the center of the table as possible. The second-best position would be the Head of the table if I had that choice. Wherever you sit, it should ideally face the panelists.

8. **Can we take a particular point of view on a subject in the GD and then later on during the GD, switch over to another point of view?**

   It is avoidable to do so, but yes, at times situations do arise which may necessitate this. For example, another candidate has obviously proved your point of view wrong. Now, instead of arguing continuously, it is better to accept graciously that while the other person was right, you were not completely wrong. And go on to explain a minor point where you were right.

   Obviously, it is better not to take a position on any particular argument unless you know the facts of the case first. Don't blindly take sides unless you are sure how to proceed.

9. **If we do not understand the meaning of the topic, should we ask the moderator to explain it to us?**

   No. Please do not ask anyone in the room the meaning of the topic. Instead of displaying your ignorance, it is better to wait for some other candidate to explain the meaning of the topic. Let the discussion start, listen carefully for the first few minutes, and when you have figured out the meaning of the topic, start participating in the discussion.

10. **If I feel strongly about an issue, should I voice my feelings?**

    The GD is not a place to display your emotions. You need to appear Cool, professional, neutral, and objective. You need to have control over your emotions and feel whatever the provocation. But keep in mind the religious and cultural sentiments of others.

    Remember the rule: Logic wins over emotion in a GD

11. **What is the right time to enter a GD to ensure that I am heard properly?**

    In any GD, there are highs and lows: The highs are when the discussion is heated, and everyone is speaking. The lows are when the noise lowers, and the candidates pause to take a breath. That's the best time to enter the GD. However, it is not advisable to wait for a low as GDs are generally very competitive and there is constant talking. Look out for an idea that you agree with, latch onto the discussion, and jump straight in!

12. **How do I participate when the noise level is too high?**

    Assume that the noise level will be constantly high. It is pointless to keep waiting to speak. Instead, when one person is dominating, agree with them and start talking. That person will support you because you have supported them, and the two of you can then proceed to influence the GD.

13. **Is it beneficial to be the first speaker in a group discussion?**

    This is both risky and rewarding at the same time. Your start will determine not just the course of the GD but your own first impression with the panel judges as well. If the start is great, then the first impression will be so. If not, then it will badly affect their judgment of you. So, speak first only if you feel you can make a great start, which will provide you with the perfect launch platform.

    Being the first speaker is a high-risk, high-return strategy

14. **How critical is my fluency in English to my performance?**

    Fluency in Spoken English is a valuable asset, and one must constantly keep practicing it. However, what matters most is what you say, rather than how you say it. The content of your talk is very important. The panel judges are looking for new, fresh, creative, and sound ideas from you. Don't get distracted by your lack of good spoken English. Rather, focus on speaking well, logically, and listening properly. You should try to speak in English as much as possible, but it is Ok to slip into another common language like Hindi to drive home a point. But keep coming back to English. The rest will follow.

15. **How much or for how long should I speak?**

    There is no hard and fast rule for this. A judicious mix of speaking and listening is what the judges are looking for. For example, in a 25-30-minute GD with 10-12 participants, you should try to participate at least 5-6 times, with each entry lasting at least 90-120 seconds. However, this is only an illustrative example. One must stay in the center stage as much as possible while giving the others respect and displaying leadership in assigning speaking roles.

16. **What if another candidate has already said what I wanted to say?**

    You have two choices:

    1. Agree with the point made by that candidate and add on to it by displaying your knowledge of the subject by giving some examples or case studies. Make it short and simple, and then go on to the next point.

    2. Just think of something totally different to say on that same point of view. To avoid this situation, make sure you speak up in the first 2-3 minutes for the GD, else someone else will have already started your point.

17. **What level of aggression is acceptable in a GD?**

    There is a very fine line between aggression and assertiveness. You should always try to sound assertive and not loud or stubborn. The moment you notice people reacting to you with extreme emotions, either negatively or strongly, or picking fights with you, you may take it that you are being too aggressive. Assertiveness involves an element of win-win, but at the same time, the final call is yours. How you respond to others, whether in a cool manner or with irritation, determines the level of aggression.

    There is no excuse for shouting in a GD. Maintain a strong voice but not so loud that it hurts to listen!

    (illustration 64a)

18. **Are GDs an equal opportunity platform?**

    The GD is an equal opportunity platform; open to all, with the rules and regulations the same for all. No special treatment or privileges need to be extended to members of any particular sex. Being rude is not acceptable whether to a male or a female. So, the same common-sense rules and etiquette must be exhibited towards everybody, without exception.

19. **Is it all right to ask direct questions to other candidates during a GD?**

    It is all right to ask questions if you didn't understand a point or wanted clarification. But not for the purpose of making another person look bad. Your question could bring disharmony and unsettle the group, turning them against you. So, try to avoid this as much as possible.

20. **How should a group select a topic if asked to?**

    You could initiate a brainstorming session and reach an agreement on a topic. Or you could give out three topics, ask others to list them in order, and choose the most popular. Remember, this is a golden opportunity to display initiative and leadership, so grab it.

15.8 Summary

The job interview is a subjective process of candidate selection. However, it is the most widely used. Whether phone or video, face-to-face or group, the outcome of the interview is clear for both the interviewer and the interviewee. For the candidate, it is the opportunity to make the best first impression and convince the organization of their potential as the best candidate. For the interviewer, it is an opportunity to assess whether the candidate is the right fit and has the necessary skills and requirements. In this, the interview is like a marriage or a partnership. Good communication, timing, and honesty result in success in an interview.

Group Discussions need assertion, not aggression.

Knowledge Check:

1. What is the importance of the job interview?
2. What are some of the traits that interviewers want in successful candidates?
3. Name the different types of interviews with one example question of each not mentioned in the chapter.
4. Make your own checklist for your next job interview.
5. What are your biggest strengths and weaknesses? Name 5 of each?
6. What is your dream job? What makes you suitable for your dream job?
7. Write a description of the appropriate dress for the job. Give reasons for the type of clothing choices.

Get Ready for the Real World.

MOCK Interview for admission to a top Business Management Program

Candidate: Good Morning

Member 1: Good Morning. Please sit down.

C: Thank you, sir.

M1: You seem nervous. Would you like to have water?

C: No, thank you, I am good, sir.

M1: Tell us something about yourself.

C: Yes, sir. My name is Vihaan. I have done my B. Tech and I are waiting for the results of the final semester. My schooling was in BCS, Shimla. I have recently finished an internship with the Wipro Software Division, sir, and was involved in a very exciting project there.

M1: Your internship was in software, whereas you have pursued Electrical engineering. Why?

M2: Your resume says your mother is a Doctor. Didn't you want to pursue medicine?

C: Let me answer one question at a time. Sir, I will take up the second question first. I am not interested in Medicine, sir. I was always interested in Project Management. That is why I pursued Engineering, as that instilled in me the discipline of logical reasoning. And I did my internship with Wipro Software, sir, as that would have given me valuable exposure to Project Management. As regards your first question, my father passed away when I was very young, and my mother always encouraged my brother or me to pursue our dreams. Hence, both of us chose our vocations in consultation with her, but the decision was ours.

M1: Why only MBA? After B.Tech., you can pursue any technical field.

C: I feel that an MBA will add to my skill set by giving me critical thinking and Emotional Intelligence skills, which I may have lacked in my B. Tech hardcore number-based education. I will be more equipped to deal with people's problems and solve complex management problems with the management and leadership exposure that I will get in your institute.

M3: What do you think are the qualities that a good manager should not possess?

C: A good manager does not confuse the issue with the individual. For a good manager, the person and the problem are separate. A good manager does not get personal and views problems objectively and proactively.

M2: Where did you learn all this?

C: I have seen this in my professors at college. I have also seen this by observing my mother at the hospital where she works. It is a government hospital that faces severe staff and resource shortages. However, the entire hospital team works in coordination and does not get into conflicts on a routine basis. I also follow a lot of blogs and writings by gurus of their respective fields.

M2: What are your hobbies?

C: I like to write and tweet regularly on issues related to technology. I am also socially aware and try to engage with social change agents, not just politics or politicians. I am a keen observer of people and love to act out different characters on stage. Public Speaking and compering are my other hobbies.

M1: Suppose we had only one seat left. Should we take you or your best friend?

C: Ideally, I think you should take both of us, as we both are meritorious and capable. But if there is only one seat, you are the best judge to decide. May the best person win, though I am confident of getting admission this year.

M1: Do you have any weaknesses?

C: Yes, sir. I think everyone has weaknesses. I think I am a perfectionist, which sometimes creates problems as I tend to over-focus. I am trying to strike the optimum balance between always doing the right thing and doing things right.

M1: Well, thank you, Vihaan. **We are pleased to offer you the** admission seat.

C: Thank you.

Applied Knowledge

1. What did you think of Vihaan's performance?
2. Which question could you have answered better? Why?
3. Why do you think Vihaan got the admission?
4. Can you think of an alternate answer to each of the questions asked of Vihaan?
5. Pair up with a peer or use AI tools like Prepfully or Interview Warmup. Take turns being the interviewer and interviewee. Record the session and evaluate:
    - Clarity of answers
    - Confidence and tone
    - Body language
    - Depth of examples

This reflective practice sharpens your performance dramatically.

Chapter 16 Performance Storytelling and The Art of Promoting Yourself

Neuromarketing & Human Psychology, positioning your strengths for career advantage

LEARNING MILESTONES

This chapter will enable you to:

- Master performance storytelling by activating your creative side.
- Practice performance storytelling to sell your skills effectively.
- Use basic human psychology to influence leaders and clients.
- Use Neuroscience to help others notice and favour you.
- Determine how recruiters and clients make decisions.
- Align your strengths with the industry needs and vacancies.
- Recognize opportunities and openings before the competition.

Expert Quotes

> *"Your main selling point is what others say in praise about you.... in your absence."*
>
> *-Coach Prashant*

16.1 Selling your Skills

When you step into the professional world, or get newly promoted, the universal truth is: 'only that which can be seen is sold.' It's not just *what* you do, but *how* you present what you do that is the differentiator. Competition is continuously increasing, and those who can prove their visibility get noticed. In this unfair world, Introverted or shy individuals often get left out, and it often becomes essential to make behavioral changes in one's personality to remain in the notice of those who matter.

You may have the best technical skills among your peers, but in the absence of good soft skills, these tech skills are like gold and cash kept inside a locker. They are valuable only to you, but of no value to anyone else.

Increasingly, candidates are becoming like products who are in demand only when they have the necessary skills that employers seek to choose from a large population. In such a competitive scenario, how do you sell your skills? How do you get noticed in a crowd? The answer is Performance Storytelling.

16.1.1 What is Performance Storytelling?

Performance Storytelling means telling stories that shape the narrative of your successes and achievements in a way that does not sound like bragging. When you are able to explain to another person your life's challenges, how you overcame those challenges, and your learning journey, they are able to understand your true potential. Performance storytelling is the art of making another person appreciate you and the value that you can bring to them and their organization without sounding boastful or self-centered.

Performance storytelling is not telling lies or fictional accounts about made-up events. Rather, these are small, real-life, true anecdotes or incidents from your life where you exhibited some special skills. Or when you went above and beyond the ordinary.

While Data Storytelling involves using visuals and graphs to convey messages in a simple form, performance storytelling is a more human and personality-based approach. It requires activating your creative side and understanding human behavior to tell the right stories at the right time.

16.1.2 Benefits of Performance Storytelling

Talking about oneself does not come naturally for many of us. The author has worked with thousands of corporate professionals. One of the patterns in good professionals who don't get promoted or are unable to advance in their careers despite their excellent technical skills is their inability to talk about their own work. While it is true that many of us work in teams and the benefits accrue to the team, it is also true that individual excellence gets rewarded. Through stories, we are able to express our thoughts and showcase our work with pride. We gain confidence in talking about ourselves and how our presence made the difference between success and failure. How other people reached out to you and how you were able to add value and innovate for the larger good.

1. Stories answer a question that almost every influential person in your life asks: WIIFM = What 's-In-It-For-Me? Whether you are raising money for your start-up, appearing for a job interview, or trying to convince a friend, you need stories to close the pitch. Why should anyone care about you or your product or service?

2. Stories help you focus on the personal element that evokes emotions. Too often, people get lost in technical details when they speak about their work. Others who are not from the same field or industry find it hard to understand. But emotions are universal. People feel similar emotions, and stories can help in creating an emotional connection.

3. Performance storytelling helps others visualize future success and potential. While everyone makes similar claims and pitches, performance storytellers can create a mental visual for the other person

where they are able to `see' what success looks like. They can then make the connection between the claims made in your annual report or CV and what you are actually capable of.

16.1.3 STAR Framework for Performance Storytelling

So how does one develop this skill? The STAR frameworks remain one of the simplest and powerful techniques for performance storytelling. The STAR narrative is a 4-step process wherein you take the listener on a short narrative right from the situation up to the end result.

The STAR is an acronym that stands for:

S= Situation	T= Task
A= Action	R= Result

Let's go through the STAR framework in detail:

1. S = Situation.

This sets the context of the story. This tells the listener what was happening. Where did it happen? Who were the stakeholders involved?

Example, "Last June, when I was working on a project, the client was unhappy with the code that was being delivered so far. My managers and I were at our wits' end.

2. T = Task.

This showcases responsibilities and accountability, and the challenges related to the same. The purpose of talking about challenges and problems is to make the other person understand the depth and gravity of the problem that you were in.

Example: " The client kept raising tickets, and there were multiple escalations. The delivery team and the sales team seemed to be at odds, and the client was threatening to move to the competition."

3. A= Action

This is the heart of your Performance Story. What you actually did to address the challenge. This is when your role in removing the problem gets highlighted. This is where you get the other person to appreciate the importance of your presence and the value that you added.

The purpose of this level is to showcase your knowledge, skills, and attitude.

Example: "I had recently taken a certification: 'AI in Data Analytics'. I used the knowledge that I had acquired in this course to pitch to the client an alternative solution. While this new solution had not been tested before, the client heard me out and appreciated my initiative in thinking out of the box."

4. R = Result

This is where you showcase the outcome. What happened when you jumped into solving the problem? What would have happened if you were not present? How does your presence result in savings of time, money, and effort? This part of the story makes the listener aware of concrete and tangible positive changes that occurred as a result of your actions.

Example: "Since the new AI-based solution had not been tested before, it was more expensive to implement. However, the client was very interested, and we were able to increase the project value by 20% resulting in a healthy improvement to the bottom line. We were also able to use four more resources with AI domain expertise who had been on the bench up to then. I was given the achiever of the quarter award by the MD."

Case in Point (the context is from the IT industry)

Interviewer: "Tell me about your AI skills."

Standard Answer: "I've worked with tools like Python, TensorFlow, and scikit-learn during my projects. I've also worked with basic neural networks in TensorFlow and Keras, experimenting with different activation functions and optimizers like ReLU and Adam to minimize loss."

STAR Answer: "Over the past few months, I've completed certifications in Artificial Intelligence. I observed client feedback, wherein the need of the hour was to innovate using AI. I attended the training workshops organized by the L&D Teams. I applied for projects where I got hands-on exposure to topics like supervised and unsupervised learning, neural networks, and natural language processing. I've also worked with tools like Python, TensorFlow, and scikit-learn during my coursework." "For example, during my AI certification project (Situation), we were asked to build a model to predict customer churn and high attrition rate (Task). I took the lead in data preprocessing and feature selection (Action), and our model achieved about 87% accuracy using a Random Forest classifier (Result). That experience helped me understand how data quality directly affects model performance." "Since then, I've been exploring how AI applications like recommendation systems or conversational bots can enhance customer experience — I even tried building a simple chatbot using an open-source NLP library." So while I'm still early in my AI career, I'm comfortable working with end-to-end model development — from data preparation and algorithm selection to evaluation using metrics like precision, recall, F1-score, and ROC-AUC." I've been experimenting with small AI applications, like a chatbot using open-source NLP tools. I'm still learning, but I'm confident about my fundamentals and really excited to bring that AI knowledge into a business setting — using it to solve real problems and improve processes."

16.1.4 Performance Storytelling Practice prompts

Performance Storytelling can be practiced through these AI prompts. One can input these prompts into an AI tool, giving the context of the job or project being pitched. Each of these prompts will generate a response that can be the foundation of your Performance Story. Once the prompt is more detailed, use the response generated by the AI to personalize it to your own life using names, places, and dates in the story to make it sound more credible and authentic.

Sample prompts:

1. Hey AI: Tell me about A time when you jumped in to solve a problem, without your seniors, manager's, or client's guidance.
2. Hey AI: Tell me A time when you had to interact with a difficult person
3. Hey AI: Tell me A time when you learned from a mistake.
4. Hey AI: Tell me A time when you had to work on a difficult team.
5. Hey AI: Tell me A time when you were unfairly criticized and how you handled it?
6. Hey AI: Tell me A time when you taught someone how to do something new.
7. Hey AI: Tell me A time when you had to say 'no' to a professional request from a senior, professor, a leader, or a client.
8. Hey AI: Tell me A time when you saved your client/leader money or made them money.
9. Hey AI: Tell me A time when you developed a new or improved process at work.
10. Hey AI: Tell me A time when you disagreed with a client or manager, and how you resolved it.

When you combine storytelling with human psychology and neuroscience, you gain mastery of the skill of Neuromarketing. You gain a powerful toolkit for gaining visibility, recognition, and growth

16.2 Neuromarketing as a Tool for Influencing Leaders

Have you ever wondered:

- Why do some people get selected in interviews while others do not, despite having the same degrees and experience?
- Why do managers select specific people for projects and promotions while ignoring the others?
- What will it take to persuade your client and leader to give you an appointment for a crucial discussion?

- Why is it that some people get instant feedback on their presentations and reports, while others are constantly in suspense over the outcome?

The answer lies in the fact that making decisions is both a conscious and non-conscious process in the brain. It is important not only to work and interact with managers and clients, but also to understand their motivations and the reasons why they behave and act the way they do. This involves aligning your intentions with their agenda. This is exactly what neuromarketing aims to do. By triggering positive feelings and emotions in others, it compels them to look at you in a positive manner.

It is important for candidates to have a working knowledge of human psychology and neuroscience, which helps in determining how employers make conscious and subconscious decisions about hiring and buying. By reading others' body language, saying the right words, and using the correct visual mediums, we can get an insight into what the other person is thinking. What do they want? Because once we understand what the other person wants, we can modify our own behavior to match that want. This is how a successful sale is made, whether it is the sale of a product or service or selling yourself in an interview.

Neuromarketing is a derivative of neuroscience, which is a combination of human psychology, consumer behavior, and marketing research. The objective of applied neuromarketing is to determine what motivates influencers and leaders to make their decisions and how our efforts can influence them to choose favorably towards us.

While neuromarketing employs tools, such as VR, Eye tracking, EEG, and FMRI, facial coding, and other technological tools, it also provides an insight into basic human behavior and motivations through basic psychology.

16.3 Using Neuromarketing and Psychology to Get Ahead

It is a simple matter of demand and supply. The successful candidates are those who can supply the correct information or product to the right person at the right time. Neuromarketing helps prospective candidates and sellers to achieve their goals and targets by understanding the motivations of their target market.

Neuromarketing is also used in Social Networking, AI, and Big Data for understanding and influencing internet search behavior and website design. Through neuromarketing, a prospective job hunter or supplier can see where the demand is. What skills do they need to work on to get hired? What courses should they take so that their knowledge and skills are up-to-date as per the latest industry requirements? Accordingly, they can direct their efforts precisely in the right direction without wasting time.

16.4 How do Recruiters and Clients make Decisions?

Anyone looking to get hired, promoted, wealthy, or just plain lucky can use Neuromarketing for their personal gain. Research has shown, and advertising

and marketing have proven time and time again, that buying or hiring decisions are taken not just on the basis of data or information but also on the basis of emotion.

Where data fails, emotion always wins!

People who can understand how to read other people's minds can get their work done. But how does one master this art of reading minds? Simply by using logic and emotion in the same discussion or pitch. Logic makes people give you a chance in a meeting to talk about yourself. But in a situation where most others have the same skills or education, how do you convince the recruiter or buyer? By sharing experiences and stories with them, you bring them into your world. Through your stories and shared experiences, you can demonstrate to people:

- What they will gain by hiring you or using your product
- What they will lose by not hiring you or buying your product

Either argument or pitch involves a clever use of different kinds of emotions.

The following case studies with their analysis demonstrate how a psychology-based approach can be used for personal success in the interview scenario:

Case in Point

Interviewer: "How good are you at this task or technology? How long have you been using this technology or software?"

You: "When I was in school, I saw a movie called Artificial Intelligence by Steven Spielberg. That was the first time I had felt the impact of Science fiction and Machine Learning on our lives, but I was too young to understand it completely. However, that love for Computers and Technology stayed with me, and I knew I wanted to make a career in Data Science. When I was in college, Big Data Analytics was a concept just coming into fashion. I took courses related to Big Data and ML. In fact, in college, I collated all the data through a piece of software I created and made a database for the library based on user data, and even received a commendation certificate from the founder! I am very passionate about this technology."

Analysis:

With the above answer, you left an impression on the interviewer's mind. You could have answered by having a boring, technical discussion of the technology and the projects that you have done with this technology. But that's just another routine answer.

Instead, you used basic human psychology. You told a story about a college library that had many problems. You took the interviewer on a mental tour of the campus. He/She visualises the library systems getting transformed, thanks to your software. He/She visualises books being issued and returned on time, and reminders and fines being managed seamlessly. He/She visualises a

thankful administration, and you are the reason for their happiness. And the interviewer thinks, "This is the kind of candidate I want in my team!"

That's what your objective should be in an interview, especially a job interview — to create a movie about you that plays in your interviewer's mind long after you've left the room! You should not just provide the information given in your CV about your skills. Instead, you should tell a story about how you used your skills to add value to a situation.

Case in Point

"When I joined the cross-functional team as a process coordinator, we had a new product launch delayed by 6 weeks because of misalignment between design and manufacturing. Team morale was slipping, and leadership was asking tough questions.

I convened the design, manufacturing, and supply-chain teams for a "handoff workshop". I created a visual map of the hand-off steps, identified five major bottlenecks, introduced a weekly sync meeting, and a hand-off checklist.

We brought the launch forward by 3 weeks, improved on-time delivery from 60% to 85% and reduced rework cost by 12%. The customer experience improved, our cost base lowered, and we avoided the penalty clauses. Leadership described this as "model behaviour" in the post-launch review. For this organisation seeking faster time-to-market, this is exactly the type of initiative that adds value.

Next step: I am now looking to apply this hand-off discipline across other product families and scale these gains globally."

Analysis:

Through this answer, you showed many qualities which are important for recruiters and managers: Leadership, initiative, creative thinking, and people skills. These are the qualities that you get selected for. Your technical skills and education are important, but may not be unique to you. But the ability to get things done is very valuable to any decision maker.

Your interviewer knows you did not work alone and that you worked in a team. But you do not have to keep bringing up your teammates in this story. The objective is to make yourself look good. And be proud of yourself when you tell such incidents. The interviewer will connect the dots and remember you at the time of selection.

16.5 Three steps to use neuromarketing for a successful life

In daily life,, decisions are taken based on certain variables. Irrespective of your vocation, the following are some ways in which neuroscience and neuromarketing can help you attain professional success:

16.5.1 Attention

This is perhaps the most crucial part of business communication. In a CV, a good headline to describe yourself gets the attention of recruiters. In a presentation, a good opening grabs the attention of the audience. In a job interview, a firm handshake and a good self-introduction give a positive start to a new engagement.

In advertising media, FMCG packaging, specially designed logos, colours, and fonts are chosen after extensive research to grab eyeballs.

16.5.2 Emotional Connect

Business Storytelling combines data, emotion, and context to influence the listener. In a job interview, telling the interviewer about your experience and involvement in a crucial project, where you were able to solve a major problem, helps them get an insight into your capabilities. Storytelling helps the interviewer remember you after you have exited the room. A good story about your success in a particular college or a professional project is like a movie about you that plays in your interviewer's head long after you've gone. Stories help you establish common ground with the listener, change someone's mind, motivate and energize, or caution someone against making a mistake.

For example, when you are thinking of buying a new smartphone or a gadget, you go online and look at reviews. But what are reviews? Reviews are stories. They are not just facts, features, and specifications. They are stories about the experience of others who have used a similar gadget.

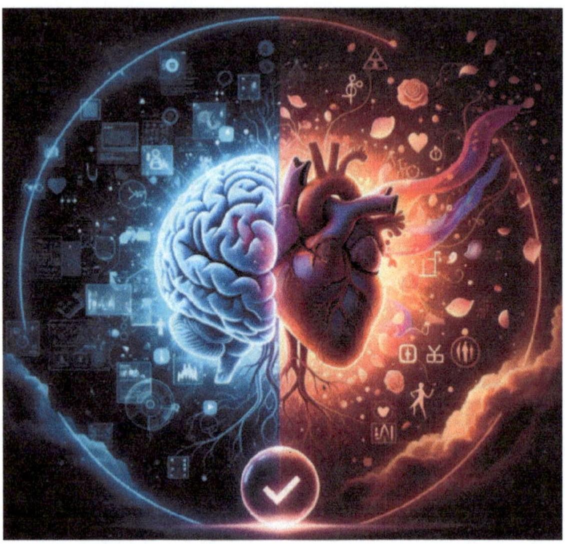

***Figure 16.1**: Two engines, one mission: better decisions*

Case in Point

A 75-year-old, well-educated, well-read senior citizen lady had been suffering from progressive hearing loss. Over the years, her son got her the best medical treatment, but her hearing continued to decline. Her hearing loss was also a cause of miscommunication and conflict in their house. He and his wife tried their best to convince their mother to wear a hearing aid, but she was totally against the idea. They would show her catalogues and fliers and information on the latest hearing aid solutions, but she would not agree. She would argue, "What would my friends think?" Embarrassed at the thought of her friends laughing at her hearing aid, she continued to suffer due to declining hearing but refused to wear an aid.

After some time, the son took his mother to the doctor for a check-up. The doctor was his friend. While examining her ears, he casually turned to the son and asked, "So when is your wife due for her delivery of her second child?" The son replied, "In 3 weeks." The doctor casually turned to the mother and said, "But Aunty, so sorry, you won't be able to participate in your grandchild's happiness." The mother got angry and said, "Why are you talking like this?" The doctor replied, "When the child cries or calls out to you, you won't be able to hear the child".

The mother was silent all the way to the home. As soon as she reached home, she told her son to order the hearing aid immediately! She kept on insisting for many days and did not rest till the hearing aid came. And she has not taken it off since! All because she did not want to miss out on hearing her grandchild's voice!

Where data and logic could not convince her, emotion did!

16.5.3 Perception and Reputation

Successful candidates work on how others perceive them. How others talk about you and think about you, and how that information is absorbed by the leaders, contribute significantly to your success. If someone gives good feedback about your presentation skills to your leader, then it can influence their mind towards you. In this case, even your below-average presentation will look good to them. It is very important to cultivate an image and persona where others speak well of you. Due to social media and other channels, this reputation, whether positive or negative, reaches the ears of decision makers very quickly. So pay attention to your professional image and reputation. Someone is always watching!

Case in Point

Recommendations about you or client testimonials of your product are far more effective than your qualifications. Others who have had a good experience dealing with you are the best ambassadors for you. It is always beneficial to ensure that your professional profile on social media platforms, such as LinkedIn, has good recommendations from credible people who can vouch for your technical and professional ability. Recommendations and testimonials build your reputation.

16.6 Recognize opportunities and openings before the competition

The two easy ways in which you can recognize and capitalize on opportunities before others are:

1. Observation
2. Matching Yourself with Your Leaders

16.6.1 Observation

In this age of hypercompetition, a keen observation of your immediate environment can help you get ahead. Successful people have an in-built alert system to detect when something around them has changed. It could be a physical change in their leader or non-verbal cues. Either way, through observation, these people can take immediate action to align themselves with the leaders. If some event happens regularly in your life but does not happen one day as per schedule, it is important to know why. For example, a leader who greets you daily suddenly starts ignoring you, or a co-worker who is always on time suddenly starts coming late. It is important to know why it is occurring and to evaluate how and why this change in pattern can affect you. This evaluation then enables you to take steps accordingly.

***Figure 16.2**: The more you learn, the more you earn*

Case in Point

Shaurya is a software engineer in a global IT company. He has been on good terms with his manager and clients, and quite popular with his colleagues. Since last month, Shaurya has been noticing that the client has been delaying responses to his queries. A number of dependencies have cropped up, and the backlog is growing. Shaurya has also noticed that lately his manager is not making much eye contact with him.

Shaurya initially ignored these signals, but when these became a pattern, he decided not to ignore them any further. He sought an appointment with his reporting manager and asked him if there was any matter.

The manager dropped a bombshell that the project was going to be scrapped, and their division may close. Shaurya did not waste time and immediately

started looking for opportunities in other groups. He got absorbed in a long-term project that had just been ramped up. Sure enough, after a fortnight, Shaurya's previous project was ramped down, and his other colleagues are on the bench. Shaurya's alertness to his environment saved the day for him.

16.6.2 Influencing Skills

Robert Cialdini has been called the Guru of Influence. The reader would do well to familiarize themselves with Cialdini's book: *Influence: The Psychology of Persuasion.* First published in **1984**, it became a **classic in behavioral psychology, marketing, and ways to influence others**.

Here are **Robert Cialdini's 6 Principles of Influence** with **one-line explanations**:

1. **Reciprocity:** People feel obligated to return favors or kindnesses.
2. **Commitment and Consistency:** Once people commit to something, they strive to act consistently with it.
3. **Social Proof:** People look to others' actions to decide what's right or appropriate.
4. **Authority:** People are more likely to follow credible experts or leaders.
5. **Liking:** People are easily persuaded by those they like or find similar to themselves.
6. **Scarcity:** People value things more when they perceive them as rare or limited.

16.6.3 Influencing leaders by matching yourself

The principle of matching is that we like to work with people who we think are like us.

Matching is a framework that can be used for ensuring that you are prepared for any eventuality. Nothing will then come as a surprise to you, and if there are any serious issues, you will be prepared and equipped to handle them.

Matching is done on two levels, Behavioral and Physical.

i. Behavioural — Understanding the Leader's Agenda

During meetings or in a group, observe the kinds of questions leaders or recruiters ask. That will give you an idea as to what is important for your leader. What are their priorities? You may realize that your priorities are different from your leader's. Matching your agenda with that of your manager or recruiter will help you focus on what is important for your leader as well.

Case in Point

Raghu regularly reads the financial newspapers and blogs. In one Podcast, he heard an interview with his company's MD who said that he is very interested in the EV automobile sector, and their main focus in the next 3 years will be

on AI in the EV automobile sector. Raghu immediately started updating himself with technologies related to driverless cars and automobile security. In the next town hall, in the presence of the MD, he asked a question related to whether their project could be extended to include drones in the e-commerce vertical. The MD was impressed and asked Raghu's reporting manager to include him in an important on-site project related to self-driving cars.

ii. Physically Matching Yourself

Match your pace, walking style, talking pitch, speed, and volume with the others. You will find leaders responding better to you. For example, if your leader bends towards you to talk, it's a good idea to mirror that posture. In a call, if your voice volume is much lower or higher than the others, then there is a chance you will not be heard.

***Figure 16.3**: Mirror the vibe, match the energy*

16.7 Summary

Performance storytelling is essential because it helps professionals turn their achievements into engaging, memorable narratives rather than dry facts. It allows others—like recruiters, leaders, or clients—to clearly see your impact and value. By framing experiences through stories, you connect emotionally, build credibility, and make your success resonate with your audience.

A basic knowledge of Neuroscience and Neuromarketing: human psychology can help to give you a winning edge. Modern marketing methods, such as neuromarketing combined with Data Analytics, Machine Learning, and AI, enable professionals to beat the competition. Advertising works on tapping into our psychology. Sports coaches instill a sense of commitment and urgency in their troops by invoking a spirit of winning. Leaders in the Defense forces brace their troops by invoking a sense of sacrifice and patriotism. Good leaders motivate their staff not just by monetary incentives but also by giving praise, encouragement, and feedback at the right time. Doctors are able to provide hope and motivation to their patients by saying the right thing at the right time.

We too can use a combination of Data and Emotion tools, such as Storytelling and Matching, to make ourselves look good in the eyes of the leaders and ensure our visibility when they make decisions related to our future.

Knowledge Check:

1. How can Performance Storytelling help in communicating your value?
2 .Why is it important to have a basic knowledge of human psychology to promote yourself?
3. What is neuromarketing? How can we use it to gain a competitive edge?
4. How do recruiters make hiring decisions for reasons other than technical competence? Discuss in 40 words.
5. What are the three steps for using neuromarketing to influence others? Give one example of each.
6. Mention the two ways in which you can recognize opportunities for professional growth. Give one example of each.

Get ready for the real world

"So Aishwarya, tell me about yourself. What are your strengths?" asked the interviewer."

Aishwarya replied, "Umm, I was born in Vijayawada in the year 1997. I have heard so many times that it was the hottest year ever. My father is a manager at Honest Bank, which is 25 minutes from our house. He generally drops me off at college on his way to the office. My mother is a teacher, and my sister is in college, pursuing her Master's in Fine Arts. I live with my parents and grandparents in our ancestral house. I got 84%marks in my class X exam, and then I was wondering which subjects to take and...."

"That will be enough, Ms. Reddy," said the interviewer to Aishwarya. She was surprised as she had just sat and begun the speech that she had practiced many times. This was a make-or-break interview for her, as there were no other companies for campus placements. Dejected, she came out of the interview room where her best friend Yudi, who was also the Student Placement Cell in-charge, asked her, "How did it go? How come you came out so soon?" She started crying and rushed away without speaking.

The next week, Yudi came to know that Aishwarya had not been selected. He was on good terms with the recruiter and called him for a general report, and then asked her about Aishwarya.

The recruiter said, "Oh, she has no idea what she is talking about. I asked about her strengths, and she started to give me her personal family history! Sorry, but we cannot have such unprofessional candidates working for us."

Yudi shared this feedback with Aishwarya, who replied, "But what should I have said?"

Yudi replied, "Recruiters want to get an insight into your personality. They want to know that they are selecting candidates who will fit perfectly into their company. You must tell them about projects that you have been part of, your professional interests, what you have been doing to educate and upskill yourself in the latest technologies, etc. Tell them about a situation where you showed leadership or initiative. They want their employees to use these skills at work as well. You need to match your skills with what the recruiters want. Only then will they be able to judge whether you have the right soft skills required for the job.

Anyway, I have lined up one more interview for you. Make sure you are prepared this time."

Aishwarya went totally prepared with 2-3 short case studies from her life where she displayed excellent organizational and communication skills. She spoke about her involvement with extracurricular and community service projects, and the recruiters were impressed. She was surprised that the recruiters discussed these projects as much as her technical knowledge in the interview.

She is now confident of getting the job

Applied knowledge

1. What is the mistake that Aishwarya made in her first interview?
2. What do recruiters want to hear when they ask you to tell them something about yourself?
3. What advice from Yudi would you follow while trying to promote yourself in front of recruiters or clients?

Build your vocabulary

Learn and use the Words and Business phrases mentioned in this chapter to improve your Spoken English Skills:

- **Competitive edge:** To have an advantage over others due to the presence of some skill
- **Align yourself:** To become part of the other person's project or plan by doing or thinking what they want.
- **Insight:** Knowing what is in the other person's mind and making your plan accordingly
- **Seamless:** Something that happens or is done without interrupting the normal workflow or schedule
- **Perfect fit:** A skill or thought that exactly matches what your leader wants at that point in time